# ILLUSTRATED HISTORY OF
# CENTRAL OTAGO
### AND THE QUEENSTOWN LAKES DISTRICT

# ILLUSTRATED HISTORY OF CENTRAL OTAGO
## AND THE QUEENSTOWN LAKES DISTRICT

GERALD CUNNINGHAM

Published by Reed Books, a division of Reed Publishing (NZ) Ltd,
39 Rawene Rd, Birkenhead, Auckland.
Associated companies, branches and representatives throughout the world.

This book is copyright. Except for the purpose of fair reviewing, no part of this publication may be reproduced or transmitted in any form or by any means, electronic or mechanical, including photocopying, recording, or any information storage and retrieval system, without permission in writing from the publisher. Infringers of copyright render themselves liable to prosecution.

© 2005 Gerald Cunningham
The author asserts his moral rights in the work.

National Library of New Zealand Cataloguing-in-Publication Data

Cunningham, Gerald, 1945-
Illustrated history of Central Otago and the Queenstown Lakes District / Gerald Cunningham.
Includes bibliographical references and index.
ISBN 0-7900-1023-2

1. Central Otago District (N.Z.)—History. 2. Central Otago District (N.Z.)—History—Pictorial works. 3. Queenstown-Lakes District (N.Z.)—History. 4. Queenstown-Lakes District (N.Z.)—History—Pictorial works. I. Title. 993.94—dc 22

Front cover: Queenstown, Rees Street, 1 October 1878. Hocken Collections E2062/35. University of Otago, Dunedin, New Zealand
Back cover: Opening of a fruit-canning factory in Roxburgh, 1905. Hocken Collections SOS-064F.

Cover design: Steve Russell
Editor: Gillian Kootstra

ISBN 0 7900 1023 2
Printed in New Zealand

# CONTENTS

*Author's note* — 7

1. Introduction — 9
2. First footsteps — moa and Maori — 13
3. The explorers — 21
4. The early runholders, 1857–1910 — 27
5. Gold! Gold! Gold! — 43
6. Chinese miners in Central Otago — 56
7. Rabbits — the scourge of Central Otago — 62
8. Transport and the Otago Central Railway — 67
9. World War I and Private Andrew McBreen — 76
10. D Company — 23rd Battalion and the Battle of Crete — 81
11. Beginnings of the wine industry — 90
12. Origins of the fruit growing industry — 92
13. The stock and station industry — 100
14. Alexandra from the nineteenth to the twenty-first century — 107
15. Roxburgh and the Teviot District — 115
16. Life in Macetown 1862–1900 — 123
17. The rise and fall of St Bathans — 132
18. From Blacks to Ophir — 140
19. Wanaka and Hawea — lakes and mountains — 147

| 20 | Naseby and Kyeburn | 157 |
| 21 | Ranfurly — art deco on the Maniototo Plain | 167 |
| 22 | Cromwell and Bannockburn | 176 |
| 23 | Clyde and the Dunstan — the first 10 years | 187 |
| 24 | The road to Skippers | 194 |
| 25 | Electricity — from Bullendale to the Clyde Dam | 201 |
| 26 | Hayes Engineering Works — Oturehua | 213 |
| 27 | Folly of the Kawarau Falls Dam | 218 |

*Bibliography* 225

*Index* 227

# AUTHOR'S NOTE

This book is not an academic work that will send the reader glassy-eyed with boredom. It is a story of Central Otago and the Queenstown Lakes District, written with the purpose of bringing alive the history of the region through the use of photographs and text. In the pages that follow the reader will gain an insight into this unique area and its people, from the time of the first Maori to the present day. Much thought has gone into the selection of the best of the old photographs that are available, many of which have been obtained from different and often obscure sources throughout New Zealand. A large number of these photographs have not been published previously. Many of the historic parts of Central Otago still exist today, either unchanged or restored to their former state. Where possible, I have taken my own photographs of these historic sites, and these are also included in the chapters that follow.

My thanks to senior editor Gillian Kootstra and the team at Reed Publishing. Without their encouragement and support, this book would not have been written.

*Gerald Cunningham*
*Lauder*

*For Susan*

# 1
# INTRODUCTION

The boundaries of Central Otago are vague, the reason being that the name Central Otago, or Central as it is more often referred to, evolved in the mid 1800s to identify an area that was the interior of the province of Otago in relation to the city of Dunedin.

Otago is a modern name. Maori called the area Araiteuru, after the ancestral canoe of the same name that was wrecked off Shag Point, near modern-day Palmerston. The name Otago evolved from Otakau, the title given to a channel in Otago Harbour. From that humble beginning, Otakau came ashore as a name given to a block of land centred on Dunedin in 1844 called the Otakau Block. Finally, with revised spelling to reflect the local dialect, it became Otago, the name eventually given to the entire province.

For the purposes of this book, Central Otago and the Queenstown Lakes District are considered to be all that area of land bound by the towns, villages or districts of Lawrence, Hyde and Kyeburn in the east, the remote Lindis Pass in the north, lakes Hawea, Wanaka and Wakatipu in the west and Kingston in the south. Not included are the townships and villages of Middlemarch, Dunback and Macraes Flat, which are inland from Dunedin but either have a climate that is more influenced by the ocean on the east coast or fall under the jurisdiction of the Dunedin City Council.

## THE CLIMATE

The Mediterranean-style climate that Central Otago enjoys makes the area unique in New Zealand. With the prevailing weather coming from the direction of the Tasman Sea, most of Central Otago lies in the rain shadow of the mountains of Fiordland and the Southern Alps. Moisture-laden air, unable to lift over these mountain ranges, drops its moisture as rain on the west coast and then continues as a warm, dry wind over Central Otago.

Referred to as the nor'wester, this wind often reaches gale force, especially in the spring and summer months, and is similar to the Santa Ana that blows in California and the Mistral in France.

With most of the rain falling on the western side of the mountains, very little is left to provide moisture to Central Otago, and as a result much of the area has a semi-arid climate. The average annual rainfall of only 300 mm in the interior of Central Otago is very low when compared with other parts of New Zealand, where up to 6000 mm of annual rainfall is possible. The Queenstown Lakes District has a higher rainfall than the interior of Central Otago, being influenced by the mountains and broad sheets of water. Its annual figure is twice that of the interior, in locations such as the Maniototo Plain, but still very low by New Zealand standards.

Low rainfall means few clouds, so skies in Central Otago are clear, summers are usually very hot and severe droughts are common. These clear skies have the opposite effect in the winter, when temperatures regularly drop below freezing, savage frosts are the norm and snow is a regular visitor, especially to the high country.

This climate makes for extremes. The village of Ophir in Central Otago holds the record for the lowest temperature ever recorded in New Zealand: minus 21.6°C on 3 July 1995. Hot summers and frigid winters also place Ophir in the record books as the location where New Zealand's largest temperature swings take place. One massive swing saw the town's temperature vary by 55°C from the hottest day to the coldest day over a 12-month period.

## GEOGRAPHY, VEGETATION AND GEOLOGY

Central Otago is an upland basin surrounded by several ranges of mountains: the Kakanui Mountains, the Hawkduns, the Remarkables and the Old Man Range. This basin is in turn divided roughly north to south by other, lower ranges of hills, such as the Rock and Pillar, the Raggedy, the Old Woman, Rough Ridge, Pisa and the Knobby.

The three large lakes, Hawea, Wanaka and Wakatipu, were created by glaciers that have long since melted. These ancient glaciers scooped the three lake beds to a depth well below sea level and, when at their peak, Queenstown had 900 m of ice riding over it. Smaller lakes, such as Lake Dunstan, have been created by man as a by-product of the need to generate electricity, while even smaller ones, such as lakes Onslow and the Manorburn and the Poolburn reservoirs, were built to provide water for irrigation.

Central Otago is drained by four substantial rivers. The largest, the Clutha, is also New Zealand's largest river by volume. Its name is derived from the Gaelic word for one of Scotland's great rivers, the Clyde. The other three large rivers that drain Central Otago, the Kawarau, the Manuherikia and the Taieri, like the Clutha, finish their journey to the sea on the east coast.

Some 15 million years ago Central Otago was a low-lying area of lakes, billabongs and wetlands, similar to the ecology of present-day Kakadu in Australia's Northern Territory, or the Florida Everglades in the United States. Fossil evidence and large deposits of coal in Central Otago point to the fact that during this same period the area was covered in forest. Climate change, fire, human habitation and introduced animals, many of which are now pests, have led to the almost complete disappearance of this forest. A fraction still remains in the higher rainfall areas around the lakes, but the dominant landscape is now open tussock land, grassland, schist rock outcrops and large areas that have fallen victim to the recently introduced pest plants of sweet briar and thyme.

Early photographs of Central Otago show an area devoid of trees, but it is difficult today to imagine places like Arrowtown, Queenstown, Alexandra, Naseby, Macetown and Lawrence without trees. The early settlers were careful to plant trees throughout the area, and the present-day inhabitants and visitors reap the benefit of these plantings of mainly English trees. Only one native woody plant exists: matagouri, the low, thorny plant that covers large areas and thrives on the fertiliser applied to the land to aid modern-day farming.

Schist rock dominates the Central Otago landscape. Millions of years ago areas of sandstone and mud were buried and compressed, subjected to intense volcanic heat and chemical action, then folded. Schist rock was the result. It lies in flat sheets that crumble and break off in slabs, making it a very useful building material. The process that produces schist also produces quartz, a stone that often contains gold, antimony and scheelite (tungsten), all valuable minerals that were to influence the history of Central Otago.

## THE PEOPLE AND THE ECONOMY

The first known human inhabitants of Central Otago were the Maori who came to hunt moa. The descendants of these people form part of Ngai Tahu, a tribal name still in use today. A further 600 years were to elapse before the first European explorers, whalers, sealers, adventurers, and settlers began to arrive. The first settlers to venture into Central Otago were sheep farmers who leased large properties called runs, initially raising sheep for their wool, as refrigeration of meat for export did not begin until 1882. When gold was discovered at Gabriels Gully near Lawrence in 1861, and on the Clutha River close to the present-day town of Cromwell in 1862, hordes of gold seekers arrived from all over the world, and today the scars they left on the landscape in their search for gold can still be seen throughout Central Otago. Many of these goldminers remained after the gold ran out, to farm, open businesses and plant orchards. Today agriculture, tourism and horticulture are the basis of the local economy.

# 2
# FIRST FOOTSTEPS — MOA AND MAORI

The first people known to have set foot in Central Otago were the ancestors of Maori, who arrived possibly in the thirteenth century during an era of widespread voyaging across the South Pacific. Although these hardy travellers' exact points of departure remain unknown, the Society Islands and the Cook Islands stand out as likely homelands because of similarities in tools and other artifacts found both in those islands and in New Zealand. The reasons for departure are also speculative, although pressure on resources, food shortages and a culture of exploration and expansion may all have played a part.

It seems likely that New Zealand was found by East Polynesian explorers during a voyage of discovery and then settled in a planned migration by colonists travelling in small groups aboard double-hulled canoes. Using the skills developed over generations, they navigated by the stars, the moon, the clouds, wave action and migratory birds to find their new home. The

In order to test the theory that Polynesians migrated to New Zealand from the Cook Islands, this double-hulled canoe was built using a design copied from an early drawing completed by an artist who sailed with Captain Cook. The vessel sailed from the Cook Islands to New Zealand and back several times without incident during the last decade of the twentieth century, relying solely on the ancient Polynesian methods of navigation. These voyages were proof that such trips were feasible and added weight to the theory that the early Maori were capable of regularly moving to and from New Zealand.

deliberate nature of this settlement seems to be confirmed by the number and variety of plants that the voyagers brought with them. The timing of their arrival has been the source of some debate over the years, and some studies have put the date as early as the eighth century. Recent studies, however, put the date at around the thirteenth century as no hard and indisputable evidence of the presence of humans before then can be found.

## THE MAORI IN CENTRAL OTAGO

After reaching New Zealand, the new arrivals began to spread out over both islands to locate places to settle that were rich in resources. In the South Island, one such area of settlement was on the south-east coast, where seals, fish, shellfish and birds were plentiful and where the climate was relatively warm. These early inhabitants lived a mobile, nomadic lifestyle, moving from location to location to make use of the resources available at different times of the year. During the spring and summer months, they moved inland to Central Otago as the temperature rose and the snow melted to hunt one of the greatest gifts the new land had to offer: the moa.

Early Maori employed dogs to ambush the giant birds and then killed them at close range. The hunters were after the prized leg meat, because the moa was a ground-dwelling bird and had no need for wing muscles, which in turn meant no breast meat. The hunters would discard the rest of the bird. They would then preserve the meat by surrounding it in its own fat and packing it into bags made from split bull kelp for transporting back to the

Muri Lagoon, Rarotonga, Cook Islands — the only safe anchorage on the island and the departure point for many early Polynesian voyages. Once through the deep passage in the reef, as shown in middle picture, the sailors would have picked up the trade winds that blow steadily in the direction of New Zealand, particularly during the winter months.

FIRST FOOTSTEPS — MOA AND MAORI

coastal settlements via the Clutha and Taieri rivers.

Physical evidence of these hunting practices is spread all over Central Otago, mostly in camps set up as places where the meat was butchered and preserved. Several of these sites are in the Cairnmuir Mountains near Bannockburn, the northern fringe of the Old Man Range, the Manuherikia and Ida valleys, the Maniototo, the Teviot, Kyeburn and Hawkesburn. In one hectare on the valley floor beside the south-east branch of the Hawkesburn, a large concentration of flake knives, adzes and a slate knife were found, along with remains of large ovens and middens. Moa bones have been regularly unearthed throughout the region, as have gizzard stones swallowed by the birds to help grind up their food. In addition, Oturehua, Wedderburn and Waipiata all have deposits of quartzite that Maori quarried for use in the manufacture of flake tools.

One feature of the moa bones found throughout Central Otago and in the butchering camps is that most of them had been broken open. The explanation given for this is that Maori found the bone marrow a rich food source and may have also used it as an ingredient in the preservation process they had developed.

Central Otago was never closely settled by Maori but largely remained a stopping-off place to other destinations and a moa hunting ground, until the

Examples of stone implements used by the Maori. These were tools of convenience, made from the limited materials that were available. Oturehua, Wedderburn and Waipiata were important sources of the quartzite used in their manufacture.

ALEXANDRA MUSEUM

giant bird became extinct. Close settlement was made difficult by the harsh climate and by the fact that the kumara, a fleshy sweet potato that was a staple of the Maori diet, would not grow successfully in the lower part of the South Island.

However, this did not mean that Maori were not intimately familiar with the geography and topography of Central Otago. They were certainly aware of the Lindis Pass as an entry point to the area. Maori living in the more northern areas of the South Island were also aware of the presence of precious greenstone (nephrite) deposits both on the West Coast and at the head of Lake Wakatipu, and used the pass to access them.

Life for early Maori remained hard. They were a strong, tall and vigorous people, but their average life expectancy was only 28 years, as they fell victim to illnesses such as pneumonia and to degenerative diseases. The former was a consequence of living in damp, cold, windy conditions and as hunter–gatherers, often being immersed in cold water for long periods of time. The degenerative diseases were more than likely a result of heavy lifting and general body strain caused by leading a very active outdoor life in the battle to survive.

Over time, however, the nature of Maori society changed. Although Maori in the South Island retained their nomadic lifestyle for longer than their North Island counterparts, who had generally formed into tribes by the sixteenth century, they eventually adopted a tribal social structure and moved away from living in small, mobile communities. The delay in developing tribal structures was the result of a lower population density in the south, which meant less competition for resources and therefore less of a need to seek strength and protection within a tribe. When the inhabitants of the lower South Island did form into a tribe, it may have been in part the result of influence of people who had migrated from the North Island, where tribal affiliations had formed. The tribe that arose in the South Island was called Ngai Tahu, and its members were the most scattered people of any group in the South Pacific. When the first Europeans arrived in the early 1800s, it is estimated that there was only one inhabitant for every 50 square kilometres of Otago.

These settlement patterns had the effect of lowering the occurrence of warfare in Otago. In fact, there is no evidence of warfare among Maori in Otago until the seventeenth century. This is in spite of the fact that the name 'Maniototo' in Central Otago is a derivative of the Maori word Maniatoto, meaning Plain of Blood. With no warfare to spill human blood, it is more likely that the name refers to the blood of the moa.

**OPPOSITE LEFT** When the first Europeans began to arrive in New Zealand at the beginning of the nineteenth century they found the Maori to be a proud, warlike race, confident of their ability to survive in an often harsh environment. Many of the men wore heavy facial tattoos as seen in this painting from the 1800s. The Maori were expert guerilla fighters who did not give up their land easily to the new settlers. Because of the low population in the South Island, Central Otago was never the scene of Maori fighting Europeans, as was the case in the North Island.

HOCKEN COLLECTIONS S04-272S, UNIVERSITY OF OTAGO, DUNEDIN

**OPPOSITE RIGHT** A portrait of Hariata Rongowhitiao showing the chin tattoo or moko that was worn by Maori women until the early twentieth century. The practice became unfashionable but is now undergoing a revival as Maori embrace their culture.

HOCKEN COLLECTIONS S04-272T UNIVERSITY OF OTAGO, DUNEDIN

FIRST FOOTSTEPS — MOA AND MAORI

By the time the early European runholders began to enter Central Otago in the 1850s they found an open country devoid of human settlement. This may have been the result of war parties from the North Island either killing or intimidating the few Maori who once lived around the Queenstown Lakes District. It may also have been the result of the extinction of the moa, which removed the need for Maori to travel into Central Otago to hunt this food source. Whatever the reason, absence of close settlement by Maori made the European settlement of Central Otago and the South Island very different from that of the North Island. The south did not experience the painful wars that resulted from the competition for land and power that characterised the history of the North Island, particularly in the 1860s.

## THE MOA

The extinct moa was New Zealand's link to ancient Gondwanaland. The bird's ancestry dates back tens of million of years to a time when New Zealand was part of that great continent. As a member of the ratite family of birds, the moa was closely related to the African ostrich and Australian emu. Like these two species, it was a flightless bird of great strength that preferred bush or scrub-covered country and did not move in large flocks but in small groups of four to five birds. It slept standing on one leg, laid only one or two eggs at a time and did not move around at night. The larger ones could kick like a horse with enough force to disembowel a human and often defended themselves by attempting to trample an enemy. Over the millennia they evolved into 11 different species that ranged in size from that of a goose to a huge bird that weighed 250 kg and stood 2 m tall. Central Otago was at one

OPPOSITE Skeleton of a moa found in Canterbury and assembled by its discoverer, scientist James Gault. This is a skeleton of *Dinornis giganteus*, the largest moa, a 250-kg bird that stood 2 m tall. The heavy leg bones and large feet are evidence of its ability to run very fast. As a completely flightless bird, speed was its only method of escape, but was rarely used because of a lack of predators. For thousands of years its only enemy was the now extinct Haast eagle, but this situation changed with the arrival of the Maori, and the kiore (Polynesian rats) that came to New Zealand with them in the early canoes.

HOCKEN COLLECTIONS S04-272J
UNIVERSITY OF OTAGO, DUNEDIN

LEFT Three different species of moa: *Dinornis novaezealandiae* on the left, the giant moa, *Dinornis giganteus* at centre and *Pachyornis elephantopus* on the right. Moa feathers were prized by early Maori, who wore them in their hair or wove them into cloaks.

ALEXANDRA MUSEUM

time home to seven of these 11 species, with the most common being the *Euryapteryx geranoides*, a medium-sized bird weighing some 50 kg.

Until the arrival of humans there were no land mammals to prey on moa. Their only enemy was the now extinct Haast's eagle, which with a weight of 26 kg and a 3m wingspan was quite capable of attacking and killing a moa.

By the 1700s the moa was extinct in Central Otago, and in the more remote parts of New Zealand by the early 1800s. There is no record of any European seeing a live bird. The commonly held belief is that they were hunted to extinction by the Maori, but the reasons for their demise were more complex. The moa was under stress through climatic and environmental changes long before any human set foot in New Zealand. They may have survived these changes if the kiore, or Polynesian rat, had not arrived with the Maori.

With no competition from other mammals and no predators, the kiore spread out across the South Island and the North Island in huge numbers to indulge in two of their favourite foods: moa eggs and chicks. This predation had a huge effect on the reproduction rate of the moa as the bird nested on the ground and was slow to reproduce. Coupled with this devastation was the change in environment brought about by Maori, who regularly set fire to the native vegetation on which the moa depended. The end was of course hastened by hunting. Paradoxically, the kiore was in turn devastated by the ship rat and the Norway rat, introduced into New Zealand by Europeans. The kiore is no longer found on the New Zealand mainland, now being confined to a few offshore islands. It was the first, but definitely not the last, introduced pest to devastate the ecology of Central Otago. Worse was to follow in the nineteenth century with the introduction of the feral rabbit, which in turn led to ferrets and stoats being released in an effort to control them.

# 3
# THE EXPLORERS

The first humans to see and explore Central Otago and the Queenstown Lakes District were the Maori. Several centuries were to elapse before the first European looked out over these expanses of water. His name was Nathanael Chalmers and the year was 1853. However, it was a Maori by the name of Reko who was his guide and who must be given the credit for Chalmers' success.

## NATHANAEL (NAT) CHALMERS (1830–1910)

Nathanael Chalmers was a man who happened to be in the right place at the right time. Two things came together that would help him make a name for himself as an important part of the history of Central Otago: his chance meeting with the Maori Reko, who would show him the way; and a sense of adventure. Chalmers was not a man who had an ambition to discover large areas of open grassland on which to graze mobs of sheep, nor did he have the money to finance such a project. It was simply the adventure of being the first European to explore the area that lured him into Central Otago.

Nathanael Chalmers and his brother Alexander were attracted to Otago in 1848 by the Otago Free Church Settlement, established by Captain Cargill that same year in his position as agent for the New Zealand Company. In 1848 Otago and Southland were one province and William Chalmers, Nathanael's father, had purchased for each of his sons one of the 20-hectare blocks of land that had been made available for settlement in the Clutha District. After spending time breaking in the land, both brothers were drawn to Australia by the recently discovered goldfields of Victoria, but failed to make money there as gold prospectors. Nathanael ended up in Sydney, where he bought 450 sheep in the Hunter River area, and along with a friend who owned the 70-tonne schooner *Otago*, he shipped these sheep to Oreti in Southland in 1853. These would be the first sheep in Southland,

Portrait of the early explorer, Nathanael (Nat) Chalmers (1830-1910). He was the first European to explore Central Otago, a journey that would not have been possible without the local knowledge and expert survival skills of the Southland Maori, Reko.

HOCKEN COLLECTIONS S04-272W
UNIVERSITY OF OTAGO, DUNEDIN

21

which in 1853 was called the Murihiku block — a large parcel of country the government had purchased from local Maori for 2600 pounds.

It was at this time that Chalmers met Reko, who was making a living carrying travellers across the Mataura River on his reed mokihi, or raft. Reko was familiar with the district and offered to guide Chalmers 'to look at the country up the Mataura River, as far as we could go in the direction of the Waitaki Valley', through an area as yet unseen by Europeans. Reko's price for this service was a metal cooking pot. Chalmers had no idea of the distances or the heights involved in such a trip and may have thought twice about the wisdom of the journey had he been aware of them, as he was definitely not a seasoned explorer.

In 1853 Chalmers and Reko left Southland in the company of another Maori named Kaikoura. They headed up the Mataura River, living off eels and ducks as they went, until they reached the Nevis Valley. Here they climbed the Hector Mountains and Chalmers saw what he described as a lot of water and snowy mountains a long way off. This was Lake Wakatipu, and he was the first European to see it. The men then followed the spine of the Carrick Range to its summit at Mt Difficulty, descended into the Kawarau Gorge and crossed the Kawarau River via the natural bridge, the only easy crossing point on the river, located upstream of the present-day Roaring Meg Power Station. By now Chalmers was beginning to suffer. His boots were worn out and he was covered in lacerations from the tough, sharp speargrass, wild spaniard and matagouri. More seriously, he was suffering from bad diarrhoea, which was a common ailment in early Southland, where drinking water was often swampy and the settlers were not aware of poor water as a source of infection.

Once over the Kawarau River, the three men followed it downstream to where Cromwell is now located. There they changed direction and headed for Lake Wanaka. Crossing the Clutha at Wanaka using a koari (flax) raft, they reached Lake Hawea. By now Chalmers was in such poor physical condition that his only desire was to return home by the fastest possible route. This meant using the Clutha River, and Reko built a raft from hundreds of dry flax flower stems gathered on the shores of Lake Hawea. The wild ride down the Clutha and through the Cromwell Gorge stunned Chalmers by its speed. Four days

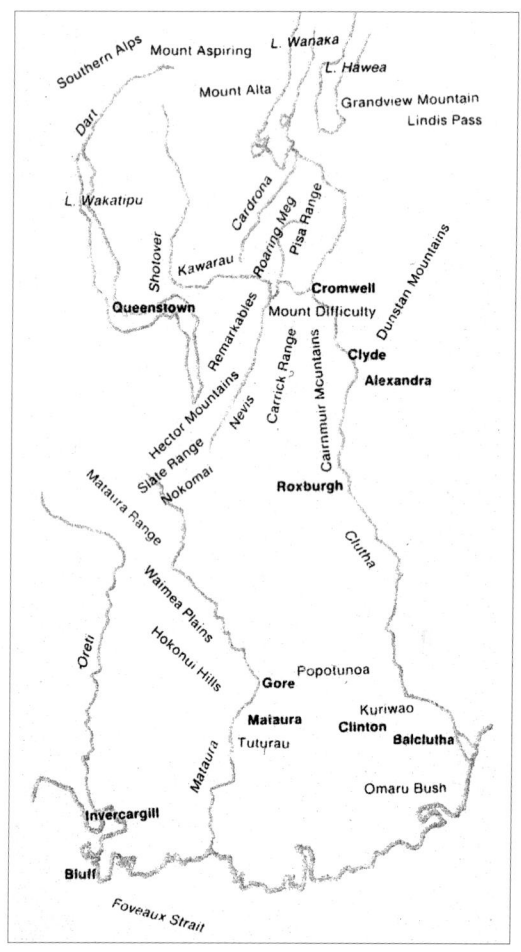

This small map shows the main points on the route taken by explorers Reko, Nathanael Chalmers and Kaikoura during their journey through Central Otago in 1853.

LAND INFORMATION NEW ZEALAND

later the three men landed at Te Houka, a few kilometres upstream from Balclutha. In three weeks the small party had made a round trip of 500 km. The credit for the success of the trip must go to the experience and knowledge of Reko, with Chalmers just following along, but it was the latter who is remembered for the achievement.

This was Nathanael Chalmers' first and last exploration. Within 10 years the whole of Central Otago would be surveyed and taken over by sheep runs and goldminers. In 1856 he married and took up a share in a sheep run, and then moved to Invercargill, where he became involved in provincial politics as Southland's first treasurer. In 1864 he left New Zealand to begin cotton growing and sugar milling in Fiji. He finished his working career as a stipendiary magistrate and died there in 1910.

Reko simply returned to his old life ferrying travellers across the Mataura River. In 1856 he drew a map on the dirt floor of his whare showing the way to Central Otago for the explorer and surveyor John Turnbull Thomson, and this mud map began a new stage in the exploration of the area.

The rock formation and natural bridge on the Kawarau River, located a short distance upstream from the Roaring Meg Power Station, between Cromwell and Queenstown. The entire flow of the river once passed through a channel 2 m wide at this point. With its span widened by later floods, this rock bridge was once an important crossing point for Maori and European explorers.

CROMWELL MUSEUM

## JOHN TURNBULL THOMSON (1821–1884)

John Turnbull Thomson, or Mr Surveyor Thomson as he was often called, was a man who had an enormous influence in the formation and identification of early Central Otago. Appointed chief surveyor of Otago and Southland in 1856, he was to survey the then unmapped interior of Otago. While carrying out this task he found himself in a position to name many of the features of the area. Most of those names have withstood the test of time and are still in use today.

Thomson was born in England in 1821 at Glororum farm, Northumberland, which overlooks the castle of Bamborough. To the west of the farm lay the ancient, holy island of Lindisfarne. His grandparents were from the Scottish Lowlands and owned a farm called Earnslaw, located north of Coldstream. His grandfather, James Thomson, was the Laird of Earnslaw, who in the 1790s developed a popular breed of sheep called the Border Leicester. Young John Thomson spent a number of holidays on Earnslaw and came to know it well. At other

THE EXPLORERS | 23

times he also visited his mother's family home in the valley of Abbey St Bathans. These names will be familiar to those who know Central Otago. St Bathans in the Maniototo, the Lindis Pass at the northern edge of Central Otago and Mt Earnslaw to the north of Lake Wakatipu are all places named by Thomson. Although it did not exist in Thomson's time, the old steamer *Earnslaw*, which still operates today as a tourist craft on Lake Wakatipu, would have been so named as a result of Thomson's earlier influence.

Trained as a surveyor and engineer at Aberdeen University and the Newcastle School of Engineering, Thomson left England for Malaysia at the tender age of 16. His intelligence is obvious from the fact that he held these qualifications at such a young age. At 21 he was appointed government surveyor of Singapore and was responsible for mapping and laying out much of that island city. His health suffered in the tropics, and in 1856, while looking for a cooler climate, he arrived in Auckland, where he was offered the position of chief surveyor of the new province of Otago at an annual salary of 600 pounds. From Auckland he travelled by ship to Dunedin, which in 1856 was so undeveloped that it was referred to as Mud-edin. Thomson would spend the greater part of his life in Otago and Southland, marry and raise a family of nine daughters.

When he arrived in Dunedin to take up his new position his first task was to decide on sites and then lay out the proposed towns of Invercargill and Bluff. From his papers, which are now in the National Archives in Wellington, it can be seen how seriously he took his work and how important it was for him to make an initial reconnaissance of the area to be surveyed. On his first trip to Invercargill Thomson met Reko, the man who was able to explain the unmapped interior of Central Otago to the new surveyor.

The year 1857 was a busy one for Thomson. In October he travelled inland to Central Otago, stopping at the now defunct Taieri Lake, once located at the confluence of the Taieri and Kyeburn rivers near Waipiata. By November Thomson had ventured as far inland as the Manuherikia River, before returning to Dunedin at the end of that month. From this trip he estimated the area of pastoral land in the interior that he was required to survey to be around six million hectares. On 7 December 1857 he left Dunedin to explore the headwaters of the Clutha and Waitaki rivers. Following directions given by Reko, he set off up the Waitaki Valley and 10 days later crossed into Central Otago by way of the Lindis Pass, which he named. He camped on Black Knob mountain, which he renamed Grandview. The latter name was appropriate because from where he stood he had a grand view of lakes Hawea and Wanaka. In front of him lay the plains of the Upper

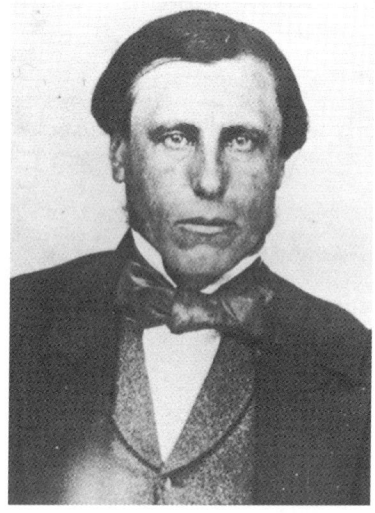

John Turnbull Thomson (1821–1884), explorer, surveyor, artist, engineer, architect, father of nine daughters and the man who had a huge influence in the surveying, naming and development of early Central Otago.

ALEXANDRA MUSEUM

Clutha and a high mountain, which he named Pisa because it had a huge leaning rock on its summit that reminded him of the leaning Tower of Pisa. After Thomson tried unsuccessfully to cross the flooded Clutha River, he backtracked through the Lindis Pass, travelled further north and became the first European to see Aoraki Mt Cook. He also named Mt Aspiring and the Twizel River.

When he had completed his survey of the Waitaki Basin, Thomson tried to cross back into Central Otago via the Hawkdun Range but ran into bad weather, which delayed him and forced his return to the coast for provisions. He then headed inland to the Taieri River. This last trip gave him enough information to compile his reconnaissance map of Otago, so he left it to his assistants, Alexander Garvie and James McKerrow, to fill in the gaps. Garvie surveyed Central Otago while McKerrow completed a survey of the Queenstown Lakes District. Thomson's explorations were published in two Otago newspapers, and the details he gave encouraged settlers to stock large areas of Central Otago with sheep, thus leading to the establishment of the early runs. Although he did not do the survey work, Thomson was responsible for naming the newly surveyed area, and it was at this point that a large number of the present-day Central Otago names came into being. Many related back to his childhood home in Northumberland.

Mt Ida and the Idaburn stream he named after Ida, a legendary chief who once lived in Bamborough Castle. The Lammermoor Range was named after St Cuthbert, the shepherd boy from the Lammermuir Hills, who became the bishop of Lindisfarne. The name of the Dunstan Mountains was derived from Dunstanburgh Castle, while Beaumont relates to Beaumont Water.

When it was time to name the tributaries of the Taieri River, Thomson wanted to preserve names the Maori had given them: Te Aruhe-a-hope, Te Awa-kauru, Wai-pakurakura, etc. The European settlers objected because they thought these were too difficult to pronounce. It is a common misunderstanding that Thomson took this rejection badly and reverted to using the names of farm animals instead, but this is unlikely as many of the animal names were also in use in the Border Country of England. If they had not been appropriate, the names could have been vetoed in the same manner as the Maori ones. Thomson named 12 of the 14 streams that flow into the Taieri River after animals: Eweburn, Fillyburn, Gimmerburn, Hogburn, Horseburn, Houndburn, Kyeburn, Mareburn, Sowburn, Stotburn, Swinburn and Wetherburn. The Poolburn was named after its appearance, while the name Manorburn came from a parish of the same name in Northumbria.

Not content to stop there, Thomson named Blackstone Hills for their appearance and Corbies Rock in the Hawkdun Range after an area in the Borders where a raven is called a corbie. The name Hawkdun itself is also a Border name meaning Hawk Heights. Chatto (Creek) was a residence in Roxburghshire, Earnscleugh a stream in Berwickshire and Lauder a village in the same location. Roxburgh, Ettrick and Cardrona are all villages on the Scottish border. He also named the Raggedy Range, Rough Ridge and the Rock and Pillar after their appearance. The Styx is, in mythology, the name of one of the five rivers in the underworld. Lawrence and Clyde were named after English generals involved in the Indian Mutiny, while Cromwell was a general in the English Civil War and Naseby was a battle in that war, as well as being the name of an English town. One name that people are still trying to figure out is that which Thomson gave to Tiger Hill, located some two kilometres south of Omakau. Thomson himself is remembered at Thomson's Gorge, the gorge that runs through the Dunstan Mountains from Matakanui to Bendigo. Mt Turnbull and Mt Thomson in the Southern Alps are also named after him. Further recognition was given to his work when a waterfall at the base of Mt Aspiring was named the Turnbull Thomson Falls in 1980.

Thomson also reported on the farming and mining potential of the land he had surveyed. As a trained observer he discovered gold in the Lindis River, four years before the official discovery of gold in Central Otago by Gabriel Read. He was also chief engineer of Otago, and in this capacity laid out the main roads of Central Otago and was responsible for designing bridges to span the Taieri, Clutha and Shotover rivers. Thomson was a gifted artist, and many of his survey sketches became subjects of his later paintings. He was also an accomplished architect and writer.

In 1876 Thomson accepted an invitation to become surveyor general of New Zealand, based in Wellington. In this capacity he toured New Zealand extensively putting a national survey system in place. Thomson experienced tough conditions while surveying Otago and elsewhere in New Zealand. He describes these conditions thus: 'after being wet all day in crossing the swollen creeks and making our way through high wet grass and scrub, we had to camp on the wet ground at night' (in John Hall-Jones, *Mr Surveyor Thomson*). He retired in 1879 to his home near Invercargill, and by 1884 he was dead, his early demise possibly hastened by those tough conditions

# 4
# THE EARLY RUNHOLDERS — 1857–1910

In 1857 large areas of Central Otago were wide open for settlement. The land was mainly covered in native tussock and grassland with some fern and matagouri, ideal sheep country for those with the capital and skills to take it on and farm it successfully. The Waste Lands Act of 1855 set the guidelines for the issue of grazing licences of large open areas that were and are still referred to as runs. Each run was given a number, and anybody could apply to take up a run of their choice provided they were prepared to pay a small annual fee plus a tax per 1000 head of livestock over and above an initial 5000. Tenure was poor, poorer than leasehold, and is best described as grazing rights for a period of 14 years. These rights could be cancelled with compensation at any time if the run was required for closer settlement. Anybody settling on a run was able to freehold only 32 hectares of land of their choice on which to build a homestead and a further 4 hectares as an outstation. Size and boundaries of the properties were vague, fences were mostly non-existent and stock had to be kept from straying by shepherds. Once runs were taken up, the runholders had to stock the land in order to show that they were genuine pastoralists and not simply speculators looking to on-sell the grazing rights. If the runs were not promptly stocked, the grazing rights lapsed and the land went back into the common pool.

In spite of these conditions, there was no shortage of applicants to lease the runs. Those who were successful, however, required capital to purchase stock, erect buildings, pay wages and often initially support themselves and their families without an income. Because of these costs, many of the runs were taken up by wealthy absentee landlords or partnerships in order to provide the necessary capital. As a result, large areas of Central Otago ended up in the hands of a few, and it was not until the late 1800s that the government began to take steps to break up these runs for closer settlement.

Although hundreds of runs were settled, four names stand out among those involved in the history of the early runs in Central Otago: William Rees, Nicholas von Tunzelmann and the brothers John (Jock) and Allan McLean.

## THE FOUNDER OF QUEENSTOWN — WILLIAM GILBERT REES (1827–1898)

William Rees, or King Wakatip as he was often called, was the first European to settle the area that is now the modern tourist town of Queenstown, where some of New Zealand's most expensive real estate is currently located. His influence was such that he is remembered today by a large statue located at the lake end of the mall in Queenstown where his homestead and woolshed once stood, and also by a plaque on the stone wall that fronts Lake Wakatipu at this point.

Rees was born in Haverfordwest in the United Kingdom in 1827, into a talented but relatively poor family, whose occupations included barrister, painter, dramatist, naval officer, writer, headmaster, mathematician and historian. His naval officer father died from yellow fever while at sea when Rees was only 12, and his widowed mother moved to Bristol, where he was educated at the Royal Naval School. When Rees left school, he worked as an engineer's apprentice and then as a teacher. In March 1852, at the age of 25, he joined the thousands of English, Scots, Welsh and Irish who were flooding out of the United Kingdom seeking a better life, when he emigrated to Australia on the ship *Mary Anne*. On arrival in Australia, he tried his hand unsuccessfully at gold prospecting and then became manager of a sheep and cattle station called Stonehenge on the Darling Downs near Toowoomba in Queensland. It was here that he met the son of a wealthy squatter, George Gammie, who in turn introduced him to a London-based investor, Colonel William Grant. These two men became Rees's partners, and this partnership would eventually take up all the sheep runs on the eastern side of Lake Wakatipu.

Now aged 31, Rees returned briefly to England, where he married his cousin, Frances Gilbert. The couple then left for New Zealand aboard the *Equator* to seek their fortune, arriving in Wellington on 22 January 1859. His long career in New Zealand began when he and Frances moved immediately to the South Island. In the years that followed, Rees

William Gilbert Rees (1827–1898) was the first European to settle the site that would become Queenstown. With a homestead and woolshed located on the shores of Lake Wakatipu, he and his family were forced to move on when the land they occupied was required to establish Queenstown to cater for the miners who flooded into the area when gold was discovered nearby in 1862.

HOCKEN COLLECTIONS S04-272X, UNIVERSITY OF OTAGO, DUNEDIN

was to found, rule and then lose a pastoral empire. His ambitions lay in the relatively unknown and unexplored tract of country south of Lake Wanaka, and he began to plan a trip into this part of Central Otago while living in a cottage near Waikouaiti, which he rented from the legendary whaler turned businessman, Johnny Jones. Local Maori had told the settlers of the existence of the large area of water that came to be known as Lake Wakatipu, but which had not been explored by Europeans.

In January 1860 Rees, with his brother-in-law, Nicholas von Tunzelmann, left Dunedin in the company of four other men and headed inland via the Waitaki Valley. Von Tunzelmann would eventually become the other person to feature in the early settlement of Lake Wakatipu. His father was a wealthy major in the Russian army and the mighty Czar Nicholas I was his godfather. These two fell out over the young von Tunzelmann being sent to Germany to be educated. The power of the czar was such that the family was forced to abandon their estates and was given 24 hours to leave Russia. Von Tunzelmann was educated in Paris and Edinburgh. By the time he landed in New Zealand and joined forces with William Rees, he was a qualified veterinarian.

The party crossed into Central Otago via the Lindis Pass on 4 February 1860. Four members were not impressed by the country they were entering and left to return to Dunedin. Rees and von Tunzelmann carried on until they came to a fast-flowing river, which Rees named the Shotover after his partner George Gammie's English residence, Shotover House. From there both men explored right up the lake to Glenorchy and while retracing their steps began to set fire to the fern to clear the way for the sheep they intended to drive into the area.

On their return to Dunedin they faced the problem of gaining a grazing licence for the area, as there were prior applications for the Wakatipu runs. The fact that they had visited the area gave them an advantage, and each man was successful in securing the run of his choice. Rees and his partners, Gammie and Grant, were granted grazing rights of Run 346 at the top of the eastern side of Lake Wakatipu and Run 356, which included present-day Queenstown and Arrowtown, a total of 62,000 hectares. Von Tunzelmann secured a run on the western side of the lake. There is a common misconception that the choice of runs by the two men was settled by the toss of a coin, but this is not the case as both applied for and secured the land they preferred.

Once the grazing rights were granted, Rees and von Tunzelmann

A pencil drawing of Frances Rees, completed in October 1858 while she was on board a ship bound for New Zealand. As the wife of William Rees she was the first European woman to settle at Lake Wakatipu. Her nickname was Frank, and Frankton — the area that would become a suburb of Queenstown — was named after her.

HOCKEN COLLECTIONS S04-272Y, UNIVERSITY OF OTAGO, DUNEDIN

THE EARLY RUNHOLDERS — 1857–1910

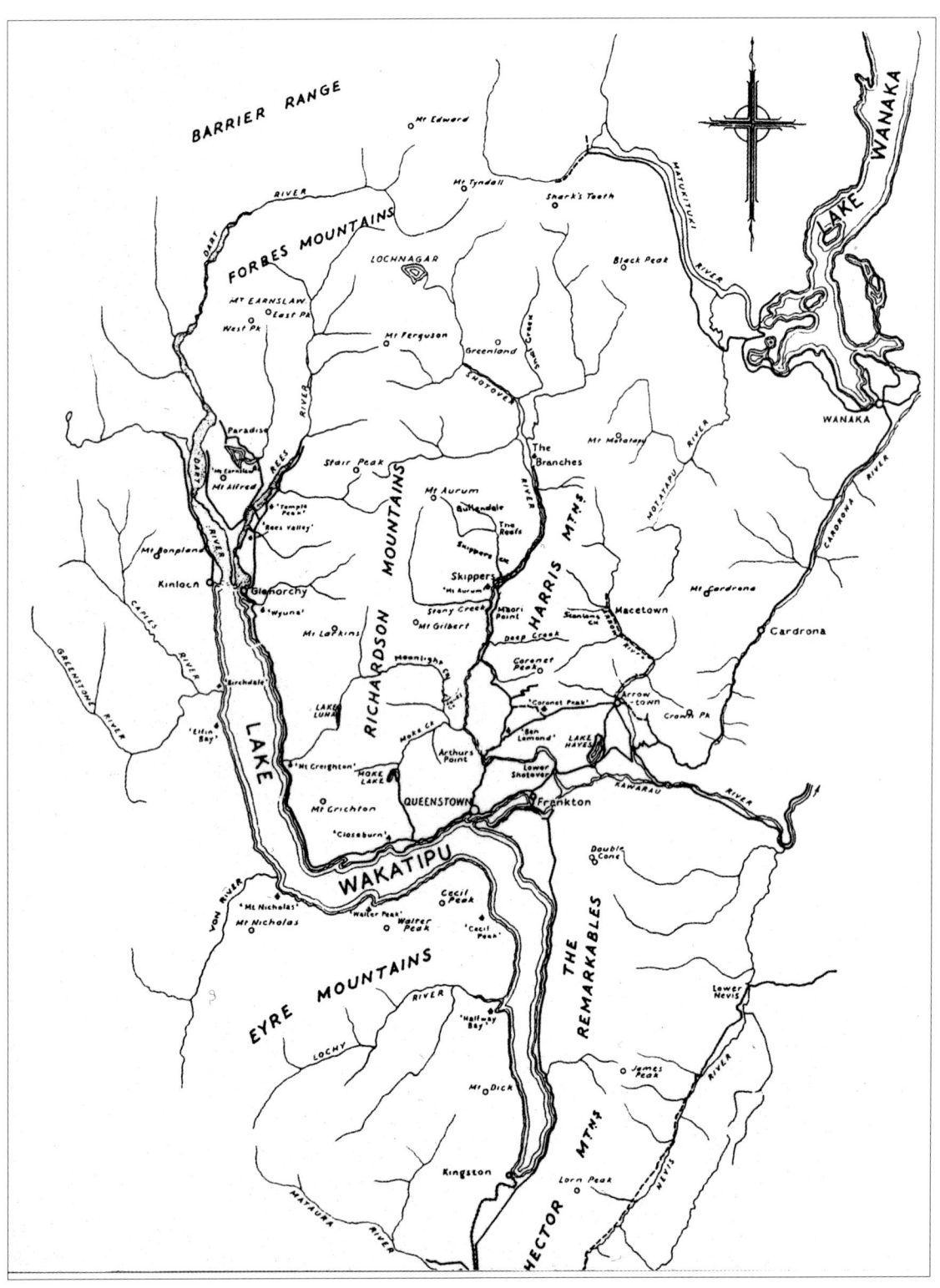

OPPOSITE Map of lakes Wakatipu and Wanaka. When Rees and his two partners' landholdings were at their height, they held the grazing rights of all that area on the eastern side of Lake Wakatipu, from the Rees River at the head of the lake to Kingston at its tail. Von Tunzelmann's run was on the west side of the lake, near the Greenstone River.

ALEXANDRA MUSEUM

ABOVE Nicholas von Tunzelmann, son of a Russian aristocrat, veterinarian, brother-in-law of William Rees and a runholder in his own right, with interests that included dancing, singing, playing the violin and yodelling. It was he who explored and settled the Wakatipu District with William Rees. Von Tunzelmann's preference was for the western shore of Lake Wakatipu where he established a run near the Greenstone River. Like William Rees, his tenure as a large runholder was a short one.

OTAGO SETTLERS MUSEUM 017, DUNEDIN

made arrangements to drove in 3000 merino sheep that Rees and his partners had imported from Australia to stock the runs. The two men moved these sheep overland via the Maniototo Plain, Thomsons Gorge and Cardrona, swimming the large, cold rivers as they went. On arrival, Rees built his house and outbuildings at what is now the end of the mall opposite the wharf in present-day Queenstown. Von Tunzelmann set up on the other side of the lake, taking the grazing rights of Run 350 near the Greenstone River. His property comprised some 20,000 hectares, and a lavishly furnished two-storied house he called Fernhill was built in partnership with his brother John. Sadly, the run did not prosper. Scab — an infectious disease that badly affects sheep — broke out, and rabbits later infested the land. The brothers lost thousands of sheep to scab and eventually went bankrupt. John became a schoolteacher, while Nicholas, after spending time in Australia where he attempted to establish an orange and banana plantation, returned to an 80-hectare property near Walter Peak, on the western side of Lake Wakatipu, and eked out a living there until he died in 1900. He was known as a gentle person, with a charming personality, completely unsuited to life as a runholder. His interests lay in singing, playing the violin, yodelling and dancing. Today the Von River, Mt Nicholas and some descendants are all that are left to remind people of the exploits of Nicholas von Tunzelmann.

Over the three years following the time he stocked his first run, Rees and his partners bought up other grazing rights, until their pastoral empire spanned the whole eastern shore of Lake Wakatipu from Glenorchy to Kingston, a total of four runs covering 97,000 hectares. Rees and his wife Frances must have thought they had found paradise, but their peace did not last. The discovery of gold at Gabriels Gully in 1861 and on the Clutha River near Cromwell in 1862 had extreme consequences for Rees and his family. By 1867 their golden days were over, and in the same year Rees quit Lake Wakatipu to work as a stock inspector for the government. He was still working for wages when he died in Marlborough at the top of the South Island in 1898, of gallstone complications and peritonitis, aged 71.

The fact that Rees died in obscurity does not detract from his enormous contribution to the successful settlement of Queenstown. When the goldminers rushed to the area in 1862, they did so with little thought as to how they were going to survive. Rees supplied them with meat and used his three boats to transport provisions, building materials

THE EARLY RUNHOLDERS — 1857–1910 | 31

and other necessities of life up the lake from Kingston. This was not an act of charity, as he was quick to profit from the miners' needs and was often accused of running an overpriced monopoly. However, without his help it is doubtful if the miners would have survived long enough to establish Queenstown.

Rees was also a prolific name-giver, and many of the names he gave to various locations in the Wakatipu area are still in use today. The Arrow and Dart rivers were so named because of their swiftness; Diamond Lake for its clear sparkle; Moke Creek and Moke Lake after an old mule that he owned; and Simpson's Creek after the run's cook, who must have been a good one to be so honoured. Coronet Peak he named for a rock formation and the Crown Range for the group of rocks on the summit. The Rees River he named after himself. Other features in the district were named after the Rees family. Cecil Peak and Walter Peak on Lake Wakatipu were named after Rees's infant son Cecil Walter, by the surveyor James McKerrow. Frankton was the name given to the area by Sir John Richardson, superintendent of Otago, in 1861, after Frances Rees, whose nickname was Frank. Three of the best known names in the area came from other sources. Queenstown was named at a public meeting

**BELOW LEFT** The *Earnslaw* as it appears today. Designed and built as a workhorse to carry cargo and passengers, this steam-powered vessel has been refitted and now caters for tourists wishing to cruise Lake Wakatipu and visit various attractions on its shores.

**BELOW RIGHT** A bronze statue of William Rees has been erected in his memory in Queenstown, close to the wharf and a few metres from where he built his woolshed in the 1860s. Standing beside him is a merino ram, the hardy, fine wool breed of sheep that he and von Tunzelmann introduced to the area.

RIGHT ABOVE Kawarau Falls, the point where the waters of Lake Wakatipu leave the lake to form the Kawarau River and begin their journey to the sea on the east coast. This is how the falls would have appeared to William Rees, before a dam and bridge were built there in the early twentieth century in an abortive attempt to stem the flow of the Kawarau River, to aid the search for gold.

HOCKEN COLLECTIONS 505-045B,
UNIVERSITY OF OTAGO, DUNEDIN

RIGHT BELOW Queenstown in the 1870s was a far cry from the modern, vibrant resort it is today. This street is now a mall of smart cafés, souvenir and specialty shops located in the heart of Queenstown.

HOCKEN COLLECTIONS S04-2720
UNIVERSITY OF OTAGO, DUNEDIN

convened for the purpose in 1863 and The Remarkables for their unusual shape, by the surveyor Alexander Garvie. Lake Wakatipu was a name given by the local Maori long before the arrival of the European, and comes from waka tipua, trough of the giant.

The influx of goldminers and the attractiveness of where Rees had built his homestead were the beginning of the end of his pastoral empire. The land was wanted for settlement, and as a result the grazing right of

THE EARLY RUNHOLDERS — 1857–1910 | 33

**ABOVE** The retail area of Queenstown was flooded when Lake Wakatipu rose on 1 October 1898. This was something that William Rees and those who followed him did not allow for when choosing to build on this attractive but flood-prone shore of the lake. This section of Queenstown has been flooded many times since the photograph was taken and continues to flood at regular intervals.

HOCKEN COLLECTIONS S04-272A'

**LEFT** Queenstown in the 1880s, looking from the direction of the wharf. At the front right is Eichardts Hotel, which was built on the site of William Rees's woolshed. With only part of that building now operating as a hotel, the façade has been retained but the interior has been changed and renovated.

HOCKEN COLLECTIONS S04-272P'

Run 356 was cancelled. Compensation was paid, but after the amount given had been split among the three partners, Rees received very little. Rees tried to freehold the 32 hectares he was entitled to under the terms of the grazing right as that area around his homestead, which would have included the developing village of Queenstown, but this proposal was rejected. He was now faced with the decision and costs of re-establishing himself and his family on one of the other runs, but by 1866 these grazing rights had only a few years to their expiry date, with no automatic right of renewal.

Rees and his partners must have weighed up the financial wisdom of remaining with the status quo and decided against it. This decision was probably hastened by the harm done to their runs by rabbits, a slump in wool prices and the presence of scab among the flocks. The formal partnership was dissolved and the three partners went their separate ways.

All Rees had left was a homestead, located near where his statue now stands in Queenstown. This he sold in 1866 to the wealthy merchant Bendix Hallenstein for 80 pounds.

## MORVEN HILLS STATION FROM 1858 TO 1874

Morven Hills Station was the combination of four runs on which grazing rights were granted in 1858 to members of the McLean family. At its peak Morven Hills comprised 143,000 hectares that extended from the Ahuriri River in the north, to the shores of Lake Hawea and the banks of the Clutha River in the west, the Dunstan Mountains in the east and Leaning Rock Creek in the Cromwell Gorge in the south. Within its boundaries lay Bendigo, Logantown and Welshtown, which included the site of one of New Zealand's richest quartz mines. In 1874, before the rabbit plague took hold, Morven Hills ran a total of 135,000 sheep. Numbers varied as it was not unusual for a run of this size to lose 40,000 sheep to snow in a bad winter.

Morven Hills was to have a big influence on the development of Central Otago. Many of the settlers

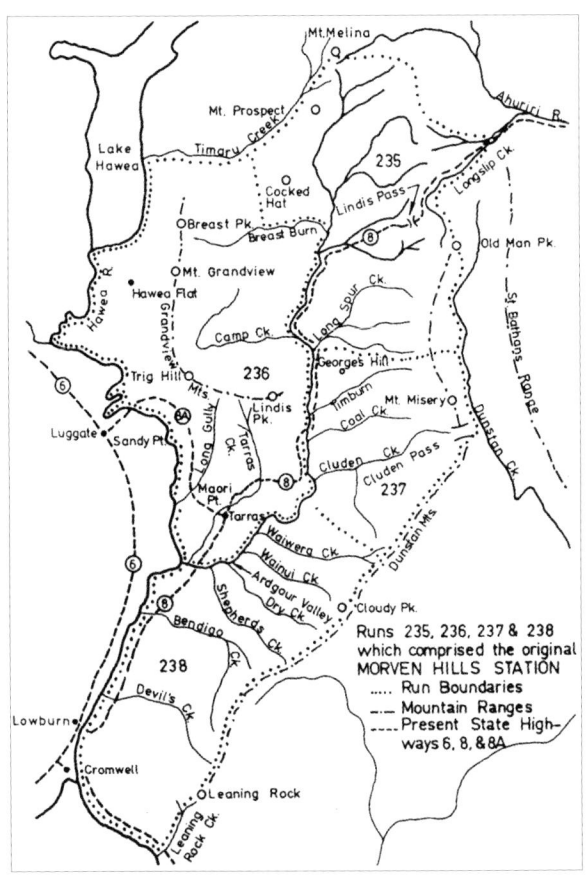

Four runs, numbered 235–238, were combined by the McLean family in 1858 to form the mighty Morven Hills Station, a property which ran merino sheep and whose boundaries stretched from the Ahuriri River in the Waitaki Valley through to the Cromwell Gorge in Central Otago. It was on the extreme southern edge of the property, in the Cromwell Gorge, that Hartley and Reilly made their now famous gold discovery in 1862.

LAND INFORMATION NEW ZEALAND

THE EARLY RUNHOLDERS — 1857–1910 | 35

who went on to farm their own properties on the area gained their basic training while working on the property. John McLean, using the profits he made from the run, built a home near Oamaru that would eventually become St Kevin's College, the Catholic boarding school where young people from Central Otago are still educated.

## JOHN (JOCK) MCLEAN (1818–1902)

This man was the driving force behind the establishment of Morven Hills Station. He followed closely in the footsteps of the surveyor John Thomson when, in the autumn of 1858, he stood on the slopes of Grandview and saw for the first time the land that would become Morven Hills. Impressed by what he saw, he made an application for a grazing right in the area on his return to Dunedin.

John McLean was born in 1818 on the island of Coll in the Scottish Inner Hebrides, where his father was a crofter. When his father died, John took over the family farm but faced a life of poverty and hardship. To escape this depressing future, he and his mother, along with his two brothers, packed up and emigrated to Australia. In Australia the family's fortunes began to change for the better, but being used to the wetter climate of Scotland they never felt comfortable dryland farming in their adopted country. In 1852 they sold their Australian property and bought two substantial farms in Canterbury. When a Maori told John of the existence of the great tracts of unsettled land in Central Otago, he set out with a packhorse to see for himself.

ABOVE The Honourable John (Jock) McLean (1818–1902), reluctant politician and wealthy part-owner of Morven Hills Station from 1858 to 1874. When he died at his home, Redcastle, in Oamaru in 1902, his house was inherited by a nephew and later became part of St Kevin's College, a Catholic school that educated several generations of Central Otago youth.

OTAGO SETTLERS MUSEUM 02, DUNEDIN

LEFT Horses were the only means of transport and power on the early runs, and much time and effort went into growing chaff and hay to feed them. A run could not survive without some flat land to grow these crops, which were also required to feed sheep in the winter when the ground was often covered in snow for weeks at a time.

Allan McLean, brother of John McLean and co-owner of the huge 143,000-hectare Morven Hills run in Central Otago between the years 1858 and 1874. Born in 1820 into a family of crofters on the island of Coll in the Scottish Inner Hebrides, he became one of early New Zealand's wealthiest men.

OTAGO SETTLERS MUSEUM 026, DUNEDIN

**LEFT** Morven Hills Station woolshed was an impressive building, pictured here in 1902 when Frederick Dalgety leased the run. Built of stone, it had indoor holding pens (on the left of the photograph), which were used to keep sheep dry overnight so that shearers could make an early start after a night of heavy dew or rain. Seventeen openings can be seen on the long section of the shed, which meant that there was room for the same number of shearers to work inside at the one time. Once a sheep was shorn it was let go down a chute. Each lower, square opening seen here is an exit for one of these chutes.

HOCKEN COLLECTIONS S04-272N, UNIVERSITY OF OTAGO, DUNEDIN

The Waste Land Board was unwilling to grant John the sole grazing rights of such a large area of land, so each member of the McLean family made a separate application and were granted the grazing rights of four adjacent runs that were then amalgamated to make up Morven Hills Station. John and his brother Allan took the responsibility of managing the huge station. Temporary corrugated iron buildings were constructed as living quarters, followed later by a large stone homestead and a 34-stand stone woolshed. Shepherds were employed to look after the flocks of sheep, and in its early days Morven Hills employed 16 shepherds, all from the Scottish Highlands, who spoke only their native Gaelic. Wages for a shepherd were one pound a week, plus free tea, salt, sugar, flour and meat. Oddly, vegetables were not included; they were expected to grow their own.

Farming was not easy in this remote location. Heavy snowfalls had to be contended with and many sheep were killed through eating tutu, a poisonous plant that grew wild on the property. Others fell victim to wild dogs that were left behind to fend for themselves when their goldminer owners moved to new discoveries. Then there were the rabbit plague and low returns for wool, which combined during the depression of the 1880s to put many of the runholders, especially the ones who were heavily mortgaged, out of business. Those who could not cope with the rabbits simply walked off their properties, and it was often left to the stock firms in Dunedin, who held the mortgages, to sort out the problems left behind. As a result, the stock firms became unwilling runholders themselves.

In 1862, life on Morven Hills was complicated by the discovery of gold in Central Otago. Miners swarmed all over the property in their search

**ABOVE** A typical Central Otago shearing gang in the 1860s. Shearers were not employed full-time by the runholder, but moved from station to station, hoping to secure work during the season. The men in the middle of the photograph with watchchains and nonchalant postures are not shearers but foremen or run managers. The Maori shearer in the middle of the front row is interesting for the 1860s. Maori embraced modern shearing as an occupation and now make up the majority of the shearing gangs in Central Otago.

HOCKEN COLLECTIONS S04-272E, UNIVERSITY OF OTAGO, DUNEDIN

**LEFT** A portrait of a typical musterer who worked the high-country runs in the late 1800s. Musterers still do this work today, though their mode of dress is more casual. Their working dogs have changed very little, however. Willing, loyal and affectionate, the intelligent breeds now seen throughout Central Otago look exactly the same as those pictured here.

HOCKEN COLLECTIONS S04-272H, UNIVERSITY OF OTAGO, DUNEDIN

**OPPOSITE TOP** Hand-clippers like these were one of the most important pieces of equipment on the early runs. Without them it would have been impossible to relieve sheep of their wool. Laborious to use, they were replaced by electric clippers that sped up the process and clipped the wool closer to the sheep's skin.

for the precious metal, stole the runholders' sheep, grazed their own stock without permission, lit fires and generally disrupted station life. John McLean resented their intrusion to the point where he forbade his staff to give any food or shelter to the intruders.

John entered political life in 1867 when he was elected to the Legislative Council, and he gave up the day-to-day management of Morven Hills to spend time in Wellington when the council was sitting. It was during these years that he built the house in Oamaru that would become St Kevin's College. In 1874 the McLean clan decided to sell Morven Hills and dissolve the family partnership. Allan McLean eventually retired to Christchurch, where he built a palatial home called Holly Lea. He died there in 1907, leaving this house 'to become a home for women of refinement and education in reduced or straitened circumstances'. John McLean gave up politics and retired to Oamaru, but kept an active interest in local affairs. He died in 1902 at the age of 84.

RIGHT Holly Lea, the house built in Christchurch in 1900 for Allan McLean, one of the owners of Morven Hills Station, contained 54 rooms, and included a great hall that was 14 m in height. It was sumptuously furnished with Sheraton furniture and the internal walls were decorated under the supervision of a French fabric expert brought from Paris for the purpose. With an arcade gallery, rising through three floors, all linen used throughout the house carried the McLean crest. Two hectares surrounded the house, bounded by brick walls and iron gates. Allan McLean had no wife or family to enjoy the opulence he created and on his death willed the house 'to become a home for women of refinement and education in reduced or straitened circumstances'.

CANTERBURY MUSEUM, CHRISTCHURCH

**LEFT ABOVE** Merino, the fine-wool sheep imported from Australia, was the breed the early runholders used to stock their runs. Originally from Spain, it is a unique breed, well able to handle rough high country, poor pasture and difficult conditions. Merinos have two weaknesses: they are prone to a debilitating infection called footrot if their pasture is constantly damp; and ewes will often abandon their newborn lambs for trivial reasons, such as the weather being too cold. The merino was the breed responsible for bringing the once fatal disease of hydatids into New Zealand. With vigilant dosing of dogs in the latter half of the twentieth century, to break the lifecycle of the hydatid worm, the disease has now been eradicated from this country. This merino ram has the characteristics of his breed — strong curved horns and neck folds.

**LEFT BELOW** Forty-six bales of wool, part of the clip from Morven Hills Station on its way to Kurow via the Lindis Pass. Bullocks, although slower, were stronger than horses and were often used to pull a wagon of this weight over a rough track. They were also calmer than horses, less likely to take fright, and could be controlled by one man walking beside the wagon wielding a long whip. The whip was not used on the bullocks, but was cracked in the air. This, plus the use of a loud voice and a strong vocabulary of swear words by the bullock driver, was usually enough to keep the animals focused.

MANIOTOTO EARLY SETTLERS MUSEUM

## MORVEN HILLS STATION FROM 1874 TO 1910

The new owner of Morven Hills Station, a Colonel Whitmore, bought the property from the McLeans in 1874. He held it for only a few weeks before selling it to a man named Cogle who also owned Lauder Station on the opposite side of the Dunstan Range from Morven Hills. A year later the property was sold to Frederick Dalgety and his associate, Charles Nichols, and for the next 34 years Morven Hills was to remain part of what came to be known as the Dalgety empire.

Frederick Dalgety was a Scotsman who had made a fortune in Australia. He was the founder of the well known stock and station company that operated in New Zealand and Australia until recent times. Under Dalgetys' ownership, Morven Hills had a succession of managers, who in turn reported to the manager of Dalgetys in Dunedin. By the early 1880s the rabbit plague had begun to seriously affect the profitability of Morven Hills and after a number of years led to the abandonment of large parts of the station. The situation was not helped when half of the sheep on the property were killed in a huge snowstorm in 1895.

ABOVE With little in the way of timber available in Central Otago to fence the early runs, other materials had to be used. Here a flat piece of schist rock has been used as a fencepost with holes bored for the wire. This unique use of stone was commonplace on Central Otago properties well into the twentieth century and today they can still be seen throughout the region.

RIGHT Horse power provided by a team of horses such as these fine Clydesdales was vital on the early runs. Without them it would have been impossible to harvest the fodder crops needed to sustain sheep through the Central Otago winters. No longer used commercially, these gentle and intelligent animals are today kept by enthusiasts and paraded in full harness on special occasions.

THE EARLY RUNHOLDERS — 1857–1910 | 41

A camping party on Morven Hills Station in 1903, a few years before it was broken up for closer settlement in 1910.

HOCKEN COLLECTIONS S04-2, UNIVERSITY OF OTAGO, DUNEDIN

For several decades, political pressure had been building on the government to legislate for the break up of large properties like Morven Hills into smaller blocks for closer settlement. For Morven Hills this was the beginning of the end. In 1910 impending forced subdivision saw the flock of 68,000 merino and half-bred sheep mustered and sold at a clearing sale at nearby Tarras. The disposal of the stock and chattels of Morven Hills Station took only three hours. When it was over, one of Central Otago's earliest grazing properties no longer existed.

Under government legislation the property was subdivided into smaller units, which were in turn balloted and taken up by the successful ballot winners. The name Morven still exists today on land that was once part of the station. Morven Downs was one of the smaller properties created by the subdivision. It was purchased by Hector Gibson in 1916 and stocked with merino sheep from New South Wales in Australia. Today his descendants still own the property.

# 5
# GOLD! GOLD! GOLD!

At sunset on 20 May 1861 the history of Central Otago was changed for ever when the Tasmanian Gabriel Read discovered commercially viable gold deposits at a place now called Gabriels Gully. What followed, slowly at first, but frantically as it gathered momentum, was a goldrush in which fortune seekers from all over the world descended on Central Otago. Gold had been found previously but had either been ignored by those who discovered it or had not been found in quantities that made it worth exploiting. In the following year, 1862, an American, Horatio Hartley, and Christopher Reilly, an Irishman, turned up in Dunedin to cash in 47 kg of gold they had washed from the Clutha River. The rush that had started with Gabriel Read's discovery now took on gigantic proportions. By the turn of the century, gold was being panned, sluiced, dredged and mined all over Central Otago where there was sufficient water to work the claims. If no water existed it was brought in by water races dug by hand over huge distances. Goldfields spread from Lawrence to Clyde, to the Nevis Valley, to Glenorchy and up the Shotover River to Skippers. Gold was mined at Bendigo, sluiced at Matakanui, Naseby, Hamiltons, Bannockburn, Roxburgh, Skippers and St Bathans and dredged from the Clutha River around Roxburgh, Alexandra, Clyde and Cromwell. Central Otago became a name and place that was known around the world. Otago became New Zealand's richest province and Dunedin its wealthiest city.

### GABRIEL READ (1824–1894)

Gabriel Read, the man who started it all, was a wanderer who suffered from a serious mental illness for the better part of his life. He was a religious and educated man who was prepared to use the skills he had acquired in other goldfields around the world to find gold in New Zealand. Once he had found the precious metal he showed others how to extract it from the ground and

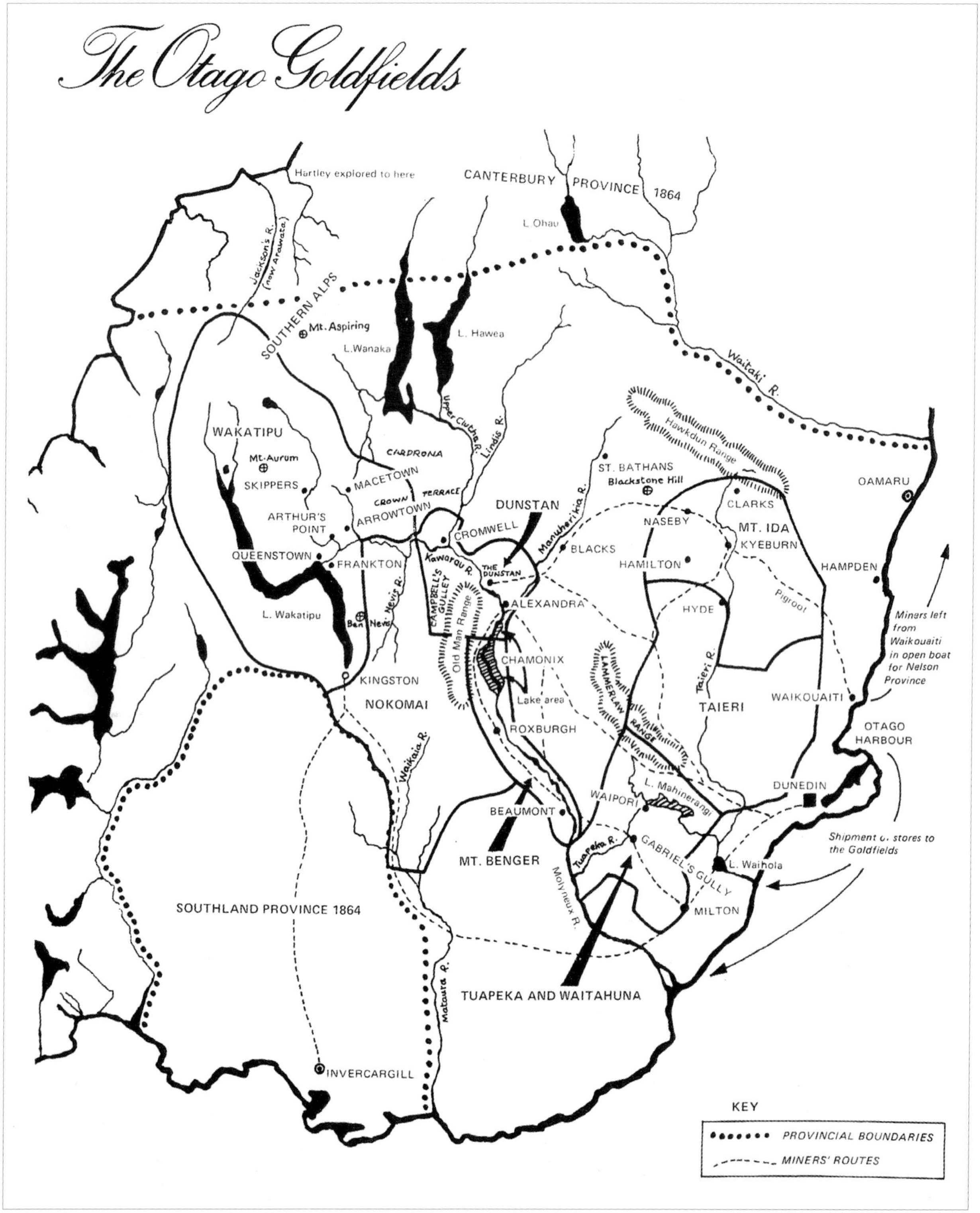

The Otago Goldfields
Hartley explored to here
CANTERBURY PROVINCE 1864
L. Ohau
Jackson's R. (now Arawata)
SOUTHERN ALPS
Mt. Aspiring
L. Wanaka
L. Hawea
Waitaki R.
Upper Clutha R.
Lindis R.
Hawkdun Range
WAKATIPU
Mt. Aurum
SKIPPERS
CARDRONA
MACETOWN
CROWN TERRACE
ARROWTOWN
ARTHUR'S POINT
QUEENSTOWN
FRANKTON
CROMWELL
DUNSTAN
THE DUNSTAN
Kawarau R.
CAMPBELL'S GULLY
Manuherikia R.
BLACKS
ST. BATHANS
Blackstone Hill
NASEBY
CLARKS
MT. IDA
KYEBURN
HAMILTON
OAMARU
HAMPDEN
Pigroot
HYDE
ALEXANDRA
Old Man Range
L. Wakatipu
Ben Nevis
Nevis R.
CHAMONIX
LAMMERLAW RANGE
Taieri R.
Miners left from Waikouaiti in open boat for Nelson Province
KINGSTON
NOKOMAI
Lake area
TAIERI
WAIKOUAITI
OTAGO HARBOUR
ROXBURGH
Waikaia R.
DUNEDIN
L. Mahinerangi
WAIPORI
BEAUMONT
MT. BENGER
Tuapeka R.
GABRIEL'S GULLY
L. Waihola
Shipment of stores to the Goldfields
Molyneux R.
MILTON
SOUTHLAND PROVINCE 1864
Mataura R.
TUAPEKA AND WAITAHUNA
INVERCARGILL
KEY
PROVINCIAL BOUNDARIES
MINERS' ROUTES

**OPPOSITE** A map of the goldfields of Central Otago and the Queenstown Lakes showing the gold discoveries that had been made throughout the region by the mid 1860s.

ALEXANDRA MUSEUM

**ABOVE** Peter Edward, an Indian from Bombay who was given the name 'Black Peter' in a less sensitive age, was the first man to take gold from Gabriels Gully for his own use, long before Gabriel Read arrived there in 1861. Peter Edward was never interested in keeping the discovery to himself, but the people he mentioned it to did show interest in following up. It was the knowledge of his find that led Gabriel Read to the area that would eventually be named Gabriels Gully.

HOCKEN COLLECTIONS S04-2721, UNIVERSITY OF OTAGO, DUNEDIN

then moved on. His payment was a reward of 1000 pounds offered by the then Otago Provincial Government to the first person to find a payable goldfield. He was initially attracted to Gabriels Gully by stories of a man, an Indian from Bombay, with the racist name of Black Peter, who had been taking small amounts of gold from the area for his own use. Gabriel Read was also aware that local Maori knew gold existed all over Central Otago but initially did not bother washing it from the rivers as it had no value in their culture. The gold existed, but it was a matter of finding it. This was where Gabriel Read was able to use his skills and stake for himself a permanent place in the history of Central Otago. His find at Gabriels Gully would eventually produce a total of 12,000 kg of gold before it was abandoned, and today the gully is retained as a heritage park with public access.

## HORATIO HARTLEY AND CHRISTOPHER REILLY

Horatio Hartley and Christopher Reilly met on the California goldfields and were known as 'forty-niners', a name used to describe people who had worked the American goldfields discovered in 1849. When they arrived in Central Otago, chasing the goldrush at Gabriels Gully, they, like Gabriel Read, brought very valuable skills with them that had been acquired in California.

Too late to secure a decent claim at Gabriels Gully, the two men set out to prospect the western bank of the Clutha River. Encouraged by what they found but short of food, fuel and equipment, they returned to the coast and purchased enough of these necessities to see them through the coming winter of 1862. When they returned to the Clutha River, they began to prospect the eastern bank. Their experience told them that winter was an opportune time to work the river because, with moisture locked up in snow and ice, the Clutha was low, exposing beaches and other sandy areas that might contain gold.

Both men were correct in their assumptions, and under harsh winter conditions they struck a bonanza in the Clutha just south of Cromwell. When they had washed enough gold, and fearful of their find being discovered by others before they could claim a reward offered by the Otago Provincial Government, they packed up and returned to Dunedin. On 15 August 1862 they deposited their gold with the Chief Gold Receiver and agreed to show others the location of their find for a reward of 2000 pounds. This reward carried a proviso that their find would produce 500 kg of gold over a period of three months. Hartley led a party back to the Clutha River

**ABOVE** Twenty-one ounces of Central Otago gold. Much of the gold found in the Clutha River was in the form of nuggets and flakes as shown here. It was round and smooth, the result of the abrasive action of water and gravel over thousands of years.

ALEXANDRA MUSEUM 96/582

**LEFT** Officialdom was in place before gold was ever discovered in Central Otago. The Gold Fields Act of 1858 required all miners to hold a Miner's Right before they could legally prospect for the precious metal.

HOCKEN COLLECTIONS S04-272U, UNIVERSITY OF OTAGO, DUNEDIN

in the Cromwell Gorge. They washed the required 500 kg, and the Dunstan goldfield was officially proclaimed on 23 September 1862.

Little is known of Hartley and Reilly's movements after they made their find public. Reilly undertook survey work for a deepwater port at Port Molyneux, while Hartley explored other parts of Central Otago. Both men then left New Zealand, and it is believed that Reilly died in Dublin in 1887, while Hartley died in San Francisco in 1903.

## THE CENTRAL OTAGO GOLDRUSH

The rush that followed the early discoveries was huge. Thousands of local men left Dunedin and headed for Central Otago. There were no restrictions on immigration into New Zealand at the time, and dozens of ships brought hopeful prospectors to Port Chalmers, near Dunedin, from all over the world. Many men left for the goldfields unprepared and poorly equipped, with no idea how they were going to live or eat in Central Otago. They fanned out all over the area, prospecting the rivers and creeks for the easily won alluvial gold that had washed out of the surrounding hills over the millennia.

ABOVE Jim Richardson, one of several goldminers who only ever made small returns from prospecting. In his old age he lived in a well kept hut, located beside one of the piers of the old Alexandra Bridge.

ALEXANDRA MUSEUM

RIGHT Banks were quick to follow the goldminers and set up facilities where the latter could cash in their gold. This gold office once belonged to the Bank of New South Wales and is today located in the main street of St Bathans. It was removed to Oturehua some years ago, where it was restored and eventually returned to its present site.

Many who were from Australia and California had no concept of how vicious a Central Otago winter could be. They were given an expensive lesson in 1863 when some 500 prospectors lost their lives. Severe flooding of the rivers in early winter that year washed away dozens of miners while they slept in their tents along the riverbanks. Many more casualties followed when men were cut off at high altitude by blizzards and froze to death before they could reach safety. Food was scarce and expensive. Fuel was almost non-existent in the treeless tussock and grassland that was Central Otago.

In spite of all the drawbacks, while the alluvial gold lasted, many of those who escaped death and starvation made money. Sadly, many more did not. Their numbers swelled the small rural villages that already existed in Central Otago, while other settlements were hastily constructed to cater for their needs. Many of these villages faded into obscurity once the alluvial gold ran out, while new ones were built to accommodate sluicing, the next method used to recover gold.

**ABOVE** Sluicing in the foreground and elevating in the background, at John Ewing's Kildare Hill Claim, St Bathans in 1881. The elevator shows the height to which the spoil was lifted using water pressure. The deep hole that has begun to take shape is today filled with good clean water and forms the Blue Lake, a feature of St Bathans. This picture was obviously taken while a tour party was being shown around, as the working men of the era did not wear bowler hats or carry rolled umbrellas.

ALEXANDRA MUSEUM CCE/15

**LEFT** Extensive sluicing and elevating were carried out near Roxburgh. This is the Roxburgh Amalgamated Company's sluicing claim on the eastern side of the Clutha River, opposite the town of Roxburgh, in 1905.

ALEXANDRA MUSEUM

The last standing poppet head in Central Otago, located at the site of the abandoned Golden Progress Mine near Oturehua in the Ida Valley. Built to provide access to and from the mineshaft, the winch was driven by steam from two coal-fired boilers located nearby. Men and equipment were lowered into the shaft via a cab attached to wire ropes running through the wheels shown at the top of the structure. Gold-bearing material was removed from the shaft by the same method and taken to a site 100 m from the poppet head, where it was crushed to extract any gold. The Golden Progress Mine was finally abandoned in the late 1930s, when the quartz-bearing reef was lost, but at one time it employed 30 men working in shifts.

By 1866 the easily won alluvial gold was gone. The hard drinking and hard living alluvial miners were then left with two choices if they wanted to stay: become involved in sluicing, which required capital, or work for wages paid by the sluicing partnerships or companies. Those who chose the latter found there was a strong demand for their labour to work the sluice sites or dig the water races to bring in water to operate the sluice guns. Where sluicing took place villages often sprang up nearby or increased their population and facilities. Many of these villages still exist today, usually with a much-reduced population base. Cambrians was one such village. Populated mostly by Welshmen, it now serves as a holiday village. Ophir survived to gain a new lease of life, as did Bannockburn, St Bathans, Naseby, Lawrence and Cardrona. Others like Hamiltons, Kyeburn, Matakanui, Bendigo, Welshtown, Skippers and Macetown eventually became ghost towns with little left in the way of signs of occupation other than the odd cemetery, many fine trees, or the ruins of rough stone and mudbrick huts.

## QUARTZ MINING

Those miners involved in sluicing knew from experience that the gold they were chasing originated from seams of gold eroded from the surrounding hills. Because of the cost involved in mining this gold, which was usually bound up in quartz rock, they were not interested in mining it while more easily won alluvial gold existed. As sluicing sites became clogged, worked out or exhausted, miners' interest began to turn to quartz mining. As the quartz seams often lay deep in the ground, were notoriously difficult to follow and needed specialised equipment to extract the gold, large amounts of capital were required to develop a quartz mine. Companies were formed and often floated on the stock exchange to raise the necessary capital. Shafts were sunk and mines were developed all over Central Otago. The Invincible Mine north of Glenorchy was one, Bullendale near Skippers was another, Bendigo was a third. There was quartz mining at Bannockburn, Oturehua, Waipori, Macetown and right to the very edge of Central Otago at Macraes Flat. Rock mining is still carried on today at Macraes Flat by Oceana, using the open cut method. This operation now produces 50 percent of New Zealand's gold.

Once a shaft was sunk a poppet head straddling it was installed to lower and lift men and materials. A stamper battery was needed to crush the quartz, often powered by an expensive waterwheel. Quartz mining was financially risky because a good yield was one ounce of gold to every tonne of quartz mined and crushed. The shafts sunk were often very deep and the

**LEFT** Water was used in early quartz mining to drive the stampers which crushed the gold-bearing quartz. This waterwheel belonged to the owners of the Young Australian Mine located high on the Carrick Range behind Bannockburn. It was driven by water brought in over a huge distance by water race from the Nevis Valley. The building of this water race bankrupted many of the contractors brave enough to become involved in its construction and was eventually mostly paid for by the government. When the mine closed, the waterwheel fell into disrepair, but it was recently renovated by the Department of Conservation and can be seen today at its original site. The water to power the wheel is now used for irrigation.

HOCKEN COLLECTIONS S04-272C, UNIVERSITY OF OTAGO, DUNEDIN

**BELOW** Thomas Logan (1836–1897). With three partners he developed the rich Cromwell Quartz Mine at Bendigo in 1868. He took a fortune from this mine but died a pauper as a result of bad investments after he quit Bendigo.

ALEXANDRA MUSEUM

quartz vein containing the gold could suddenly disappear or go too deep to mine. Given all these factors to contend with it is not surprising that the majority of the early quartz mines were only marginally successful. The most successful was the Bendigo Mine, and this was largely due to the skill of one man, Thomas Logan, who set up and managed the Cromwell Quartz Mining Company.

### THOMAS LOGAN (1836–1897)

After a shaky start, John Logan made a fortune from quartz mining in Bendigo in the 1860s. He was experienced enough to know that the quartz he found there was very rich, but he lacked the capital required to mine it. In 1865 he managed to interest some Dunedin investors in joining him in opening up a claim in the Bendigo area. However, when he felt that he was being treated unfairly by his partners he purposely lost the gold seam, until his partners gave up and withdrew. In 1868 he set up the Cromwell Quartz Mining Company with three other shareholders and began mining. Little did he and his partners know that they were about to make one of the biggest fortunes from goldmining in New Zealand. They sank a shaft, which still exists today, very deep but half-filled with water and closed off by heavy steel mesh, on the hill behind Bendigo, between Logantown and Welshtown.

**BELOW LEFT** The climate of Central Otago was something that the dredge operators had to cope with. Here the elevator of the *Dunstan Lead* is covered in icicles during the winter of 1904. The pond on which the dredge is floating also appears to be frozen over, making for difficult, if not impossible, working conditions.

ALEXANDRA MUSEUM

**BELOW RIGHT** Nothing stood in the way of the miners when they thought they could tap a gold source. The early miners knew that the riverbeds in Central Otago were full of gold, but did not have the technology to gather it in any quantity until the dredges began to invade the rivers. Here an early attempt is being made to dive for gold in the Clutha River near Cromwell, as one way of overcoming the river's depth and current. It is not known whether any gold was recovered by this method, as diving was not a widely used technique.

HOCKEN COLLECTIONS S04-272F, UNIVERSITY OF OTAGO, DUNEDIN

The four partners made enough money from their mine to retire quite young, but they seemed unable to cope with their wealth. Logan launched himself into a life of opulence, owned several slow racehorses and made some bad investments in other mining ventures. He died a pauper in 1897. Another of his partners, William Garrett, was killed when he fell from his horse after a big night at a local hotel. The third, George Goodger, jumped to his death off the old Cromwell Bridge. The only partner who made good was Charcoal Joe Hebden, a humble charcoal burner before he invested in mining. He returned to England with his money, spent it wisely and lived to a solid age.

## DREDGING

Mining for gold in the beds and on the banks of the rivers was the last method used in Central Otago to obtain the precious metal. The experienced alluvial miners knew that the riverbeds were full of gold, but they had no way of getting at it in the swift currents. To overcome this problem they began to use a dredge, which was really a floating platform on the river that housed the machinery required to scoop the gold-bearing gravel from the river. The first dredge developed was the spoon dredge, which with the aid of the river's current lifted loads of gravel out of the river using a large spoon-like device. These were mostly unsuccessful as they were not able to penetrate far enough to reach the deeper parts of the riverbed and, when they did reach it, the spoon often snagged, threatening to tip the platform.

**LEFT ABOVE** One of the early current-wheel dredges on the Clutha River near Roxburgh. Each had a belt of buckets that was driven by the river's current, but were never very successful. Their failing lay in the inability of the buckets to reach the river bottom, where the gold lay, when the dredge was in mid river. They were able to reach the gold-bearing gravel closer to the riverbank, but in that location there was often not enough current to drive the buckets. Current-wheel dredges were soon replaced by the more successful steam dredges.

ALEXANDRA MUSEUM

**LEFT CENTRE** The *Golden Treasure* dredge, shown in the Clutha River at Millers Flat in 1910, was a steam-driven machine, using coal mined at Roxburgh. The *Golden Treasure* was an early version of the steam dredge, dozens of which would work the Central Otago rivers in the early twentieth century. They were later replaced by the more successful electrical dredges.

ALEXANDRA MUSEUM

**LEFT BELOW** Larger dredges operated around the clock and took several men working in shifts to ensure that the huge floating machine ran smoothly.

ALEXANDRA MUSEUM

RIGHT Dredging meant huge investment in the equipment required to build a dredge and large amounts of working capital to operate it. Capital was usually raised by floating a company that was formed with the honourable intention of making money for its shareholders from gold dredging. Here is the prospectus issued by a sharebroker in Dunedin in 1897 to raise 7500 pounds by offering investors 7500 shares in the Golden Reward Gold Dredging Company, which would eventually operate dredges both in Central Otago and on the West Coast. The names of the dredging companies and the dredges always held the promise of riches. Not all dredge companies or the machines they owned were successful, making this method of goldmining financially risky and not for the faint-hearted.

HOCKEN COLLECTIONS S04-272V, UNIVERSITY OF OTAGO, DUNEDIN

---

A thoroughly well-prospected Dredging Claim on the Molyneux River, next to the Golden Gravel Gold Dredging Company, Ltd., the capital of which Company was recently very largely over subscribed, and there are now buyers of the Shares at a premium.

# PROSPECTUS

OF THE

# Golden Reward Gold Dredging Co.,

LIMITED.

(To be incorporated under "The Companies Act, 1882.")

**CAPITAL - - - - £7,500,**

IN 7,500 SHARES OF £1 EACH.

Of which 1,500 Fully Paid-up Shares are to be allotted to the Vendors in payment in full for their property; the remaining 6,000 Shares are now offered to the public for the purpose of providing capital to build and place on the property a powerful and modern type of Dredge suitable to work the Claim.

**TERMS OF SUBSCRIPTION.**—One Shilling per Share on Application, and One Shilling per Share on Allotment; the balance to be called up as required, in Calls of not more than One Shilling per Share at intervals of not less than One Month.

SHARES WILL BE ALLOTTED IN THE ORDER OF PRIORITY OF APPLICATION.

Copies of this Prospectus and Plan of the Claim may be obtained by applying to any of the Brokers.

DIRECTORS:

The number of Directors shall be five, of which only one of the Vendors may act as a Director, and only in terms expressed in Articles of Association. The other four shall be elected by the Shareholders at the First Statutory Meeting, which will be held as soon as possible after registration of the Company.

BANKERS:
BANK OF NEW SOUTH WALES.

SOLICITOR: CONSULTING ENGINEER:
Mr. W. C. MacGREGOR. Mr. ED. ROBERTS.

BROKERS:
Mr. J. A. CHAPMAN, A.M.P. Buildings, Dunedin    Messrs. FAITT & CO., Gore
Messrs. ACLAND & DUDLEY, Christchurch    Mr. ROBERT THOMPSON, Oamaru
Mr. W. R. PEARSON, Lawrence    Mr. W. G. DUNSFORD, Timaru
Mr. HENRY SYMES, Alexandra South    Mr. C. S. BOOTH, National Chambers, Wellington

SECRETARY:
Mr. J. J. RAMSAY, Dunedin.

Dividends will be paid on all Shares alike, irrespective of the amount called up.

THIS Company is being formed to take over from the vendors the Special Dredging Claim, No. 42a, on the Molyneux River, which is **next to and below the Golden Gravel Dredging Company's Claim** (which was floated a few days ago, and the capital was **very largely over subscribed**), and extends one mile down the river, and comprises 61¼ acres. **The Claim has been proved beyond all doubt to be a highly payable property.**

The Engineer who reported on the Claim writes—"The Claim is shown on the plan accompanying the report, and from it you will see that the width of the river in this locality is about one hundred and sixty yards. The current is very steady and consequently the amount of drift carried along is very small here, and this is a most advantageous feature from a dredging point of view. **The banks of the river along the boundaries of this Claim have been sluiced and cradled for gold, and auriferous gravels are showing all along the water line and in the places where the miners have worked down,** until the percolation of the water into the holes from whence they were taking out the auriferous gravels became so great as to defy all their efforts to pump it out. Generally it is a most difficult matter to get down more than a few feet below water level. From walking along the banks of the river in this Claim it must be apparent to any experienced person that the very many indications of mining everywhere point conclusively to the fact that the gravels contained a very remunerative quantity of gold. I have examined miners who have worked along the banks of the river, and from what they earned when working, can say that from a dredging point of view the gravel deposits along and under the bed of the river **on this Claim are of a very payable nature.** If you will examine the plan you will see about half way down the western bank are some old Chinese workings, and from this place, after they had finished working as deep as they could, seven Chinamen went home to China. Now, seeing that Chinamen do not go away, as a rule, with anything less than from £300 to £700 per man, they must have made an excellent profit from working at this place. From indications I am of opinion that the false bottom on which the richest stratum of gold wash lies is deep in this Claim—probably from 30ft to 40ft deep. Still there are, no doubt, here as elsewhere, small patches where it is much shallower, and it was one of these patches the Chinamen dropped upon. The class of stones left behind by the Chinamen in the bottom of their workings point to the wash as having been of a very payable nature."

The fact that miners found this ground remunerative under such difficulties and the primitive mode they had of working it, speaks volumes for the quantity of gold a modern type of dredge would win, for it must be borne in mind that two men with an ordinary cradle could not treat more than three to five cubic feet of wash a day; and it will be seen by Mr. Donaldson's report that six men who worked a spoon dredge on the beaches of this Claim could not raise and treat more than 10 tons of wash a day, and yet they made **over £3 per week per man,** and that Mr. Donaldson was one of a party that obtained 64oz of gold in 10 days.

The Claim, like that of the **Golden Gravel Company's** property, is situated on that part of the river that runs through the **Beaumont Flat.** About a mile and three quarters above the claim is a long narrow gorge, and as the river is **very wide below the gorge,** the golden wash that has been rushed down it during floods has settled from the Beaumont Bridge **downwards in the more tranquil water and flat country.**

## STEVENSON & POOLE

### New Zealand Engineering and Electrical Works...

Makers of Gold Dredges in latest style and of any capacity.

Present Output about One Dredge per Month.

We have Built more Dredges than any other makers in New Zealand.

ONLY FIRST-CLASS WORKMANSHIP AND MATERIAL SUPPLIED.

STEEL CASTINGS MADE & SUPPLIED.

Strict Attention and Punctual Delivery.

THOMAS STEVENSON.    ARTHUR H. POOLE.

CASTLE STREET, DUNEDIN, N.Z.

---

**ABOVE** Because of their size, most of the gold dredges that worked the Clutha and Kawarau rivers at the height of the dredging boom were manufactured locally. This was a huge spin-off for Dunedin and Central Otago firms that manufactured the dredges, which were then carted to where they would operate and assembled on site. Because of poor returns, many of the dredges never became fully operative; the machinery was eventually either sold or broken up for scrap, or sometimes just left to rot in the river.

ALEXANDRA MUSEUM

**LEFT** The *Molyneux* was a large electrical dredge that worked successfully in the Cromwell Gorge and off Scotland Point in the Kawarau River for several years.

HOCKEN COLLECTIONS S04-272B, UNIVERSITY OF OTAGO, DUNEDIN

During the depression of the 1930s many of the unemployed were encouraged, with the aid of a small government subsidy, to prospect for gold. One of these men is pictured with a cradle on the bank of the Clutha River. Very little gold was found, but the reason behind the idea might have been psychological, as this victim of the unemployment that haunted the decade appears to be enjoying himself in the open spaces and sunshine of Central Otago.

HOCKEN COLLECTIONS S04-272D, UNIVERSITY OF OTAGO, DUNEDIN

The next style of dredge tried was the current-wheel dredge, which was of similar design but had a chain of buckets instead of a spoon to scoop the river gravel. These dredges were not very successful as they also had trouble reaching deep enough, and there was often not enough current to drive the chain of buckets when the dredge was working closer to the riverbank,.

Dredging did not really become a viable option until the introduction of coal-fired steam dredges in the late 1800s. These in turn were followed by electrical dredges, which operated in Central Otago until 1963. All dredges were noisy, ugly and rather offensive machines, working in a lake of muddy water while making a terrible noise. Capital was also a problem in the use of steam dredges as they took large sums of money to build and then run. Again companies and partnerships were set up to invest in steam dredging, and at one time there were dozens of dredges working the bed and banks of the Clutha River from Cromwell through to Roxburgh. The later invention of a dredge elevator that could stack the tailings away from the dredge meant that the machine could then create its own pond of water in which to float while working. When these became operative, dredging moved away from the riverbanks into the paddocks that lined the rivers. It is these dredges that shaped most of the huge area of dredge tailings that exists today on the southern side of the Clutha River near Alexandra. If properly capitalised and with a bit of luck, dredging proved to be very lucrative and brought wealth into Central Otago over many years, while providing much-needed employment.

During the depression of the 1930s alluvial goldmining enjoyed a brief and mostly unsuccessful revival in Central Otago. As one way of trying to relieve the unemployment problem, the government encouraged the unemployed to prospect for gold, offering a small measure of financial assistance to get the hopeful prospectors started. In the main this proved unsuccessful, with only small amounts of gold found, as the areas had been worked and worked again by the early European and Chinese miners. When the depression ended, this alluvial prospecting came to a halt, and it is now the reserve of hopeful weekend amateurs.

# 6
# CHINESE MINERS IN CENTRAL OTAGO

As the easily won alluvial gold became more difficult to find in the late 1860s, a large number of the European miners left Central Otago for new fields on the West Coast. Members of the Otago Provincial Government, facing a loss of revenue from the tax levied on gold, decided to invite Chinese miners to work in Otago. The Chinese were known for their willingness to rework old claims that Europeans had abandoned. The European miners were not as meticulous as the Chinese, and it is estimated that Europeans often missed up to half the gold on their claims.

The Chinese were initially invited from the goldfields of Victoria and California and, later, directly from China. Most of those who came to Otago were from the poverty stricken and overcrowded Pearl River Delta in

Baby and Ah Chow were the last Chinese miners to live in Cromwell. Like many other Chinese, they never made enough money to return to China. It is possible that both left a wife and family in China, intending to return when they had made enough money on the Central Otago goldfields. The unwritten rules of the time would have dictated that they live in the squalid Chinatown section of old Cromwell.

CROMWELL MUSEUM

RIGHT ABOVE Caves in the Roxburgh Gorge, alongside the Clutha River, were lived in by Chinese miners. Schist stone was used to wall up the front of the caves and to build chimneys to channel smoke from cooking fires. In spite of the attempts to keep out the weather, surviving the cold of a Central Otago winter here would have been very difficult and unpleasant. The Chinese preferred to live in solid structures such as these caves rather than the tents favoured by the European miners.
ALEXANDRA MUSEUM

RIGHT BELOW A Chinese miner's hut stands alone at the Goldfields Mining Centre in the Kawarau Gorge. Apart from the roof, it is built entirely of river stones that would have been sluiced out of the ground during the search for gold. Often a pigsty would be located close by to provide meat and a chicken run for a supply of eggs.

China's Guandong province. The Chinese miners called New Zealand Sun Kum Shan, which translated meant 'New Gold Hills'. When the provincial government extended its invitation it did not intend that the Chinese would settle permanently in Otago, and for this reason a harsh condition was attached: no women were invited, only men. Wives and families were left behind and often never seen again. This led to problems of loneliness, opium addiction and hopelessness among many of the early Chinese immigrants.

When the Chinese arrived at Port Chalmers, they were usually fitted out by Chinese merchants in Dunedin and then began a trek of some ten days to reach the goldfields, carrying their possessions. Those who came directly from China were used to close-knit communities, paddy fields, tropical fruits and fishponds. Central Otago with its freezing winters, stifling summers and shortage of water could not have been more different from their homeland. The reason most came to Central Otago was to try and make enough money, usually 200 pounds, to return home, where they would buy land. Many Chinese managed to achieve their goal and quit Otago after several years, but many more did not. Economics forced them to stay on, often alone and unwanted. In some instances this outcome was a result of a miner's gambling away his hard-won gold or his addiction to opium, which could be smoked in the legal opium dens scattered throughout early Central Otago. Many ended their days living in rudimentary huts, eking out a living as best they could and often suffering from poor physical and mental health. Incidents of aged Chinese miners starving to death in the midst of plenty were not uncommon.

Racism, based on ignorance, was the root cause of many of the problems the Chinese faced. They looked different, dressed differently, ate different food, spoke a different language and followed different religions. They even lived differently, preferring to build themselves stone or mud huts close to their claims, while the European miners opted for tents. Many occupied caves or walled-in rock overhangs that Europeans would not even consider to be living quarters. If they resided in the goldrush towns, they could be found in a segregated, less desirable area. The Chinese miners' preference for reworking old claims that had been abandoned also caused trouble. European miners often deserted their claims in order to join a rush to a new find. Many returned, disappointed, to their earlier claims, to which they no longer held the title, to find that the more meticulous Chinese, turning over every stone, had won gold and made the claim profitable.

By 1869 there were 5000 Chinese miners in Central Otago. Prejudice now demanded that this immigration be halted or slowed, and the government's answer was to impose a poll tax on every Chinese person entering New Zealand. At the same time, the easily won alluvial gold was disappearing, which meant that many Europeans were forced to work for wages on the sluicing or quartz mining sites to survive. The European miners feared an influx of Chinese would lead to a collapse in wage rates.

It was the wish of the majority of Chinese in Central Otago that if they were unable to find the money to return home, at least their bones could

With the arrival of the Chinese came prejudice. T. Daniel, the mayor of a small town on the border of Central Otago, thought nothing of calling a public meeting in the local town hall to, as the poster states, 'consider the best means to adopt to check the influx of the Chinese'.

HOCKEN COLLECTIONS S04-272Q, UNIVERSITY OF OTAGO, DUNEDIN

be shipped back for what they considered to be a proper burial. Many died and were buried in cemeteries throughout the region. At the beginning of the twentieth century, local Chinese formed a society called Cheong Shing Tong to exhume the bodies of Chinese from these cemeteries and clean and wrap the bones, which were then placed in lead-lined coffins ready to return to China. For this reason many of the Chinese headstones in Central Otago sit over graves that no longer contain bodies. The bodies that once occupied the graves now lie in lead-lined coffins at the bottom of the ocean off New Zealand's west coast, near the Hokianga Harbour. The reason for this is that the Chinese who were exhumed were loaded aboard a ship in Dunedin called the *Ventnor*. More coffins were picked up when this ship stopped at Wellington, and as the *Ventnor* left Wellington Harbour it carried a grizzly cargo of 499 lead-lined coffins. Sadly, the ship foundered and sank near the Hokianga Harbour, and its entire cargo was never recovered.

The Chinese miners left a strong legacy in Central Otago. The abundance of large stones that exist on many of the old goldmining sites today were left there by the Chinese who stacked them into neat piles. Several of their shantytowns have also been rebuilt or renovated. The shantytown in Lawrence has recently been purchased for renovation in a partnership with the Department of Conservation. A replica of the old Chinatown that once existed in Cromwell has been faithfully rebuilt at the Goldfields Mining

Centre in the Kawarau Gorge and another has been renovated in Arrowtown. However, the most noticeable and lasting legacy is the wild thyme growing in Central Otago. This was introduced by the Chinese to flavour their food. From there it went wild and now covers huge areas.

## REVEREND ALEXANDER DON (1857–1934)

Reverend Alexander Don carved out a place for himself in the history of Central Otago as a missionary appointed by the Presbyterian Church of Otago to convert the Chinese miners to Christianity. During the years he ministered to the Chinese he compiled a list of names and took a large number of photographs. By doing this, he unwittingly created a permanent record of the Chinese miners who lived and worked in early Central Otago. If Don had not done this, the Chinese would have faded into obscurity, which was the fate of the majority of their fellow countrymen who once lived in other parts of New Zealand.

Part of what was once Chinatown in old Cromwell has now been faithfully recreated at the Goldfields Mining Centre in the Kawarau Gorge, using the same layout and materials as the original. Inside each hut are examples of the rudimentary furnishings used by the Chinese miners. Both the huts and their furnishings give a visitor to the centre a good insight into how the Chinese miners lived during the latter half of the nineteenth century.

*This old man was the last of the Chinese miners in Lawrence, who spent his old age eking out a living in that town until his death in the 1930s.*

HOCKEN COLLECTIONS S04-272L,
UNIVERSITY OF OTAGO, DUNEDIN

Don was an Australian who, after being forced by family circumstances to begin work at the age of nine, was able to pay for his own education by teaching at the same time. In 1879 he began his career as a missionary in Dunedin, an occupation that would become his life's work. Sent to China by the Presbyterian Church to learn Cantonese, he returned to Dunedin with a poor grasp of the language and began life as a missionary to the Chinese, based at Riverton in Southland and later at Lawrence in Central Otago. He gained recognition through his habit of walking all over Central Otago in the summer months, carrying a rolled umbrella and briefcase, while dressed in a waistcoat complete with watch chain and sporting a cork hat. In spite of his efforts over many years, Don was not very successful as a missionary, and during all the years he ministered to the Chinese it is estimated that he only converted some 20 of them to Christianity. This was due in part to the fact that the Chinese were not interested in the religion of the European who discriminated against them and in part to Don's failings as a missionary. One positive thing to come out of it all was Don's willingness to help the Chinese, writing letters for them, fighting against their persecution and offering general help. He had an ulterior motive for this, related to their possible conversion to Christianity, but the results were positive for the Chinese and alleviated some of their suffering.

Although only mildly successful as a missionary, Don was promoted to general moderator of the Presbyterian Church in New Zealand and then to the post of Presbyterian foreign missions sectary. He spent a large amount of time in China, where he established the Canton Villages Mission and raised substantial sums of money to help ease the regular famines that occurred there. A local honour called the Seventh Council Insignia of the Excellent Crop was conferred on him by the Chinese government for his efforts.

Don retired to Ophir in Central Otago in the 1920s. He had a house built for himself and his wife, Amelia, which he called The Bungalow. This house still exists in Ophir. He died in November 1934 while travelling on a train from Omakau to Dunedin.

# 7
# RABBITS — THE SCOURGE OF CENTRAL OTAGO

Misguided early settlers released rabbits in the South Island as early as 1857, without any idea of the damage they would do to the land and farmers' livelihoods. The runholders who released the first few pairs in Southland were proud to see these rabbits thrive in their new home. By 1866 the pest appeared for the first time on Earnscleugh Station, a property that took in a large area of land on the south bank of the Clutha River, extending well into the Cromwell Gorge. At first the station owner was happy that the rabbits were doing so well on his property and made sure nobody was given an opportunity to poach them. Little did he know that within a few short years these same rabbits would become a plague that could not be controlled and would spell the ruin of his property, which he would eventually be forced to abandon.

By 1870 rabbits had crossed the Clutha River and begun their invasion of the rest of Central Otago. Rabbits love Central Otago. They thrive in the semi-arid climate of the area and produce large, healthy litters several times a year, with those progeny in turn breeding a few months after their birth. It is estimated that with no deaths, one pair of rabbits could within three years breed to 12 million. Numbers like that are testament to how quickly the rabbit problem became serious. The invasion caught runholders unprepared because they had not seen anything of this nature before. Initially, they did not have the means to even begin to control rabbit numbers, as the usual methods of shooting, trapping or using dogs were ineffective. Rabbit drives by several men armed with clubs were common in fenced paddocks. Numbers were such that, when frightened to one side of the paddock, the rabbits built up against the fence, enabling those that followed to simply run up over them and escape.

In many areas of Central Otago rabbits completely stripped the ground

The feral rabbit (*Oryctolagus cuniculus*) was the animal that ate parts of Central Otago bare. It evolved in Spain and North Africa, and was taken to the United Kingdom by the Normans. It was introduced to New Zealand in 1777 by Captain Cook, but this initial release was unsuccessful. The early settlers reintroduced the rabbits in the 1850s. They spread rapidly, with their numbers reaching plague proportions by 1890. Competition for grazing caused the reduction of sheep numbers and spelt disaster for many rural properties. Despite all the attempts to eradicate it over the last 150 years, the animal still thrives.

**ABOVE LEFT** In a misguided attempt to control rabbit numbers, ferrets were introduced in the 1880s. The ferret (*Mustela furo*) pictured here is a vicious predator that will kill just for the fun of it, often leaving prey uneaten. It is the natural enemy of the rabbit, capable of entering its burrows. Ferrets found native birds more to their taste, however, and have devastated native bird numbers since their introduction. Today, the fact that the ferret is a carrier of bovine tuberculosis is another problem for farmers, who are required to spend money to reduce ferret numbers or run the risk of having their stock rejected by the abattoirs if they test positive for TB.

**ABOVE RIGHT** Living conditions were tough for many rabbiters. Practical reasons made it more sensible to live near where they worked and this often meant makeshift accommodation. The three rabbiters shown here with their grubbers and dogs would have spent the winter months living in the sod and iron huts behind them, cooking over an open fire and washing in the local creek. Rabbit skins that have been turned inside out and stretched over wire to dry, hang on lines beside the huts.

ALEXANDRA MUSEUM

of all vegetation, leaving nothing for sheep. They also polluted the ground with their droppings and urine and dug at tussock and matagouri to eat the roots of these plants, while their burrows honeycombed large areas. Nothing was left on the land except the smell of rabbit. When this happened, the runholders whose leases had been invaded had no hope of trying to farm sheep in the face of such competition and just abandoned their properties. Those who had the capital to employ men to try and control the rabbits did so and were able to remain on their land. The costs, however, were very high. In 1882 Morven Hills Station employed 45 men whose sole occupation was to try and stem the tide of rabbit numbers. Natural predators were also introduced in 1888 when 200 ferrets were released on the station. This step was only partly successful as ferrets found domestic hens and native birds more to their taste. Ferrets would in time also become carriers of tuberculosis, which would spread to livestock. Today this is an ongoing problem, with ferrets still being trapped in many parts of Central Otago in an attempt to keep bovine tuberculosis under control.

The tide began to turn in the runholders' favour when they started using oats poisoned with phosphorous. This poison was effective but very cruel as rabbits, after eating it, suffered a long and agonising death. The runholders were further aided by the introduction of pollard poisoning, which was more effective than oats, but control of the rabbit menace was still a long way off.

Rabbit numbers were at their greatest in Central Otago during the three decades prior to 1900. The government made an attempt to be seen to be doing something when they passed the Rabbit Nuisance Act in 1876. This legislation introduced a special rate that was levied on runholders and was used to control rabbits, but it had little effect.

From 1900 onwards, rabbiting created a new industry in Central Otago. Runholders who were unable to graze sheep because of rabbit numbers began to harvest the rabbits themselves for their skins and meat. This provided employment for large numbers of men, who were paid a basic wage and a bonus on skins, but in the long term it just further aggravated the problem. It was not in the rabbiters' interest to wipe out the pest that brought them their living, so they made sure that enough rabbits remained to produce the next crop of young. In 1915 a rabbit canning factory opened in Cromwell that had an intake of 10,000 carcasses a day, giving an indication of rabbit numbers in the area. With the construction of the Otago Central Railway, rabbit carcasses were railed to Dunedin. Consignments of 13,000 rabbits a day were the norm.

In 1948 the government began to take the problem seriously by passing legislation setting up rabbit boards throughout New Zealand. This legislation was designed to completely exterminate the rabbit, and it provided for a ban on the sale of meat and skins of the pest, which took the profit and purpose out of farming rabbits for a living. The men previously involved in the industry were now employed by the rabbit boards to destroy the pest, not farm it. As the first form of attack, carrots laced with the new poison 1080 were dropped all over Central Otago by light airplane. This was followed up by night shooting and trapping. The rabbit board caring for the land once occupied by Morven Hills Station was responsible for the deaths of 83,000 rabbits in its first month of operation, so this effort to exterminate the rabbit was a serious one.

ABOVE A typical Central Otago rabbiter. He would have set the gintraps that he is carrying in his left hand the previous night, in a shallow depression grubbed out of the ground. Rabbits are attracted to freshly dug soil and are caught in the traps while investigating. The overnight catch is collected the next morning, and the traps are reset. Rabbiting was a full-time occupation for those involved. Winter was the busiest season as rabbit pelts were in top condition and of more value during the colder months. The use of traps usually indicated that the rabbiter was trapping for profit and thus possibly involved in farming the pest. For humane reasons it is now illegal to use gintraps in New Zealand.
ALEXANDRA MUSEUM

LEFT Tonkin & Co., rabbit buyers based in Lawrence, used a steam-driven traction engine to collect rabbit carcasses in their thousands from the rabbiters. Once sorted, the carcasses were railed to Dunedin, where they were processed for meat and skins.
ALEXANDRA MUSEUM

RIGHT Rabbits that have been collected by wagon have their skins graded by the man wearing a tie, who would have been either a rabbit buyer, or employed by one of the rabbit-processing companies. There is obvious interest by those surrounding him in the decision he makes on each skin, as the quality of the pelt would have determined the price paid.

ALEXANDRA MUSEUM

BELOW Staff in a rabbit canning factory which operated in Alexandra during the early 1900s. The tins of rabbit meat that surround the walls are destined for human consumption in spite of the somewhat basic conditions the meat was processed under. After some initial success, this factory, plus another in Cromwell, went out of business when it was discovered that many of the rabbits they were processing had been killed with the use of poison instead of traps. This led to consumer resistance which destroyed the local market.

ALEXANDRA MUSEUM

In this picture taken in 1917, thousands of dried rabbit skins in a warehouse in Alexandra await shipment to Dunedin, where they will be baled and most likely exported to the United Kingdom.

ALEXANDRA MUSEUM

The last rabbit, however, was never caught. In time, many of the animals developed immunity to the poison or became bait shy and would not touch it. In the 1980s the rabbit boards were dismantled by the government and farmers were again made responsible for controlling their own rabbit problems. This led to an increase in the rabbit population of Central Otago, and the pest threatened to overwhelm the area again. Local farmers took it into their own hands in the 1990s to illegally import the rabbit calicivirus disease (RCD) from Australia. This virus spreads quickly from one rabbit to another, especially in hot weather, and has proved to be very effective in controlling rabbit numbers. Other than in some areas that were always sensitive to rabbits, such as the hills behind the village of Ophir and the land around Bendigo, it is now difficult to sight a rabbit in Central Otago. However, immunity to RCD has been developing among those exposed to the virus, and the rabbit population is sure to increase unless some other method of control is found in the future.

# 8
# TRANSPORT AND THE OTAGO CENTRAL RAILWAY

A gig on show at the Moutere Station centenary near Alexandra in 2004. Moutere Station was one of the first runs to be taken up in Central Otago, but was reduced in size with the breakup of the large properties in the early 1900s. This gig is no ordinary wagon. With its leather seats and elegant woodwork it would have been built for use by the runholder or a member of his family, and pulled by a high-stepping thoroughbred horse.

The discovery of gold in Central Otago brought problems of access and transportation. The early runholders and those they employed were intrepid men and women who rode horses to travel to and from the east coast over open country. This changed in 1862 when miners set off on foot, bound for the goldfields, via the shortest route over what is now called the Old Dunstan Road. For those leaving from Dunedin, this dirt track was joined several kilometres south of Middlemarch, with the first leg crossing the Rock and Pillar Range to end at the ford over the Taieri River at Styx. After following the valley floor for several more kilometres, the Old Dunstan Road then crossed over to the Ida Valley and Alexandra. As time went on this road was used more and more by wagon drivers carting freight to the goldfields. It was also used in the reverse direction by the government-run gold escort, set up to carry Central Otago gold to Dunedin. This escort stopped overnight at Styx before tackling the second leg of the Old Dunstan Road. A hotel was built at Styx to cater for the escort and other travellers, along with a stable and a jail. The latter was mostly used to chain up the chest containing the gold being transported. These chains can be seen in the stone jail, which still exists at Styx today.

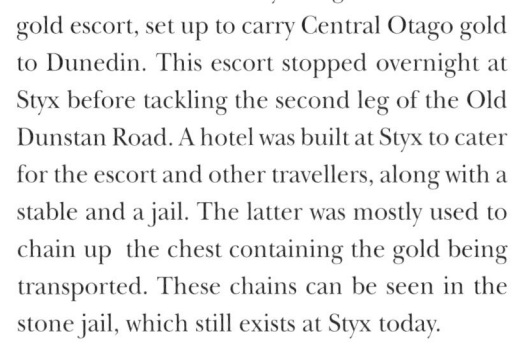

Because the Old Dunstan Road was at high altitude it was often muddy and snowbound. It was also steep and winding — far from ideal for heavily loaded wagons. Another route was needed to access Central Otago, and this was developed via what is today called the Pigroot. This track began at Palmerston on the coast and travelled inland past present-day Dead Horse Pinch, crossed the Kye Burn river at Kye Burn and accessed the goldfields via the Ida and Manuherikia valleys. It had the advantage of allowing goods to be shipped by sea from Dunedin to Waikouaiti and then taken overland to Palmerston to join the Pigroot. In time it became the more popular route into Central Otago as it was easier on horses and wagons and less likely to be closed in winter. It was, however, a very muddy track as is often seen in early photographs. In time it became the preferred track of the gold escorts, the passenger and mail coaches operated by Cobb & Co. and also the heavy wagons carrying all types of freight.

**LEFT ABOVE** The stone jail at Styx in 1935. Built in the 1860s, it is still in place today on the same site. Surrounded by mature trees and shrubs, it is now in poorer condition than it appears here. The building was used by the gold escort to store its gold consignment overnight; it is doubtful whether it was ever used as a jail. The box that contained the gold was secured to the inside wall by chains, which are still evident.

HOCKEN COLLECTIONS S04-272R, UNIVERSITY OF OTAGO, DUNEDIN

**LEFT BELOW** When gold was discovered in Central Otago the provincial government was quick to take over the responsibility of moving the precious metal safely to Dunedin via the Old Dunstan Road or over the Pigroot. With the former, an overnight stop was usually made at Styx, on the bank of the Taieri River. This stable was built in the 1860s to cater for the horses of the gold escort and other travellers, who would have stayed at the Styx Hotel located next door. The building still exists, with the original stone floor that was common in stables, along with stalls and feed boxes for the horses. In front, next to the tree, is an early Pelton wheel, used to harness the energy of running water.

RIGHT ABOVE Freight wagons travelling on the rough road through the Cromwell Gorge in 1900. In the years that followed, this road was upgraded to a highway and the Clyde to Cromwell railway line was built alongside it in 1921. When the Clyde Dam was constructed, the road disappeared under the floodwaters behind the dam. To compensate, a new highway was built much higher up, on the side of the hill, directly above these two wagons.

ALEXANDRA MUSEUM

RIGHT CENTRE Blacksmiths were a very important factor in keeping transport moving in the latter half of the nineteenth century. A fire burned constantly to heat the metal that was shaped by the blacksmith into steel rims for wagon wheels and horseshoes. A wide variety of metal objects were made by a skilled blacksmith, but it was these two items that were the backbone of his business. With the invention of the internal combustion engine, the blacksmith quickly became obsolete and is now only to be seen demonstrating his skills at a show or exhibition.

ALEXANDRA MUSEUM

RIGHT BELOW A Cobb & Co. coach stopped outside the Bendigo Hotel in Alexandra in 1909. With the advent of the motorcar and the Otago Central Railway, it is possible that this photograph was taken on the coach's last trip.

ALEXANDRA MUSEUM

As the goldfields entered the more sophisticated phase of sluicing, quartz mining and dredging, it became apparent that a railway line extending from Dunedin into Central Otago was required to carry the heavy freight that was by then moving into the area. With many ex-miners becoming involved in farming, a railway was also needed to transport stock to the abattoirs on the east coast. Vincent Pyke, the member of Parliament for Dunstan (now Central Otago), made it his responsibility to bring about the construction of such a railway. After being urged and pushed by Pyke, the government agreed in principle to a railway line being built into the area. What followed was a squabble among several different factions who wanted the line built through their part of Central Otago, and six different routes were suggested. By 1879, again with Pyke's urging, an agreement had been reached to build the line via the Taieri Gorge, the Maniototo Plain, Ida Valley, Alexandra, Clyde and finally Cromwell. On 7 June 1879 at a ceremony near Wingatui, a few kilometres south of Dunedin, Vincent Pyke turned the first sod to formally begin the construction. It would be another 42 years before the line reached Cromwell, a distance of only 236 km.

From the very beginning the construction of the line did not go smoothly for a number of reasons, and during the five years from 1879 to 1884 only 12.5 km was built. A depression that affected all of New Zealand resulted in the government cutting back on railway construction. Also, these initial 12.5 km were so difficult and so expensive that a government commission was set up to look at the feasibility of continuing the construction. When its investigation was complete, the commission recommended that 'construction should never have started and must now be stopped'. Vincent Pyke opposed this view, and it was his intervention that ensured the project kept going.

By 1891 the construction reached the small town of Middlemarch. It

A team of labourers working on the Alexandra to Clyde section of the Otago Central Railway. Compared to other sections this one was flat and easygoing. Shovels, picks, wheelbarrows and wagons were the tools used in the construction, making it very labour intensive and slow.

ALEXANDRA MUSEUM

**RIGHT ABOVE** The Number 1 tunnel in the Poolburn Gorge is shown here as the men working on it pose for the camera. This tunnel is 201 m in length and bends slightly in the middle. In this photo the tunnel is far from complete; there is still a lot of work to be done on it. The face of the tunnel on the left has to be lined with hand-shaped schist rock, a pile of which is lying at the front right of the photograph. Wheelbarrows are also evidence that the interior of the tunnel is still being excavated. This tunnel is located on what proved to be the most difficult short section of the line, the 10 km through the Poolburn Gorge from Auripo to Lauder. Dogged by floods, frost, snow and the difficult terrain, the tunnel took 300 men three years to construct.

MANIOTOTO EARLY SETTLERS ASSOCIATION

**RIGHT BELOW** In 1895 the railway bridge that spans the Taieri River at Waipiata was completed. Here the team of men employed by the contractor to build the bridge pose proudly in front of their creation. Dressed in their best clothes and without tools, it is likely that this picture was taken at the wind-up party held to celebrate the bridge's completion.

ALEXANDRA MUSEUM

had taken 12 years to build the initial 63 km of line from Wingatui to Middlemarch. Nineteenth-century engineering had been stretched to its limits by the difficult terrain of the Taieri Gorge. Workers used picks, shovels, wheelbarrows and explosives to build 10 tunnels plus 20 bridges and culverts. Stone for the bridges and culverts was quarried in the Taieri Gorge, taken by sledges to where it was required and then hand-shaped by stonemasons. Sand was collected from the river and moved by packhorse. Conditions were harsh. All food and equipment had to be brought in from Dunedin, again by packhorse. Accidents were common and living conditions very primitive.

Beginning with the next section of line from Middlemarch, the system under which it was to be built was changed. Each person working on the line was now regarded as a self-employed contractor, responsible for supplying his own tools, explosives, horses and carts. Workers were split into teams of 10, a leader was selected and the engineers gauged the value of the work to be done, which was paid for in a lump sum. From there, this payment was divided among each team member under a system based on individual timesheets for the previous month. Apart from the construction of bridges and tunnels, the balance of the line would be built using this method. By 1898 the line had reached the new settlement of Ranfurly, which was constructed in the middle of the Maniototo Plain to cater for the new railway. As the trains began to run, Ranfurly became the place where drivers and other staff were changed and passengers were given a brief opportunity to snatch something to eat.

During the construction of the line through the Poolburn Gorge,

**LEFT ABOVE** Local stone was used extensively during the construction of the Otago Central Railway, and many of its bridges, viaducts and culverts were built with local schist. Here a team of stonemasons is working on the stone for the foundations of the rail bridge that would span the Manuherikia River at Alexandra, in 1902. Unlike the line, which was built by waged labourers, bridges and tunnels were built by contractors who employed teams of skilled craftsmen, such as those shown in this photograph.
ALEXANDRA MUSEUM

**LEFT BELOW** As the railway through Central Otago was completed, hotels quickly followed, to profit from the business that the new line brought to the area. The mudbrick Railway Hotel, opposite the station in Ida Valley, was one such building. Constructed in 1903, it is still in its original form today and is used as a holiday home.
ALEXANDRA MUSEUM

**OPPOSITE BELOW** Cromwell railway station in the 1920s, shortly after the Otago Central Railway was extended through the Cromwell Gorge from Clyde. Sheepyards were a common feature of Central Otago stations. Sheep were loaded directly into the open wagons from the yards in the front of this photograph, for transport to abattoirs on the east coast. Many local farmers owned small blocks of land close to the stations, which they used to hold stock, while waiting for the arrival of the train. Many of these small parcels of land were later sold as lifestyle blocks. The houses shown are standard issue railway houses of a type once seen beside railway stations throughout New Zealand.
CROMWELL MUSEUM

Vincent Pyke, as a young man, was one of Central Otago's strongest supporters. He was the energy behind the approval for, and the construction of, the Otago Central Railway, and was deeply involved in the civic affairs of Clyde and the Dunstan. Today the area is called Vincent County in his memory.

ALEXANDRA MUSEUM

political, building and weather problems were all encountered. A large camp was established on the flats in front of the Poolburn Viaduct to house the 300 men required for three years to build two large viaducts and two tunnels through this short distance of 10 km between Auripo and Lauder. Heavy snow delayed construction and floods washed away part of the Manuherikia Viaduct. The government was again making cutbacks, but this time the construction was so far advanced that there was no question of abandoning the project. Clyde was finally reached in 1906, with the line being extended to Cromwell in 1921. This last section would in time disappear under the waters of Lake Dunstan, created when the Clyde Dam was built in the 1980s.

Vincent Pyke was correct in his assumption that a railway would be good for Central Otago. It opened up the area and gave it a lifeline to the coast that was not dependent on poor-quality roads. However, as the roads into Central Otago improved and the railway's monopoly on the transport of goods was eased, road transport became the preferred means of transport. From there it was only a matter of time before the Otago Central Railway became obsolete. The railway operated for only 69 years before it was closed. In 1990 the rails and sleepers were removed and the Otago Central Railway became a recreational facility called the Otago Central Rail Trail that belongs to the people of New Zealand and is managed by the Department of Conservation.

During its lifetime the railway was the scene of several accidents. Most of these took place without any loss of life, until the accident of 4 June 1943. On that day an accident occurred that cost the lives of 21 people and injured another 41. A train with 113 passengers on board left Ranfurly, heading for Dunedin. By the time it reached a section of the line just south of Hyde called Straw Cutting, both the driver and the guard were asleep at the controls. The train was travelling too fast, and as a result it jumped the tracks in this cutting. The shambles that followed was New Zealand's most serious rail accident until the Tangiwai rail disaster of Christmas Eve, 1953. Today a stone memorial is located on a section of land set aside near Straw Cutting that records the names of the 21 people killed on that fateful day.

## VINCENT PYKE (1827–1894)

Without the efforts and influence of Vincent Pyke it is doubtful the Otago Central Railway would have ever been built. He was an avid fan of Central Otago and had the political connections and energy to push the project through against serious opposition.

History regards him as one of the area's ablest politicians and most effective advocates. Born in Somerset, England, he emigrated to Australia in 1851 with his wife, Frances, where he became involved in goldmining and retailing. He was a short man of rather stout build with an appearance that would often result in his having difficulty in convincing people to take him seriously. He was not well educated but had an excellent memory, was a good debater and a powerful speaker. He was also interested in politics and was elected to the Victorian Legislature for two terms. While on a visit to Otago in 1862 he was invited by the provincial government to establish a new Goldfields Department and to become its first commissioner. After he had established that department, which became redundant in 1867, he was then appointed warden and magistrate for the Dunstan goldfields, based at Clyde. He stood for and was elected as member of parliament for the Wakatipu electorate in 1873 and for the Dunstan electorate in 1875. He was MP for Tuapeka when he died in 1894 at the age of 67. His health had been poor throughout his adult life, a problem that was possibly not helped by what has been described as his fondness for alcohol.

While an MP, he did not let his parliamentary responsibilities interfere with his other interests. He founded the now defunct newspapers the *Southern Mercury* in 1873 and the *Otago Guardian* in 1874, while also writing a number of books on the history of the goldfields in Central Otago and various other subjects. He also became involved in goldmining in Roxburgh,

Not everybody regarded Vincent Pyke as a popular leading figure in the development of Central Otago transport, as this early newspaper cartoon depicts.
HOCKEN COLLECTIONS S04-777G.

ABOVE Transport of sheep from the runs of the Queenstown Lakes District by boat was common before the advent of trucks and decent roads. Here a mob of merino ewes cram the deck of the steamer *Antrim* which plied Lake Wakatipu during the early part of the twentieth century.

HOCKEN COLLECTIONS S04-272K, UNIVERSITY OF OTAGO, DUNEDIN

RIGHT Before the bridge was built at Lowburn, the only option available to move sheep or vehicles across the Clutha River was the ferry that operated here.

CROMWELL MUSEUM

was a staunch freemason and an avid planter of trees. However, the building of the Otago Central Railway and his establishment of the Otago Central Land League are regarded as his greatest achievements. The latter was a pressure group set up to convince the government of the wisdom and fairness of breaking up the large sheep runs of Central Otago and other parts of New Zealand that had been established under the Waste Lands Act of 1855. He wanted to see the big runs made available for closer settlement and the land involved taken out of the hands of a privileged few, who were well on their way to becoming a landed aristocracy. Pyke, along with many other powerful Liberals of the time, in particular John McKenzie, a fellow MP, were successful in getting the required legislation passed and the runs divided, thus allowing the common man in New Zealand to become a landowner.

When counties were established in 1876, Vincent Pyke became the first chairman of the county that would carry his name, one that still exists in Central Otago today: Vincent County.

# 9
# WORLD WAR I AND PRIVATE ANDREW MCBREEN

Central Otago is a long way from France, Belgium and Turkey, but these countries are where many of the young men of the area made the supreme sacrifice between 1914 and 1918. Some were caught up in the nationalism of king and country which is encouraged when recruiting to fight a war, while others were simply conscripted. Some were simple country boys, only educated to primary level in small country schools, with no desire to fight an enemy of which they had no first-hand knowledge. Their education was such that many of them would fight and die in countries that a few years earlier they would have been unable to locate on a map, if indeed they had had any awareness of the countries' existence. There were others who were not reluctant and saw the outbreak of war in Europe as an opportunity to travel, try something different or get away from a boring job. Often their only concern was that the war would end before they got there and had a chance to fight. In many instances they were shocked when they arrived at the front lines and saw the chaos that was taking place.

Some young men who could survive anything took the war in their stride and returned to Central Otago to carry on a normal life. Many others were not so lucky. Often they returned scarred emotionally, physically or psychologically and found the family farm a good place to hide from the world. Some became addicted to alcohol and lived alone in the smaller, partly abandoned ex-goldmining towns, attracted by the cheap rents, trying to eke out a living rabbiting or cutting firewood, between drinking bouts. Often this lifestyle was the only choice they had as the problems they suffered from were not recognised as illnesses in the first quarter of the twentieth century. No help was available and they were just expected to get on with life.

King and country was the theme of recruiting posters during World War I.
AUCKLAND MUSEUM

## PRIVATE ANDREW MCBREEN — OTAGO INFANTRY REGIMENT

Andrew McBreen was born in Ida Valley, Central Otago, in 1893. He was from a large family of five sisters and three older brothers, and his father, William McBreen, was a farmer. Andrew is also described as a farmer, but possibly, being too young to have the funds to buy his own property, he worked as a farm labourer in the Ida Valley. In 1917, at the age of 24, he was conscripted and forced to join the Otago Infantry Regiment, which put him through his basic training at Tauherenikau, north of Wellington. On his final leave in May 1917, a social was held at Moa Creek in the Ida Valley to farewell him, at which he spoke of being forced to go to war. Given the choice he would certainly not have gone and he promised that if he ever came up against the enemy he would make them suffer for making him leave his lovely valley.

He suffered his first bout of illness, which may have been stress-related and required three visits of the doctor each day, in camp shortly before he left New Zealand. August and September 1917 he spent on board ship, which was probably the last time he enjoyed himself, before landing in Sling army camp, in Salisbury, England. This sojourn was a time for training, up at 6am and in bed at 10pm, having spent the day drilling, route marching and polishing uniform buttons. In November Andrew crossed the English

Private Andrew McBreen (1893–1918), Otago Infantry Regiment, World War I.

ROBYN NEWMAN, *LINES FROM CENTRAL*

Volunteers, complete with lemon-squeezer hats and kitbags, waiting to board troopship No 10 at a Wellington wharf on 24 September 1914, bound for the trenches of France and Belgium.

AUCKLAND MUSEUM

**LEFT ABOVE** New Zealand nurses, along with a male officer and a young relation, pose for their photograph on the deck of the troopship *Athenic*. As part of the fifth contingent of nursing staff, nurses travelled on the *Athenic* and the *Opawa* to England in 1916. The *Athenic* left from Wellington on 30 December 1916, carrying troops of the 2nd Draft, 20th Reinforcements, New Zealand Expeditionary Force.

AUCKLAND MUSEUM

**LEFT BELOW** A break for food in the trenches during the Battle of the Somme. Dead bodies and ruined equipment are lying about and the fact that the trench has been recently shelled is evidenced by the loose soil.

013087, ALEXANDER TURNBULL LIBRARY, NATIONAL LIBRARY OF NEW ZEALAND

**BELOW** During 1914–1918, the machine gun changed the way wars were fought. Soldiers were led by officers who lived in the past and used tactics that had been made redundant by the invention of the weapon. Men were forced to attack the enemy head-on and were mown down in their thousands. The Battle of the Somme, the fight in which Private Andrew McBreen perished, went on for several months. There were 60,000 casualties on the day the battle began.

78    WORLD WAR I AND PRIVATE ANDREW MCBREEN

Channel and was put into the front line. He described the horror of the mud in the trenches and the noise of the artillery as hell on earth and remarked that he would like to be back in Ida Valley driving the plough. He was transferred to the bombing section and took part in a battle, slinging bombs, as he put it, and managed to survive without a scratch, the only man unharmed out of five in his section.

On New Year's Day 1918, in his twenty-fifth year, he was taken out of the front line and enjoyed a late Christmas dinner of turkey, plum duff and rum. Later that month he was in hospital for the second time since joining the army, with an outbreak of trench foot and a bad dose of influenza, the latter the result of standing in a trench for three days with water over his knees. When he received news from home describing the weddings of several local girls, he passed the comment that there would be none left to marry when he returned.

Judged fit again, he was soon back in the trenches, where he learnt that he was the last of the young men conscripted from the Ida Valley who had not been killed or wounded. By May the European summer was making life a little more tolerable, but he was by now infested with lice and was then back in hospital with another bout of influenza.

On 25 July 1918 he was killed at the age of 25, a little over a year from the date he was conscripted. His body is buried at the Gezaincourt Communal Cemetery Extension in Somme, France. The only thing that now remains to remind people of the fact that Andrew McBreen existed and fought a war is the inclusion of his name on a marble sign set into the wall of the Poolburn Hall in Ida Valley. This sign is often covered in starling droppings.

BELOW RIGHT Many of the churches in Central Otago have plaques dedicating the church, or parts of it, to men lost in both world wars. This church beside the main road in Waipiata contains a dedication to Donald Mathewson and John Reid, two young men killed in World War II.

BELOW LEFT Headstones that remind of the loss of human life during World War I are scattered throughout the cemeteries of Central Otago. Many of the memorials, such as this one for John Swinney in the cemetery at St Bathans, are just that, memorials. There was often nothing to bury, as the remains of many of the casualties were never found, blown to pieces or rendered unidentifiable.

Today, there are many other reminders in Central Otago of those who fought in World War I. Many of the cemeteries have headstones that mention others who were killed. These headstones do not stand alone, but are part of that which has been placed over a parent's grave, which usually indicates that the soldier's body is not buried in New Zealand. Multiple war memorials exist throughout the region.

Andrew McBreen was lucky in that he came from a large family; three males born to the family since his death have been named Andrew in his memory.

LEFT New Zealand casualties during World War I were high compared with those of World War II. A memorial gate at the entrance of Hills Creek Cemetery in the Ida Valley, Central Otago, lists the names of locals who served in World War I. Given the small population of the Ida Valley, there were a large number of casualties, as another memorial with additional names stands at the southern end of the valley.

ABOVE War memorials such as this one in Alexandra are found in most of the towns and villages throughout Central Otago.

HOCKEN COLLECTIONS S05-037F, UNIVERSITY OF OTAGO, DUNEDIN

80 | WORLD WAR I AND PRIVATE ANDREW MCBREEN

# 10
# D COMPANY — 23RD BATTALION AND THE BATTLE OF CRETE

At 9.30pm on 3 September 1939, the prime minister of New Zealand, Michael (Mickey) Joseph Savage, with the use of the historic phrase, 'Where Britain goes, we go. Where she stands, we stand', followed that country's lead and declared war on Germany. In the space of a few minutes, New Zealand had been thrown into its second European war in 21 years. Few lessons had been learnt from the debacle of World War 1. The Treaty of Versailles, the peace agreement written to halt the war to end all wars, had been botched and, with the German Kaiser now replaced by Nazis, German aggression was once again on the move.

Within days of this declaration of war, the New Zealand government had begun to take steps to raise several battalions of volunteers to take part. At the same time, it made one important change to the structure of the New Zealand forces as a result of bitter lessons learnt during World War 1: New Zealand soldiers were to be led by their own. During that war, the New Zealand forces had been placed under the command of British artistocrat career soldiers who had little in common with New Zealand soldiers and seemingly little regard for the large numbers of casualties that resulted from their outdated methods of warfare.

## BURNHAM CAMP TO GREECE, VIA BRITAIN AND EGYPT

For the first time new battalions of volunteers were not named after the province where they were raised. Instead, each battalion was numbered, with those numbers starting at 18 to avoid any possible confusion or identification with previous battalions.

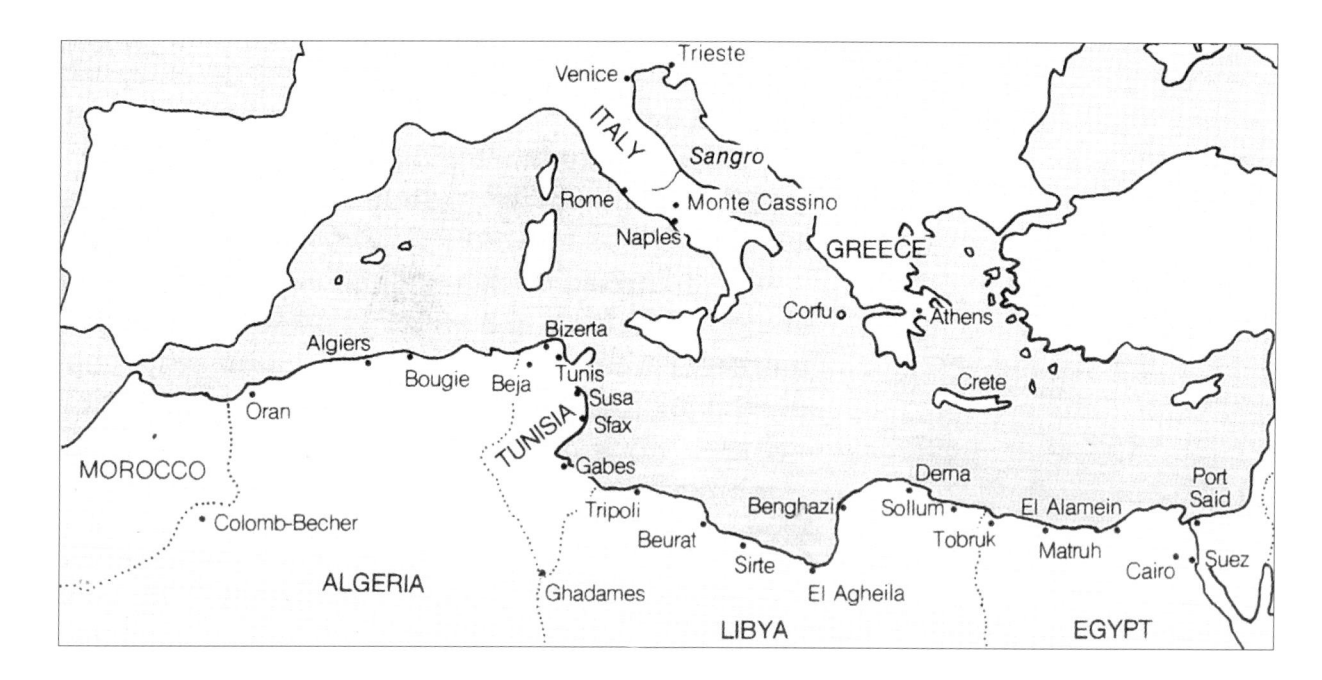

Most of the fighting done by D Company, 23rd Battalion during World War II was in Europe and North Africa, at locations shown on this map.

On 8 November 1939 a group of experienced officers who had served in World War I entered camp at Burnham, some 32 km south of Christchurch, to prepare for the training of South Island volunteers, who in turn arrived on 12 January 1940. Several battalions, including the 28th (Maori) Battalion, would eventually be formed throughout New Zealand to make up the 1st Echelon, 2nd New Zealand Expeditionary Force (2NZEF). One of these battalions was the 23rd, with ranks filled from volunteers scattered throughout the South Island. Within the 23rd Battalion itself, the various localities from which these men came were identified by companies. Volunteers from Central Otago and other areas of Otago formed D Company. This system of grouping men who were from the same province, who often knew each other, would remain throughout the entire war, from the first conflict in which New Zealand forces were involved at Mt Olympus in Greece during 1941, to the last at Idice bridgehead in Italy in 1945.

On 13 March 1940 the 23rd Battalion was placed on active service under the command of Lieutenant Colonel A.S. (Acky) Falconer, a decorated veteran of World War I who had made a living between the wars as a tobacconist. The battalion left Lyttelton on 1 May 1940 aboard the troopship *Andes*, joined a convoy in Cook Strait and then sailed via Perth and Cape Town to Great Britain, docking at Gourock, Firth of Clyde, Scotland, on 19 June 1940.

Northern Greece was where members of the 23rd Battalion went into action for the first time on 16 April 1941, in an attempt to hold defensive positions in the face of the German invasion via Bulgaria. Within days the Allies had been forced to retreat to Athens and were evacuated by the Royal Navy to Soudha Bay, Crete, on 25 April 1941.

DA-13609, ALEXANDER TURNBULL LIBRARY, NATIONAL LIBRARY OF NEW ZEALAND

The next six months were spent in Great Britain, initially living under canvas at Aldershot until being transferred to East Kent in September 1940. At East Kent the 23rd was on active service, expected to help defend that part of England where a German invasion was expected at any time. Victory in the Battle of Britain put paid to German plans for the invasion of England, and on 4 January 1941 the 23rd and the Maori Battalion left Liverpool bound for Egypt on board the *Althone Castle* via Cape Town. Several men must have had second thoughts about the wisdom of volunteering for a war because when the ship left Cape Town, 13 soldiers had deserted and were never seen again. The *Althone Castle* disembarked its human cargo in Egypt on 4 March 1941, but their stay was shortlived as a German attack on Greece was expected at any time. Twenty-one days after their arrival in Egypt, the 23rd Battalion boarded the *Cameronia* at Alexandria bound for the port of Piraeus, near Athens, Greece. From there they were transported in sheep and cattle railway wagons to Katerini in northern Greece to join a force of 58,000 British, Australian and New Zealand troops that had been ordered to help a poorly trained and equipped Greek army repel a German invasion.

The German Twelfth Army was massed on the Bulgarian border and on 6 April 1941 launched an attack on Greece. As the German blitzkrieg moved south, the 23rd Battalion was in a defensive position on the slopes of Mt Olympus, but it was not until 16 April that the battalion made its first contact with the enemy, 14 days short of a year since the 23rd had left New Zealand. During their attack on Greece the Germans held air superiority and outnumbered the Allies in both weapons and men. Thus, it is not surprising that the Allied defences of Greece were overwhelmed and forced to retreat south during this short campaign. By 24 April the 23rd Battalion had retreated to Athens and on 25 April was evacuated from D beach, Port Raffti, to Soudha Bay in Crete, on board the warships *Glengyle*, *Calcutta* and *Phoebe*. The battalion's first contact with the enemy had been unsuccessful.

Fortunately, the battalion had suffered few casualties in Greece and, although exhausted by retreat, was still a fighting unit. More serious, however, was the fact that it had lost much of its rations, clothing, camping gear and arms; equipment that would be sorely needed in the Battle of Crete, which would quickly follow the forced evacuation from Greece.

## BATTLE OF CRETE — 20–31 MAY 1941

Both the Germans and the Allies recognised the strategic importance of Crete, as the island contained three airstrips on its northern coast, which would have been very useful to the side that was successful in gaining control of them. From these landing grounds, air strikes could be launched into Egypt and parts of the Mediterranean that could not be reached from the European mainland. Following their easy victory in Greece, the German forces made plans to invade Crete, while the Allies moved to defend the island. In early 1941, the Allies had been able to crack the German codes and thus had access to the German war plans for Crete. General Freyburg, the supreme commander of the Allied forces on Crete, knew the when and where of the imminent German invasion, but was placed in the difficult position of not being able to spread his forces effectively, for fear of tipping off the Germans to the fact that their code had been cracked.

The events that took place in Crete during the month of May 1941 would be the most important of the war in establishing the reputation of the men from Central Otago who belonged to D Company, 23rd Battalion. Controversy surrounded the Allied loss of the Battle of Crete, and some of the leaders are still criticised today for what were regarded as poor decisions and weak tactics. The fact remains, however, that defeat was inevitable as the Germans had complete control of the skies over Crete, a deciding factor in the outcome of the battle. They were able to strafe and bomb Allied positions at will and land an airborne invasion fleet on Crete, unchallenged by Allied fighter planes. The Allies were unable to fortify the island owing to military commitments in other theatres of the war. The defenders were also short of the equipment required to fight a successful war, having left a large part of it in Greece. The soldiers on Crete were poorly equipped, poorly fed, poorly housed and poorly armed, while their adversaries were the exact opposite.

Once the 23rd landed in Crete, they became part of a combined force of 39,000 Greek, British, Australian and New Zealand forces present on the island and were directed to take up positions among the olive groves near the Maleme airstrip on the north coast, to the west of Soudha Bay. From 13 May onwards they were bombed and strafed daily by German Stuka aircraft as a softening-up process for the invasion that would follow. At dawn on the 20 May 1941 the invasion began when the Germans, using a large force of Dornier, Heinkel and Junker bombers, pounded the Allies' positions for two hours. The sky was then blackened by the largest airborne invasion the world had ever seen, when troop carriers began to release thousands of white, black, brown and green parachutes at various strategic locations on the north coast of Crete. Once in the air, many of the German parachutists were in the unfortunate position of being shot at from the ground and were slaughtered by the defenders before they even touched down. Those who made it to the ground safely were further hindered by not being able to locate their heavy weapons, which had been dropped by separate parachutes. Of 600 parachutists from the German 111 Battalion Assault Regiment of 11 Air Corps that were dropped in the area occupied by 23rd Battalion, a total of 400 were killed. Gliders filled with troops followed the first wave of German parachutists, and again casualties were high. Men were killed when the gliders were shot down by ground fire and crashed. Others were slaughtered en masse when Allied Bren gunners trained their sights on the exits at the rear of the gliders, killing those inside as they left the vehicle. That first day of the invasion was a victory for the Allied defenders, and it was not long before most of the men of D Company, 23rd Battalion were carrying Luger revolvers and Zeiss binoculars, taken as trophies from the bodies of German parachutists.

In the face of overwhelming German air superiority the 23rd Battalion had no chance of being on the winning side in the Battle of Crete, which was fought during May 1941. After four days of vicious fighting on the northern coast of the island they made a forced retreat over the mountains of Crete, to be evacuated from the south coast by the navy, for the second time in two months. This was a forced march, made by exhausted men over several days, with little in the way of food and water. Many could not complete the trek and were taken prisoner, destined to spend the rest of the war in prison camps in Germany.

DA-01110, ALEXANDER TURNBULL LIBRARY, NATIONAL LIBRARY OF NEW ZEALAND

In spite of the efforts of the defenders, the Germans over four days and in the face of huge casualties, eventually gained the upper hand in the Battle of Crete. Pursued by the enemy, the 23rd Battalion began a retreat to the coastal village of Sfakia, on the south coast of the island, in the hope of being evacuated by the Royal Navy. Crete is a steep country where it is possible to stand on the beaches of the north coast of the island and look up at the mountains, which are often covered in snow. The retreat over these mountains was a trek of 96 km. Men who made the trek were worn out by four days of intensive fighting and little or no sleep. With little or no food or water and with German Stuka aircraft strafing them for most of the distance, many of the Allied soldiers were unable to complete the trek. A large number simply sat down at the side of the mountain tracks, physically and mentally exhausted, waiting to be taken prisoner by the Germans. Others managed to reach Sfakia by eating flowers and drinking water from puddles to sustain them.

Those member of the 23rd Battalion who were evacuated from Crete were taken to Egypt, where their war continued in the fight against the Germans under General Rommel. This young soldier was very lucky to be part of that evacuation.

DA-01173, ALEXANDER TURNBULL LIBRARY, NATIONAL LIBRARY OF NEW ZEALAND

The 23rd Battalion lost 114 men when they were taken prisoner following the Allied defeat in Crete. Forced to spend several years in prison camps, many of the soldiers did not survive the confinement. Here a funeral of one such soldier in the prisoner of war camp, Stalag VIIIB, is recorded by Sergeant Colin Powell, who was himself taken prisoner on Crete.

HOCKEN COLLECTIONS S05-065E, UNIVERSITY OF OTAGO, DUNEDIN

It was during this retreat that a member of the 23rd Battalion, Sergeant Hulme, won a Victoria Cross. The incident took place when, on reaching the village of Stilos, two 23rd Battalion officers, Lieutenants Norris and Cunningham, made a reconnaissance while the men with them settled down for a brief rest. When these two officers reached a stone wall at the top of a nearby ridge, they saw Germans emerging from a creek bed about 400 m away. At the same time, the Germans caught sight of them and opened fire with machine guns. Men of the 23rd were summoned to the top of the ridge. Sergeant Hulme was one of the first to arrive and took up a position sitting side-saddle on the stone wall, shooting at the enemy. He killed several while firing from this exposed position, until he was himself wounded in the arm. For bravery shown during this incident, and also while acting as a sniper in the earlier fighting, Sergeant Hulme was later awarded the Victoria Cross.

D COMPANY — 23RD BATTALION AND THE BATTLE OF CRETE

Mule packer and cook, Frank Hore (left) of Naseby, Central Otago, photographed near the front line at Sangro, Italy on Christmas Day 1944. The experience he gained in the use of mules while at the same time working as a cook for the members of the Soldiers Syndicate during their annual musters on the Buster was put to good use when he performed a similar role in the army. Frank Hore survived the war and on his return to Central Otago worked for many years taking care of the water races on the Hawkdun Irrigation Scheme, which had been developed in the 1930s by the construction of the Falls Dam near St Bathans.

DA-04941, ALEXANDER TURNBULL LIBRARY, NATIONAL LIBRARY OF NEW ZEALAND

Not all those members of the 23rd who were able to complete the walk to the south coast of Crete would be evacuated by the Royal Navy. Pick-ups were made over several nights at great risk to the ships involved, but the numbers waiting were so huge that not everybody could be taken off before a halt to prevent loss of these ships was made. In spite of this conservative approach, the navy suffered the loss of some 2000 sailors in its attempt to supply, defend and evacuate Crete during May 1941. Those members of the 23rd Battalion who were left behind either became prisoners of war or hid out in the hills of Crete, waiting for an opportunity to somehow be evacuated or find their own way to Egypt.

The ranks of the 23rd Battalion were decimated in Crete. Some of their number had been evacuated directly to Egypt from Greece, but when the Battle of Crete began on 20 May, the battalion numbered 571. By the time the last pick-up was made by the navy, from the south coast, that number had been reduced to 230. Fifty-six men had been killed, 171 wounded and 114 made prisoners of war. Of the officers, none above the rank of lieutenant remained fit for active duty. However, with its numbers strengthened by reinforcements from Central Otago, D Company would remain as a vital part of the battalion until the end of the war.

In spite of the fact that the Allied forces lost the Battle of Crete, the reason that it took place would have far-reaching consequences for the Germans. By invading Crete, Hitler was forced to delay what would later prove to be his fatal mistake of opening a second front, when he invaded the Soviet Union. This delay led to the German army being caught out by the Russian winter before it was able to reach Moscow. Thousands of German troops, ill equipped for the harsh winter, froze to death and were eventually defeated. If Hitler had ignored Crete and turned his forces towards the Soviet Union a month earlier, the outcome of the invasion of the Soviet Union might have been very different. Another consequence of the Battle of Crete was its effect on the future use of paratroops by the Germans in World War II. Casualties were so high that Hitler never again used paratroops as an invading force. Instead, the men who had survived Crete as part of what had once been regarded as an elite unit, were simply integrated with the ordinary German infantry forces and ceased to exist.

Today, there is little evidence in Crete of the chaos that took place there during May 1941. A visitor is able to catch a bus or taxi out along the main road leading from Soudha Bay to the village of Galatas, where the 23rd Battalion counter-attack and bayonet charge took place. The small asphalt landing strip that was so important still exists at Maleme, but is now close to a smart tourist resort. Leaving the bus a kilometre before Maleme and walking 300 m up a side-road through olives groves brings a visitor to the German cemetery. Located on the once strategic hill that overlooked Maleme airstrip, the cemetery there contains the graves of several thousand German paratroopers. Walking among them, it is difficult to find a single headstone that names a paratrooper over the age of 28.

# 11
# BEGINNINGS OF THE WINE INDUSTRY

Central Otago's wine industry was pioneered by a man who was a native of France. His name was Jean Desire Feraud, a dapper man with a goatee beard and an appearance that confirmed his French ancestry. In the 1860s he planted the first grapes in Central Otago, on his property at Dunstan Flat, which he named Monte Christo. These vines, after a shaky start, were to produce what was referred to as 'Aromatic tonic bitter wines with excellent medicinal qualities'.

Jean Feraud, often described as a man who could be difficult, combative, intolerant and litigious, first appeared in Central Otago in 1863. He and several partners proceeded to make a fortune from gold taken at a place on the Clutha River that is now called Frenchman's Point. Located on the bank of the river, Frenchman's Point is very close to Alexandra, some 150 m downstream from where the Alexandra Bridge spans the Clutha today.

In 1864 he and another Frenchman called Bladier purchased 26 hectares of land on the Dunstan Flats and proceeded to plant the vines that would identify the property, Monte Christo, as the birthplace of the Central Otago wine industry. Monte Christo was irrigated by water from Waipuna Springs, located some seven kilometres along the present-day Clyde–Omakau road. Bladier was familiar with the irrigation techniques that were required to make the 26 hectares a successful vineyard and orchard. However, he left Central Otago in 1867 and Feraud took over his share, while at the same time purchasing a leasehold property comprising 78 hectares in the Waikerikeri Valley. Feraud purchased this second property to give himself control of the irrigation water that was vital to the success of his viticulture operation. This proved to be a bad move as he spent years arguing with neighbouring property owners over water rights. It was not until 1871, after several trips to court, that the matter was finally settled in Feraud's favour.

Jean Desire Feraud, the Frenchman who was the first person to grow grapes and produce wine in Central Otago in 1864, after establishing the Monte Cristo winery near Alexandra. Feraud was a clever man who was also a very successful goldminer, with a claim on the Clutha River near Alexandra. Today the area surrounding his former claim is called Frenchman's Point. He was also mayor of Clyde for several years from 1866. In 1891 Feraud left New Zealand, possibly to return to his native France; nothing is known of his life from that date.

ALEXANDRA MUSEUM

The stone winery built by Jean Feraud on his property, Monte Cristo, near Alexandra. He produced very acceptable wine from his locally grown grapes, wine that won several awards in Australia. The property also grew a variety of fruit trees, currants and vegetables. Monte Cristo was eventually subdivided into small blocks, many of which still support fruit trees and grapes.

ALEXANDRA MUSEUM

The litigation and lack of water had by then taken their toll on Feraud and Monte Christo. By 1873 he was in financial trouble and the lease on his property in the Waikerikeri Valley had been cancelled by the provincial government. His vines and crops at Monte Christo were also floundering under a poor water supply, and by 1873 he was bankrupt.

It seems that Feraud had other offshore funds to draw on as by 1876 he had bounced back, with Monte Christo supporting 1200 grapevines, 1200 fruit trees and 4000 small berry bushes. The wines he produced from these vines were destined to become top-quality vintages, and in 1879 and 1881 he was able to exhibit them at both the Sydney and Melbourne International Exhibitions. In these two years his wines won several First Class of Merit awards at both venues. Closer to home, he was awarded a First Class of Merit at the Dunedin Industrial Exhibition of 1881.

While all these ups and downs were happening, Feraud did not neglect his civic duties. In 1866 he became the first mayor of Clyde, was a founding member of the local hospital committee and also became a justice of the peace. In 1882 he made an odd move. He sold Monte Christo and moved to Dunedin, where he established a cordial factory. In 1891 he disappeared from the New Zealand scene and nothing more is known of his life from that date.

Monte Christo was subdivided into small rural blocks in the 1950s. The original farmhouse was pulled down, but the old stone winery still stands today as a reminder of the beginnings of the vibrant wine growing industry that exists in Central Otago today.

# 12
# ORIGINS OF THE FRUIT GROWING INDUSTRY

Although it is now a large, well established industry, fruit growing in Central Otago was something that many of the early miners just drifted into. It was certainly not their intention to become orchardists when they headed for the goldfields, but as time passed many of them realised that they were not going to make their fortunes out of gold. As they began to work for wages, many built themselves homes and planted gardens that included such small fruit as currants and gooseberries. At the same time, a small number turned to commercial market gardening, while others planted fruit trees. The fact that these plantings flourished indicated the fertility of the soil. This fertility, plus long sunshine hours in summer and the availability of a good source of water from the nearby rivers, combined to make orcharding a viable and economic proposition in various locations throughout Central Otago.

## THE TEVIOT VALLEY

The main fruit growing areas of the Teviot Valley are from Coal Creek, a few kilometres north of Roxburgh, through to Ettrick. Two brothers, John and Joseph Tamblyn, are credited with the first attempt to grow fruit commercially in Central Otago. In 1866 Joseph Tamblyn bought two cherry trees, which he planted at Coal Creek. He followed this up by importing a small number of apricot, peach and plum trees from Victoria in Australia, which the brothers then used as the basis for the first commercial orchard in Central Otago.

Their success was such that many miners began to follow suit by planting out small orchards, learning by trial and error, while at the same time continuing with their daytime jobs until the trees started to bear. Most of

A fruit canning factory, processing mainly locally grown apricots, was opened in Roxburgh in 1905 in a ceremony that was attended by a large portion of the population of Roxburgh, dressed in their finest.

HOCKEN COLLECTIONS S05-064F, UNIVERSITY OF OTAGO, DUNEDIN

them started out with imported trees, again from Australia, but this time sourced from Coles Nursery in New South Wales. Early plantings consisted of plums, apples, cherries, peaches, nectarines and quinces. A regular and honest supply of fruit trees was an initial problem until John Tamblyn established his own nursery in 1880. Once this local nursery was able to supply good-quality fruit trees, many more orchards were established, and it was not long before both sides of the Clutha River from Coal Creek to Dumbarton were covered in fruit trees.

Certain types of fruit did well in certain areas. Gold-bearing soil has always been one of the requirements for successful apricot production, with Coal Creek being the stand-out area for growing apricots. Further south at Dumbarton the environment was better suited to growing apples. Attempts were made at viticulture in this area in 1895 and were backed by government support, which paid for the services of a Signor Bragato, viticultural superintendent for New South Wales. He visited the area while on a tour of New Zealand and suggested that Roxburgh and its surrounds were ideally suited for the growing of grapes. His advice was based on a brief visit, and what he had failed to take into account was that winter frosts were too severe to allow successful viticulture in the Teviot Valley. He was partly correct in his assumption, however, as huge areas of Central Otago would eventually be planted in grapes to produce Pinot Noir wine.

Problems existed and still exist for those involved in orcharding throughout the area. Frosts, especially late frosts, were always a recipe for disaster. To combat these in the early days, oil pots were placed throughout the orchards, and when frosts threatened, the pots were lit to cover the area in black, sooty smoke. In more modern times growers still face a threat from frost, but they now have thermometers that set off a warning bell when temperatures drop. Instead of oil pots, sprinklers are now turned on to cover the crop in ice and protect it from frost. Large revolving wind blades are also used, as are helicopters hovering over an orchard or a vineyard. Both keep the air moving to alleviate frost, but use of the latter can be very expensive.

To grow successfully, especially in the hot summers, fruit in this area and other parts of Central Otago must be watered artificially because rainfall is low and often uncertain. In the early days, water was often brought in using the water races initially dug by the goldminers to provide water to their sluicing claims. Thus, it followed that fruit would be grown where these races existed, and their location was often the deciding factor in the establishment of an orchard. Following the introduction of electricity, diesel engines and modern vacuum pumps, water could be pumped directly from the rivers, and much of the modern-day irrigation is provided by overhead sprinklers using river water.

Once the first orchards began producing crops, the problem of where and how to sell the product arose. At first ripe fruit was simply hawked at such places as race meetings or, if that was not successful, house to house. A

The construction of the Otago Central Railway was a huge economic boost for the orchardists of Central Otago as it gave them access for the first time to the large markets on the east coast. In the early days, orchardists were responsible for making their own fruit cases which, when filled, were delivered to the station by cart or truck.

HOCKEN COLLECTIONS S05-0651, UNIVERSITY OF OTAGO, DUNEDIN

Strawberries being picked in a field near Roxburgh.

HOCKEN COLLECTIONS S05-064L, UNIVERSITY OF OTAGO, DUNEDIN

more sophisticated method of sale was tried in 1877 when the first consignment of 40 cases of peaches was taken by wagon to Dunedin by A. J. Tamblyn, a son of the original John Tamblyn. This was sold to a Dunedin wholesaler, Dunning Brothers. In the 1880s the Teviot and Alexandra Fruit Growers Association was formed by growers to concentrate on the marketing of fruit in Dunedin and Christchurch. A Dunedin businessman with the surname of Lorie was put in charge of all marketing, and a system of price averaging and quality control was set up. Initially, the fruit had to be taken by wagon to meet the rail at Milton, but in 1882 the railway line was extended to Lawrence, then to Beaumont, Millers Flat and finally, in 1925, to Roxburgh.

A setback to the whole system of marketing took place in 1885 when the serious pest codlin moth first made its appearance in the Teviot Valley. Growers were put under stress when many of their trees had to be uprooted and burnt in an attempt to defeat this moth. These attempts were only partly successful, however.

In 1899 the Teviot and Alexandra Fruit Growers Association was liquidated and replaced in 1901 by the Teviot Fruit Growers Association, with the ubiquitous John Tamblyn as its first secretary. This group handled the marketing for many years, until the Teviot growers voted to join forces with the government-run Fruit Control Board in 1937. This marriage provided certain advantages, the most important of which was a government guaranteed price on export fruit. By 1936 the New Zealand Fruit Growers Association also became a reality. Based in Dunedin, it made life easier for fruit growers by handling all types of equipment, supplies and trading functions. In 1939 the Internal Marketing Department was set up by the government to control the distribution of and fix the wholesale and retail prices of apples and pears. This was followed in 1943 and 1944 by the same body taking the supply and pricing of apricots, plums and peaches under its wing.

Fruit growing in the Teviot Valley today, while partly under government control, is now much more sophisticated. Science has been applied to improve everything from cultivation to packing. Orchards still line the banks of the Clutha River from Coal Creek to Dumbarton, growing the same fruits, albeit different varieties to cater for tastes to suit the lucrative Asian markets. Problems do exist in finding enough pickers to harvest the ripe fruit. This has been partly aided by district councils fast tracking temporary work permits for visitors wishing to work short term picking fruit. Apricots and cherries have become the important and profitable fruit crops, and orcharding is still a mainstay of the economy of the Teviot Valley.

## THE FRUITLANDS DEBACLE

Not all attempts at growing fruit commercially in Central Otago were as successful as the orchards of the Teviot Valley. Bald Hill Flat, the original name for the area that today bounds the main highway approximately halfway between Roxburgh and Alexandra, was renamed Fruitlands when its

Well dressed cherry pickers working in a Roxburgh orchard in 1939. As orchards grew from small beginnings into large commercial operations, the availability of labour to pick the fruit became a problem. The work was not popular because it was seasonal and wages were low; and comfortable, affordable accommodation was in short supply. Labour shortages still exist today, for the same reasons.

HOCKEN COLLECTIONS S05-065Q,
UNIVERSITY OF OTAGO, DUNEDIN

Late frosts in spring and summer are a problem that must be faced by orchardists and grape growers in Central Otago. For several decades in the twentieth century, orchardists used these pots when frost threatened. Filled with oil, they were lit to create a blanket of black smoke throughout an orchard to provide protection from frost. Although effective, the black smoke that belched from these pots was a pollutant. They are now rarely used — frost is fought using water, large fans mounted on high posts and sometimes even helicopters hovering over the area.

HOCKEN COLLECTIONS S05-045L.

potential as a fruit growing area was first mooted. Today the name Fruitlands still remains, but is entirely inappropriate as it is one of the few areas in Central Otago where fruit does not grow.

In 1914 a company called Otago Central Fruitlands was formed and 80 hectares (200 acres) of fruit trees, mainly apples, were planted at Fruitlands to supply the export market. The project was managed by an Englishman named Phillips, who had a theory that the fruit produced here would be of a special quality because it was grown at a high altitude. Enthusiasm for the scheme was such that during 1915 a further 48 hectares (120 acres) were added to the site, which then contained a total of 40,000 fruit trees.

Only one crop of fruit was ever picked and exported as the area suffered from a mini-climate that was completely unsuitable for orcharding. Fruitlands was one of the coldest areas of Central Otago and was subject to severe frosts, often out of season when the fruit was forming on the trees. The project which had started with such high hopes was a financial disaster, and many leading Dunedin families who had invested in the company lost everything they had in the fiasco. Many of the orchards at Fruitlands were owned by World War I veterans, who also went bankrupt. Those who survived turned to sheep and cattle farming, but not until they had removed the 40,000 useless fruit trees. Today not one commercial fruit tree is grown at Fruitlands.

## ALEXANDRA, CLYDE AND CROMWELL

There are five important names in the development of orcharding in Alexandra, Clyde and Cromwell: Lye Bow, Jean Desire Feraud, Andreas Iversen, Mrs Dawson and William Annan. The efforts and vision of these people, along with their recognition of the value of irrigation, set the scene for modern-day fruit growing in the area.

The first, Lye Bow, was originally from China. He was smuggled out of China after he was convicted of killing a man in a duel. He came to Central Otago in the 1860s to mine for gold, and when the precious metal ran out, he turned to orcharding and market gardening for a living. He was quick to take advantage of the two water races that existed at the southern end of what is now Butchers Dam because he realised the importance of irrigation if his efforts were to be successful. Lye Bow became a regular sight as he hawked his fruit and vegetables by horse and cart around early Alexandra. Today his orchard and garden are gone, but the area where they were located is named Lye Bow in his memory, and the outline of the two water races he tapped can still be seen running along the hillsides at the southern end of the dam.

Jean Desire Feraud, the Frenchman who is credited with being the first to grow grapes in Central Otago, was another pioneer who quickly recognised the value of irrigation. He established the orchard and market garden called Monte Christo, which was located between Alexandra and Clyde, near the Clyde cemetery. He took water from races still being used to work gold claims in the 1860s, and he was the first to become involved in litigation concerning water rights. Water was, and still is, a jealously guarded commodity in the arid climate of Central Otago, and disputes still take place over its use today, 140 years after Feraud went to court in order to secure a reliable supply for his orchard and garden.

Mrs Dawson was the wife of Richard Dawson, a goldminer. In 1863 she began to develop a garden and orchard around her home in Conroy's Gully, when by chance she was offered 12 fruit and two nut trees that had been sent from Britain to Galloway Station near Alexandra, only to be rejected

Making fruit boxes under the large walnut tree at Dawson's Orchard near Alexandra. Mrs Dawson and her husband were the couple who developed the Dawson cherry, a delicious maroon-coloured cherry that ripens just before Christmas.

HOCKEN COLLECTIONS S05-0641, UNIVERSITY OF OTAGO, DUNEDIN

ORIGINS OF THE FRUIT-GROWING INDUSTRY

Andreas Iversen was a pioneer orchardist of Central Otago, who established and managed an orchard at Earnscleugh, near Alexandra.

HOCKEN COLLECTIONS S05-064K.

on arrival by the station's owner. She shared these trees with her neighbour Andreas Iversen and, with the help of her husband, Richard Dawson, set about establishing a valuable commercial orchard. The Dawson orchard became the birthplace of the Dawson cherry, the dark red, juicy, delicious cherry that ripens just before Christmas.

The man with whom Mrs Dawson shared her fruit trees was the pioneer orchardist Andreas Iversen, a native of Denmark who came to Central Otago in 1863 via the goldfields of Australia. Initially he mined for gold at Dunstan, Naseby and Conroy's Gully, near Alexandra. When his prospecting luck ran out, he and his wife, Jane, set up house on 240 hectares (600 acres) of arid land at Earnscleugh. He had access to irrigation from miners' water races and was able to establish a large orchard in an area that is recognised today as a leading fruit growing area. Iversen was also active in local affairs. He pushed for land settlement and was the driving force behind much of the development of Earnscleugh into orchards. In later life he became the first chairman of the newly established Central Otago Fruit Growers Association and was also a member of the Acclimatization Society.

The potential of the Cromwell Gorge was not recognised until a local doctor named J.G. Hyde pointed out how similar it was to his native California, where fruit was grown extensively. In 1901 William Annan took the doctor's advice and planted the first orchard in the gorge. Again, water was the essential ingredient for success, and by 1901 the technology existed to draw water from the Clutha River, which ran through the gorge. Annan built a small cob shed and, guided by the doctor, ordered a wide variety of stonefruit, citrus and nut trees from Australian nurseries as there was no local supply at the time. Once planted, all except the citrus thrived. During the establishment years, Annan continued to work on a local gold dredge until he had made enough money to build a house on the property and move into full-time orcharding. Several other orchards were established in the Cromwell Gorge and were worked up until the 1980s, when they were inundated by Lake Dunstan, which had formed in the gorge behind the Clyde Dam.

# 13
# THE STOCK AND STATION INDUSTRY

As farming became important and gold brought wealth to Central Otago and Dunedin in the 1860s, stock and station companies became established throughout the area, and for more than 100 years they would have a huge influence on the development of the area. The industry was unique to Australia and New Zealand and was virtually unknown in Great Britain in the nineteenth century, where farmers held the responsibility for selling their own stock or wool and sourcing their own farming needs. In Australia and New Zealand the situation was different. The roads were often only rough tracks or were non-existent, runholders and farmers were concentrating on establishing themselves and farming finance was difficult to obtain because banks were reluctant to lend money when only leasehold land, animals or wool could be offered as security. Farmers needed a separate source of finance and the convenience of having their stock and wool sold for them on commission, along with a local supply of farming merchandise. As early as the 1860s there were entrepreneurs in Dunedin who saw this as an opportunity to make money as middlemen. These men included Frederick Dalgety, Donald Reid, John Ritchie, John Wright and John Stephenson, who in turn founded, respectively, Dalgety & Co., Donald Reid & Co., Russell Ritchie & Co. (later National Mortgage & Agency Co.) and Wright Stephenson & Co., business names that lasted into the final quarter of the twentieth century.

In the 1860s Dalgety & Co. began as merchants in Dunedin, calling themselves Dalgety Rattray. Russell Ritchie & Co. specialised in financing runholders, while Wright Stephenson & Co. concentrated on the sale and purchase of wool and stock on commission. Donald Reid & Co. would not become established until 1878. In time these companies would grow into large public enterprises that dealt in all aspects of business involving primary

Selling livestock on commission was, and still is, one of the valuable services provided by the stock and station companies to their farmer clients, who often lacked the business expertise to handle the sale of their livestock. This left them free to concentrate on farming. The companies owned and built yards to pen the stock on sale days. Sharp-eyed auctioneers, usually salaried staff employed by the firms, called the bids while looking for further bids in an attempt to gain the best price on the day for their employer's clients. Much of the farmers' stock is also sold direct to the abattoirs, which have their own stock buyers living in the rural communities.

production, competing with each other for business among the farmers of Central Otago and the rest of New Zealand.

Each company operated in Central Otago by employing stock agents to represent their interests to the local farmers and compete for their business through personal contact and service. Many of these stock agents were colourful characters with gregarious personalities who worked hard and also often drank hard, and the local hotels were ideal places to meet and mix with their existing or potential clients. Central Otago farmers were very loyal to the stock firms and usually channelled all their business through one firm, often over several generations on properties where sons followed fathers. This loyalty, however, was in many cases tempered by the fact that the farmer owed money to a particular stock firm and was obliged to put all his business through that company. In return, the stock firms were also loyal to their farming clients. They were slow to force the sale of farms that owed them money and had fallen behind with repayments. It is a widely known fact that without this lenient attitude of the stock firms during the depression of the 1930s, many of the local families that still farm in Central Otago would not have survived those difficult years.

The stock firms simplified farming. In addition to making stock agents available, the firms established stores throughout the area that sold farm merchandise. They built saleyards where farmers could sell their stock, and the stock agents often arrived on the farms in season, at the farmer's request, to draft and purchase fat lambs and cattle for the abattoirs. The firms built wool stores in the main centres to handle wool and skins, provided insurance cover, organised transport and offered financial advice. The firm would buy and sell all the farmer's produce on commission, meaning the firm took over any risks that existed outside the farm gate which the farmers, who were often unskilled in the ways of international business and export, were likely to face in the disposal of their produce.

## FREDERICK DALGETY (1817–1894) OF DALGETY & CO.

Frederick Dalgety left England in the 1840s to prospect for gold in Victoria, but he soon realised there was more money to be made provisioning the miners. As the gold ran out and miners turned to farming, Dalgety was there to supply their needs, while at the same time developing a large business trading in wool. In 1858 he appointed two of his brothers, Edmund and Richard, to head up his New Zealand operation, and he joined forces with one James Rattray to establish a Dalgety branch in Dunedin. In its early years this office was responsible for managing some 30 sheep stations owned by Frederick Dalgety scattered throughout Otago. This was the era of the large leasehold runs, and when the local runholders began to feel the pressures of rabbit infestation and low farming returns in the 1880s, Frederick Dalgety had the financial muscle to buy them out. He was at one time the owner of the huge Morven Hills Station that straddled the Lindis Pass and of the Hawkdun Station, near St Bathans. It was while he was the owner of this property that Dalgety made the gift of the corrugated iron Church of St Alban the Martyr to the people of St Bathans. This church still stands today in the main street of the town.

When the government moved to subdivide the large runs at the beginning of the twentieth century Dalgetys turned their attention in Central Otago to wool and livestock brokering, offering seasonal finance and supplying farm merchandise. In 1961 they took over another stock and station company, New Zealand Loan & Mercantile. This resulted in a name change to Dalgety & NZ Loan and then Dalgety Crown, until they themselves were taken over by Wrightson NMA in 1986. At that point the name Dalgety disappeared from the stock and station industry in both Central Otago and the rest of New Zealand.

## DONALD REID (1833–1919) OF DONALD REID & CO.

Donald Reid was an entrepreneur who during his lifetime went from farm labourer to cabinet minister, to stock and station company founder. He was born in Scotland and emigrated to Dunedin with his family in 1849. After working on several local properties as a labourer, he purchased land at North Taieri in 1856, which he would develop over three decades into the Salisbury Estate.

Farming, involvement in cartage and speculation in Central Otago goldmining made him very wealthy, and in 1863 he was elected to the Otago Provincial Council and then the House of Representatives as member for Taieri in 1866. His political views favoured a land settlement policy that made it easier for those with a little capital to become farmers. He described this as a belief in the notion that it was a common human aspiration to own a little bit of land. In 1872 he was instrumental in having legislation passed

Donald Reid, the founder of the stock and station business, Donald Reid & Co., was also one of the most dedicated of the liberal Otago landowners who worked for land reform. A wealthy man, he created an estate on the Taieri Plain called Salisbury, where he enjoyed the comforts of the gentry class to which he had risen. Salisbury House was built on the estate in 1872 and contained 14 rooms, embellished with marble, kauri and slate. Reid also donated 4 hectares nearby to build a Presbyterian church and manse.

HOCKEN COLLECTIONS S05-064E, UNIVERSITY OF OTAGO, DUNEDIN

that assisted settlers onto Crown land by means of a small deposit and a deferred payment. Although he achieved the rank of cabinet minister, he was never an enthusiastic politician, and in 1878 he retired from political life.

In the same year he founded Donald Reid & Co, a stock and station company that would do business in Central Otago for more than a century, trading in the latter half of the twentieth century as Donald Reid Otago Farmers Ltd, until it was taken over by the Christchurch-based company Pyne Gould Guinness. Donald Reid's main reason for starting the business was to provide employment for his family, and from 1878 to 1914 four sons, two stepsons and two sons-in-law were involved in the company. Heavy losses during the depression of the early 1880s made him cautious, and he was always content to operate the company only in Otago and then only within the bounds of the stock and station business.

Donald Reid was a short, thickset man who wore a full beard, spoke with a broad Scots accent and was taciturn and often blunt. He is also described as diligent, principled, honest and stubborn. He retired from active involvement with the company in 1918 and died the next year at Abbotsford, south of Dunedin, at the age of 86.

## JOHN RITCHIE (1842–1912) OF NATIONAL MORTGAGE & AGENCY CO.

John Ritchie was one of the most influential figures in the early development of Central Otago. Born in Glasgow, he came to Dunedin in 1865 to work for George Russell, who specialised in lending money to the big runholders, acted as a local agent for those who lived outside New Zealand and was an exporter of their wool. Ritchie became a partner in Russell's company in 1873, and the name of the business was changed to Russell, Ritchie & Co. In 1877 the National Mortgage & Agency Co. (NMA) was established in London to invest in farmland in New Zealand. To ease their entry into New Zealand, they purchased the business of Russell Ritchie, changed its name, and in 1884 John Ritchie became the general manager of NMA. He then set about transforming the firm from a finance company to a stock and station business, with its head office in Dunedin. The new emphasis was on exporting farm produce, trading in agricultural goods and lending money to farmers, using their produce as security. NMA and John Ritchie also invested directly in the freezing works industry and were involved with the first shipment of frozen meat from New Zealand on the ship *Dunedin*, which

LEFT This building in Water Street, Dunedin, began life as the head office of New Zealand's first multinational, the Union Steam Ship Company. It was later modified, by removing the pillboxes on the roof, as the head office of NMA for most of that company's life. Today the building lies empty, its decline a result of the exodus from Dunedin of the head offices of large companies.
AUCKLAND MUSEUM 995-81

BELOW George (G.R.) Ritchie, the son of the first general manager of National Mortgage & Agency Co. (NMA), was a clever and powerful businessman whose decisions had a huge effect on the Central Otago farmers who owed the company money or relied on it for their seasonal finance. On his retirement, the leadership of NMA passed to his son James (Jim) Ritchie, who led the company until it was taken over by Wrightsons (formerly Wright Stephenson & Co.) in the 1970s.
HOCKEN COLLECTIONS S05-064H, UNIVERSITY OF OTAGO, DUNEDIN

sailed from Port Chalmers in 1882. NMA became a large public company that traded for more than a century, but unlike some of its competitors, it expanded from Dunedin throughout New Zealand by purchasing existing stock and station businesses in other major centres.

John Ritchie's life was family, church and business. He was a sober man who had little interest in social contact. When he died in 1912 he left his wife Ella, six sons and a daughter. One son, George Ritchie, would head NMA, to be followed by a grandson, James Ritchie. The latter was the general manager of NMA when as a public company in 1972 it merged with Wright Stephenson & Co. and was renamed Wrightson NMA.

In time, the NMA name connection with Wrightson faded and NMA disappeared from Central Otago. The once proud NMA head office building in Water Street, Dunedin, the last reminder of the existence of the company, is now rundown and abandoned.

## JOHN WRIGHT, JOHN STEPHENSON & WRIGHT STEPHENSON & CO.

The only stock and station company that began life in the 1860s and still trades today is Wrightsons. Wrightsons began life when John Wright and

Robert Robertson started an auctioneering and merchandise business in Dunedin on 12 October 1861. Robert Robertson soon dropped out, and in 1864 John Stephenson became the second party in a partnership called Wright Stephenson. Both men were Englishmen who were to make good in a competitive business environment in Dunedin.

Wright's talents lay in the financial side of the business, while Stephenson was a successful auctioneer and a keen judge of livestock. The two partners developed a trade in horses, which were in strong demand during the Central Otago goldrush, stocked a wide range of merchandise and held monthly auctions of grain, flax and produce on behalf of their farmer clients. The partnership thrived and opened branches throughout Otago and Southland. Central Otago clients were looked after by stock agents, who roamed the countryside in horse-drawn traps.

In the 1880s the partnership came close to being taken over when John Wright offered to sell the business to NMA, but the NMA board of directors turned down the offer. In 1906 Wright Stephenson & Co. became a public

ABOVE John Wright was the financial brains behind the stock and station company Wright Stephenson & Co. Ltd, which he and John Stephenson established in Dunedin in the 1860s. In 1906 the business became a public company and, with the takeover of several of its competitors, went on to become one of New Zealand's largest businesses. It still trades today under the banner of Wrightsons.

OTAGO SETTLERS MUSEUM, DUNEDIN

RIGHT Stock and station company Wright Stephenson & Co., which served the farmers of Central Otago, was at one time heavily involved in the sale of motor cars. This Model T Ford being proudly leant on by a salesman was one of its first vehicles. The vehicle side of the business developed into Wrightcars, which traded for several decades in the retail car market until it was sold in the 1980s.

AUCKLAND MUSEUM 629.222

THE STOCK AND STATION INDUSTRY | 105

company and traded for several decades in Central Otago, offering services to the rural community in finance, livestock, bloodstock, stud stock, grain, seeds, woolbroking, meat processing, horticulture, insurance, land sales, shipping and travel. The merchandise side of the business offered, through their local stores and car yards, farm machinery, motor cars, white goods, groceries, and wines and spirits. With the takeover of NMA in 1972 and Dalgetys in 1986, the firm became New Zealand's largest stock and station company, trading under the name Wrightsons.

In the 1980s the stock and station industry changed. The use of computers brought improved business practices and record keeping, and there was no longer a need to have a stock agent in every small centre in Central Otago or, for that matter, in the rest of New Zealand. Sale of wool by sample was introduced and computers were used in the marketing of the fibre. Modern management systems were put in place and control was centralised, while many of the areas in which the company operated, including finance and the sale of motor cars, were sold or closed down. Today, the company still operates as a stock and station business but in a greatly reduced form. Wrightson is still a listed public company, but control has recently moved to a consortium of investors.

A stand erected by Wright Stephenson & Co. (now Wrightsons) at the Agricultural and Pastoral Show (A&P Show) in Dunedin displays the type of products the company was interested in selling to its farmer clients.

HOCKEN COLLECTIONS S05-064L, UNIVERSITY OF OTAGO, DUNEDIN

# 14
# ALEXANDRA FROM THE NINETEENTH TO THE TWENTY-FIRST CENTURY

The town of Alexandra began life with an identity crisis. It started as The Junction, was renamed Lower Township, then Manuherikia and was finally called Alexandra, the name that has stuck from 1863 to the present day. In that year the tiny settlement was named after Queen Alexandra, a long forgotten royal who was Princess Alexandra of Denmark before she married Edward the Prince of Wales, son and heir to the throne of Queen Victoria.

Being named after an English queen was an ambitious honour as initially there was no reason for Alexandra's existence other than as a place where goldminers bound for Clyde were ferried across the Clutha River. The first buildings were a cluster of iron and canvas huts and the streets, if they could

Tarbet Street, the first business street in Alexandra, photographed in the late nineteenth century.

HOCKEN COLLECTIONS S05-037H, UNIVERSITY OF OTAGO, DUNEDIN

be called that, were muddy tracks. When the easily won alluvial gold ran out in 1866, the population of Alexandra declined to a mere 250. It was a town that, because of its location at the junction of two large rivers, would always be prone to flooding. The Clutha carried the largest volume of fresh water of any river in New Zealand but in spite of this, Alexandra was chronically short of good clean water for many years — not a great start for a town that would become one of the showpieces of Central Otago. On the journey there, it would go through several boom and bust cycles that involved goldmining, coalmining, rabbit processing, gold dredging and, finally, fruit growing.

**LEFT** A very early Alexandra Brass Band. Hats were obviously in fashion at the time.

HOCKEN COLLECTIONS S05-037D,
UNIVERSITY OF OTAGO, DUNEDIN

**BELOW** Rough Riders, volunteers who often paid their own way in order to fight in the Boer War, being farewelled in a ceremony held in their honour in Tarbet Street, Alexandra, in 1900.

HOCKEN COLLECTIONS S05-037B,
UNIVERSITY OF OTAGO, DUNEDIN

## GOLD

The gold that existed in and around Alexandra was located in the rivers. The Clutha was too swift to be worked to any depth, but large amounts of alluvial gold were taken by enterprising prospectors who were lucky enough to own claims that included beaches on the banks of the river. These claims were better worked in winter as the level of the Clutha dropped during Central Otago's cold winters, when much of the water that fed it was locked up in snow and ice in the mountains surrounding the three lakes the river drained. Attempts were made to expose areas of the riverbed by building wing dams that extended out into the current from the bank. These dams were never very successful because of the Clutha's strong current and tendency to flood. Wing dams were more successful in the Manuherikia River at Alexandra as the current was less powerful in that smaller river. However, the full potential of gold near Alexandra was only realised when dredges began to appear in the Clutha River in the 1890s.

Dredging proved to be a bonanza for Alexandra. At the beginning of the twentieth century dozens of dredges worked the Clutha River in the immediate locality. As dredging methods became more sophisticated, the noisy machines moved inland from the riverbed, many creating their own pond of water as they went. Much of this inland dredging took place on the south bank of the river, and today a huge area of tailings, known as the Earnsleugh tailings, exists to remind people of the massive effort by man and machine that went into dredging for gold. Lanes Dam, the attractive pond that exists today high on Bridge Hill, a suburb of Alexandra, was built to provide water via pipes to dredges during the boom.

All gold eventually runs out, and Alexandra was no exception. One large dredge worked the Clutha until the 1960s, but today the river is quiet.

## CROSSING THE RIVERS AT ALEXANDRA

The Clutha River at Alexandra was not bridged until 1882. The early river crossings were made by raft and rowboat, until a punt was built and launched in 1868 by two entrepreneurs named Duly and Mackersey. This punt was two iron boats joined together and attached to a wire cable. A one-way crossing of the Clutha was priced like this: two-wheeled vehicles — sixpence; four-wheeled vehicles — eight pence; horses — sixpence; people — threepence. A daily return ticket for men and horses was a shilling. Sheep and cattle were at 'exceedingly moderate rates', which can be taken to mean prices were negotiable.

The manager and staff of McKnight's Foundry, Alexandra, in 1897, were involved in shoeing horses, building coaches and manufacturing wagon wheels, a collection of which can be seen in this photograph. All the men are wearing leather aprons, an accessory used by early blacksmiths to protect their clothing.

HOCKEN COLLECTIONS S05-037C, UNIVERSITY OF OTAGO, DUNEDIN

The first bridge built to access Alexandra was the one that today spans the Manuherikia River at Butchers Gully. Its official name was the Manuherikia Suspension Bridge, but because of the way it moved when being crossed it has always been called the Shaky Bridge. The Shaky Bridge lasted until 1942, when it was considered too dangerous to be used, especially by children, and was closed. A proposal to reconstruct it as a footbridge was mooted, and in 1952 it was re-opened.

In 1882, 700 people, one of the largest crowds seen in Alexandra for many years, witnessed the opening of the new bridge built over the Clutha River at Alexandra. A brass band led a procession to the bridge and a bottle of champagne was smashed. The new bridge was an attractive one, a single-lane suspension bridge slung between two huge pylons of hand-shaped stone, and it lasted well into the twentieth century. It was replaced by a conventional steel bridge in 1958, but today the two stone pylons remain where they were built, as a reminder of nineteenth-century craftsmanship.

A third bridge was constructed to link Alexandra with the outside world in 1899, when a railway bridge was built over the Manuherikia River a short distance upstream of the Shaky Bridge as part of the construction requirements of the Otago Central Railway.

## WATER PROBLEMS

The residents of Alexandra need water if they are to grow anything successfully during the town's hot, dry summers. From its very beginning the town was without a reliable water supply. In recent years shortages have been overcome, but the population has never been of a size to warrant large amounts of money being spent on the supply and treatment of water.

As mentioned previously, Alexandra is bisected by the largest volume of river water in the country, so it is ironic that it has suffered from a lack of water. In the latter part of the nineteenth century the technology did not exist to successfully move the water out of the Clutha into the town as the level of the river was a long way below where it was required. In 1873 much of the town water came from a water race that belonged to a man named Ovens, but supply was erratic. To maintain a reliable flow, water was imported by open water race all the way from Chatto Creek. There were, however, ongoing problems with the hygiene of water that had to flow over such a long distance. There were also problems with people poaching water from the Chatto Creek race before it reached Alexandra.

In 1907 the Chinese orchardist and market gardener Lye Bow sold his water rights to the council for 500 pounds and a dam was built that would create a reservoir called Butchers Dam, on the main road to Roxburgh. In 1919 the town purchased Joseph Lane's water rights, races and dams in the

Chatto Creek played an important role in the development of Alexandra — it was the source of the town's water supply, via a water race. This small building is the original Chatto Creek Post Office, which is close to the Chatto Creek Hotel and is still used as a place where mail can be posted or collected.

ALEXANDRA FROM THE NINETEENTH TO THE TWENTY-FIRST CENTURY

Butchers Creek, Conroys Creek and Fraser River. This move went a long way towards alleviating the water shortages, but problems still existed with hygiene. In 1939 the local health inspector reported he had found dead rabbits and sheep in Butchers Dam. In 1958 the water from the Upper Manuherikia race which supplied the town was declared unfit for human consumption unless treated first. Once again, in 1963, the medical officer of health declared the town's water to be polluted. On one occasion it had been found to contain a large concentration of vegetable matter; on another, small red worms appeared when household taps were turned on.

Disposal of sewage was also a problem until the latter half of the twentieth century. Sewage was disposed of by way of the night soil cart. Wednesday and Friday nights were set aside for night soil collection, with the carts banned from the streets until 10.30pm. These collections came to an end in 1936, when raw sewage was discharged directly into the Clutha, in spite of the fact that several small towns downstream took their drinking water from that river. This discharge had the consent of the Health Department in the mistaken belief that the Clutha flowed swiftly enough to flush the sewage straight out to sea.

Today the health issues concerning Alexandra's water supply have been solved and the town has an efficient and modern sewerage system. It is the cost of supplying water, rather than the quality, that is of concern, which in turn has brought talk of the introduction of water meters. During a dry summer, water for gardens is now restricted.

Staff pose at the door of Barry's Tea Rooms in Alexandra at the turn of the nineteenth century. Tearooms played an important role in early Central Otago, as a place where people, especially women, could meet. Today they have been replaced by cafés, and tearooms have gone out of fashion.

HOCKEN COLLECTIONS S05-037A, UNIVERSITY OF OTAGO, DUNEDIN

The old stone courthouse in Alexandra was once a candidate for demolition when the local council voted in the 1970s for it be removed to make way for a carpark. The bank manager's wife, who lived across the street, rallied support for the building to be spared. After much agitation and approaches to the government of the day, the courthouse was rescued and is now part of the Otago Goldfields Park. Today the building operates as a café. It has been tastefully renovated and its original character retained.

## TYPHOID FEVER

In 1909 there was a serious outbreak of typhoid fever in Alexandra. This illness, which can be fatal, is often the result of poor drainage or polluted water, but in Alexandra's case neither was found to be the cause. Water from the Chatto Creek water race was tested and found to be safe, but when the milk carts were ambushed on their rounds and samples tested, milk was found to be the culprit. The milk was supplied by a Mrs Lewis, who was then instructed to take certain basic health precautions that are commonplace today. She was required to thoroughly wash all milk utensils before use, her cows' udders were to be washed before milking, Mrs Lewis was to be 'in every way clean' and her young helper, Allan Lindsay, who must have tested positive for typhoid, was to stop milking immediately. It is no wonder typhoid was a problem given these serious breaches of hygiene. Alexandra was not the only town afflicted. There were other serious outbreaks throughout Central Otago, with Cromwell being hit heavily by two that involved loss of life.

## THE INSPECTOR OF NUISANCES

In 1867 Alexandra appointed its first inspector of nuisances on an annual salary of 20 pounds per year. His job, which was described as thankless and onerous, was to abate nuisance, whatever form it might take. His responsibilities included dealing with cows wandering about the town, pigs running at large in the streets, rowdy wagoners camping within the town boundaries and those inconsiderate townspeople who kept pigs in their backyards.

Goats and dogs became the issue of the day when the Goat and Dog Nuisance Ordinance was passed by the council in 1872, in an attempt to control these wandering animals. Under the ordinance, goats were required to wear a leather collar stamped with a special council seal. The year 1878 is regarded as the year of the goat in Alexandra. In that year the council became frustrated with wandering goats and put out a tender for their destruction. Tenders received ranged from threepence to a shilling per goat, and even though the lowest tender was accepted, the goats were not destroyed as the successful tenderers were not up to the task.

In 1876 the town experienced speeding problems when horses were ridden through it at an alarming rate. The matter was brought to the attention of the inspector of nuisances and the police, but it is not known if the speedsters were brought to heel. Then there were the problems of punt owners leaving their vessels stranded in Ferry Road, rowdyism at the town hall, the ferocious dog kept by a Mr Mathews, night soil being emptied in the town, the exhibition of objectionable posters, Mrs Deady tethering a cow on the streets, people cycling on the footpaths and loose wheels on the night soil cart.

Alexandra survived all these nuisances and is now an attractive, modern borough with a population of some 3500. A large number of retired people live in Alexandra. It is a conservative town, very different from places like Queenstown, Wanaka and Arrowtown, where the tourist is king, and today it performs a role as the administrative centre of Central Otago.

# 15
# ROXBURGH AND THE TEVIOT DISTRICT

Roxburgh was the location of one of the government-run free health camps that were set up in the 1930s to cater for the needs of sickly children. Shown here are staff from the Roxburgh Camp in 1942.

HOCKEN COLLECTIONS S05-045A, UNIVERSITY OF OTAGO, DUNEDIN

Roxburgh and the surrounding Teviot District have been gifted with huge natural advantages when compared with the rest of Central Otago. The area is fertile and has ample, reliable water provided by the Clutha River, which runs right through the middle of it. This water has been harnessed to provide electricity as a source of energy, gold was found to provide employment in the early days and coal has always been available locally to heat people's homes. It has a slightly higher rainfall than the drier parts of Central Otago to the north, a more temperate climate that has made fruit growing easier than in other areas and a soil type that has made it one of the few areas in New Zealand where quality apricots can be grown successfully. The first runholders to settle the area were careful in choosing the best breeds of animals to stock their properties and their runs were well managed, if not hugely successful financially. Added to these advantages is the fact that the township of Roxburgh is ideally located on a main highway, giving easy access to the port and facilities of Dunedin, and it is also visually attractive. The climate of Roxburgh also made it an ideal place for a health camp under a scheme set up by a benevolent government in the 1930s, to give sickly children a place to build up their strength during school holidays.

The Maori recognised most of these advantages long before Europeans arrived and found it an excellent place to hunt moa. They either lingered there while on their way to collect greenstone near Haast, or made special hunting trips from the east coast. The large number of Maori ovens excavated at Millers Flat is evidence of this, as are the thousands of flint chips found at Gorge Creek and the hundreds of moa bones at Ettrick.

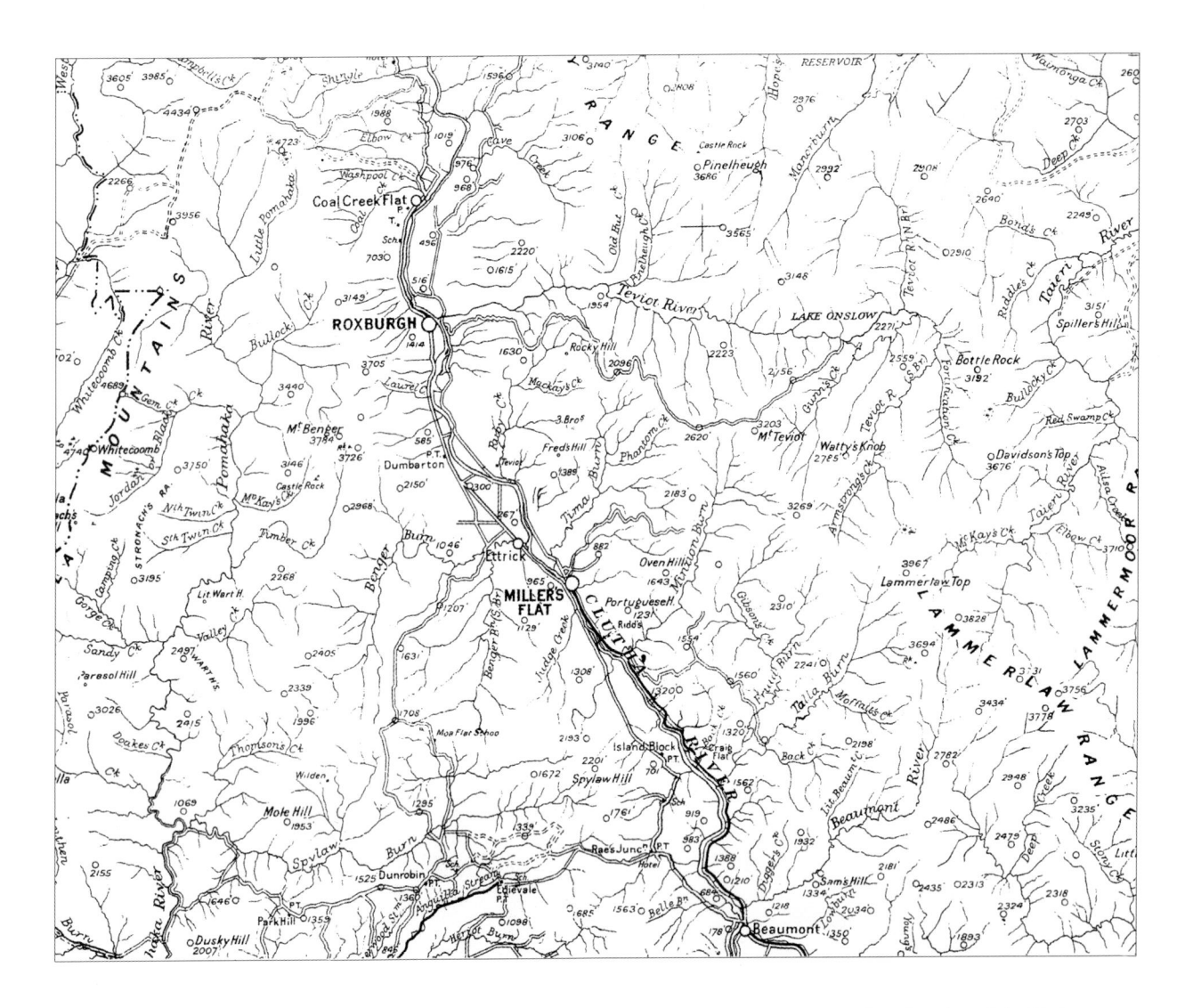

## LOCAL EXPLORERS AND RUNHOLDERS

The explorer Nathaniel Chalmers became the first European to pass through the Teviot District when he made his trip down the Clutha by raft, guided and kept alive by the talented Reko. He was followed by John Cargill and Walter Miller in 1857, who became the first men to apply for runs in Central Otago. There is also a strong theory that James Mackenzie, the man who made a living and name for himself stealing runholders' sheep, might have been the first European to travel through the district, but as his lifestyle was a furtive one this has never been verified.

Map of Roxburgh and the Teviot District.

LAND INFORMATION NEW ZEALAND

Gerit Chalmers was one of the first Europeans to move into the Teviot District when he took up the lease of Run 215, better known as Moa Flat Station, in 1858. Nathaniel Chalmers had an interest in this run from 1864 until 1868, the year he left New Zealand for Fiji. Stocking the run was difficult. It required a trip to Australia, where 2000 merino sheep were purchased and the small ship *Marbs* chartered to transport them to Port Molyneux. Unloading the sheep was not easy, nor was the trip overland to Moa Flat Station, and only 1000 sheep made it alive. Still, it was a beginning, and the station struggled on under a series of owners, in spite of financial difficulties. These troubles continued until Joseph 'Big' Clarke, the well known Australian squatter capitalist, bailed it out, took over the head lease and provided the capital to run it properly. Under his supervision it would grow to carry 120,000 sheep by 1878, and in that year the property comprised some 200,000 hectares, of which 32,000 were freehold, an unusual situation in the years when rural land was mostly leasehold.

The property was so huge that a full day's ride was required to cross it from east to west. The best pedigree Shorthorn cattle, Berkshire pigs, prize poultry, greyhounds and collie dogs were all imported to stock and help run it. Disaster was waiting in the wings, however, with the big snowfall of 1878, which lay on the ground for six months, killed 60,000 of the station's sheep and brought Moa Flat Station to its financial knees. Joseph Clarke died soon after and the lease passed to his son, Sir William, along with the huge properties his father owned in Victoria and Tasmania. In 1900 the station was again in trouble when Sir William's fortunes were affected by a depression in Australia. He offered the property to the New Zealand government at 2 pounds an acre, but the offer was declined. In 1906 it was purchased by staff members of the stock firms Wright Stephenson & Co., J.G. Ward & Co. and Murray Roberts & Co., plus several local runholders. The new owners were speculators not farmers, and in 1909 Moa Flat Station was subdivided and sold off at a handsome profit. Thus ended the reign of one of the largest rural properties in New Zealand.

## GOLD AND FRUIT

While Moa Creek Station was experiencing the vagaries of sheep farming, the rest of the Teviot District was prospering from gold, which had been discovered in various locations throughout the area in 1862. The rocky gorges and sandy beaches of the Clutha River, as it passed through the district, formed a natural tailrace that had trapped gold for centuries. As the course of the river changed over the millennia, it had laid down deposits of alluvial gold on what became dry ground, and it was only a matter of time before these deposits were found and exploited.

Andrew Young and James Woodhouse were the first people in the Teviot District to find gold when they did some prospecting while waiting for their clothes to dry after crossing the Teviot River, during the winter of 1862. This find was the reason for the beginning of Roxburgh as a settlement — to cater for the miners who worked the river and both sides of the Clutha at this point. The town began life on the east bank of the river but moved to the other side in the late 1860s. Soon gold was being taken from Gorge Creek in the north of the Teviot, through to Horseshoe Bend and Beaumont in the south. As happened in the rest of Central Otago, Chinese miners followed the Europeans, and by the 1870s there were as many as 300 camped on the outskirts of Roxburgh. Unlike other parts of Central Otago, relations between Chinese and Europeans were always cordial in the Teviot District. This is not to say that racism did not exist as, here too, the Europeans resented the presence of the Chinese as competition for gold and jobs. A man called Hong was the last of the Chinese miners, and he lived

Reverend Alexander Don, shown here on the right as a young man, was the Presbyterian missionary to the Chinese miners in Central Otago. This photograph shows him visiting several Chinese in their rudimentary cob hut at Tuapeka, south of Roxburgh.

019164, ALEXANDER TURNBULL LIBRARY, NATIONAL LIBRARY OF NEW ZEALAND

John Ewing, the entrepreneur who made and lost a fortune from gold in St Bathans, established a foundry near Roxburgh under the auspices of the Teviot–Molyneux Gold Mining Company to manufacture pipes for sluicing. The water that was brought in by pipes for sluicing was later used as irrigation.

HOCKEN COLLECTIONS S05-065J, UNIVERSITY OF OTAGO, DUNEDIN

in Roxburgh until 1938. Others, such as Ah Sue, who had been successful in their search for gold, gave generously to such causes as the local hospital when they died.

The rough buildings that comprised the original Roxburgh were all constructed from timber brought in from Tapanui by wagon. Once serious mining began, timber that could be used to build a sluice box was almost as valuable as the gold the box was designed to trap.

Sluicing and elevating was introduced to the Teviot District in 1878. Although a huge volume of water existed in the Clutha, there was no technology available to lift it. This required the construction of many kilometres of water races to provide the water needed to operate the sluice guns. The first attempt at dredging had been made in the Clutha River a short distance south of the present-day Millers Flat Bridge as early as 1863, using a spoon dredge, but this had been unsuccessful. Because of their unstable nature and inability to work in deep water, spoon dredges had had little success when tried in other parts of Central Otago. The next step up the dredge ladder was the current-wheel dredge, where a series of buckets were driven by the current of the river, and several of these were successful from 1868 to 1881 in the Clutha, operating close to Roxburgh. However, dredging only began to pay handsomely in the Teviot District when the steam dredge *Dunedin*, which began life near Alexandra, was shifted to Coal Creek in 1888. One dredge grew to several, and by 1904 there were

18 dredges working this stretch of the Clutha. Much of the money invested in these dredges was raised by public subscription, and it was an investment that appealed to the general public. Many Teviot locals invested in dredges and made or lost money, depending on the success or failure of the dredge they backed.

The last big investment in gold in the district was the Teviot Molyneux Gold Mining Company Ltd, with John Ewing, the mining entrepreneur from St Bathans, as its managing director. The company was formed to work what was considered to be an old river bed near Ettrick, but problems with the supply of water and materials during the period of World War I led to its demise in 1922. This along with other poor investments led to the loss of John Ewing's fortune, and his eventual bankruptcy.

The growing of fruit was to become the mainstay of the economy of Roxburgh, and this subject is discussed in detail in chapter 12.

When the Coal Creek mine opened a few kilometres north of Roxburgh in 1905, government representatives were given a guided tour. Here they are ready to enter the mine, well equipped with candles, either hand-held or placed in hatbands.

HOCKEN COLLECTIONS S05-037N, UNIVERSITY OF OTAGO, DUNEDIN

## COAL

Roxburgh has always produced coal, and today a substantial deposit of cheap lignite coal is still mined at Coal Creek. The first discovery of coal was made at Crossan's Gully on the east side of the Clutha in 1865, followed by a second discovery at Coal Creek a year later, a find made by two Canadian stonemasons named John Low and James Robertson. The third discovery made in 1868 by Gideon Smith at Coal Creek is the one which, along with a later purchase of another pit, still operates today under the ownership of Harliwich Holdings. The Harliwich name entered the scene when the pit was bought by the family patriarch, N.J. Harliwich, a local wagoner, in 1916. When he took over this pit, he introduced open-cut mining in place of the more time-consuming method of underground recovery. The last discovery was made by James Craig in 1887, again at Coal Creek.

The use of steam dredges was a boom time for these coal suppliers, with the three Coal Creek mines averaging a daily combined output of 100 tonnes during the years the dredges operated. When the steam dredges were made redundant by those powered by electricity, the demand for coal dwindled to domestic use only. The import of hotter-burning bright coal from Kaitangata and Linton reduced demand further, although a temporary jump in demand was caused by coal shortages during World War II.

## COMMUNICATIONS

Until the discovery of gold, there was no need for a road through Roxburgh. The runholders were mainly self-sufficient and able to travel overland by foot or on horseback. The discovery of gold and the need for supplies soon resulted in the construction of a track from Lawrence to Roxburgh, which was marked by snow poles and sticks planted at short intervals. Each of these sticks had a black flag on top, so the track would have been easy to follow in most weathers.

Communications improved in 1865 when Cobb & Co. began carrying passengers from Dunedin to Clyde via Millers Flat and Roxburgh twice a week, at the quite expensive price of 3 pounds 6 shillings one way for the Dunedin–Roxburgh leg. Crossing the Clutha was a problem in Roxburgh until a punt was installed in the mid 1860s, where the Teviot River joined the Clutha. This was followed by a second punt at Millers Flat. At the same time, the east bank of the Clutha was abandoned in favour of the west bank, with its easier contour, and this is still the route today. The punts were replaced over

*The early goldmining settlement of Horseshoe Bend, south of Roxburgh, was on the wrong side of the Clutha River when it was time for the local children to attend school. Initially they were required to pull themselves across the river by way of a box slung from a wire rope, which was a dangerous and unsatisfactory situation for young children. To overcome the problem, this bridge was built over the Clutha River at Horseshoe Bend. It still exists, renovated and deemed a historic engineering site.*

time when traffic bridges were built at Beaumont, Millers Flat and Roxburgh, although the Roxburgh crossing was carried away in a flood in 1878 and had to be rebuilt. An elaborate footbridge was also built over the Clutha at Horseshoe Bend to ensure the children who had to cross the river arrived at school safely.

As early as 1873 a railway to Roxburgh via Lawrence had been suggested, but it would be another 55 years before construction was under way. A line as far as Lawrence had been completed by 1876. Locals pushed for it to be extended, even travelling to Wellington to nag the then prime minister, Richard Seddon. Seddon agreed to build the line, but only as far as Beaumont, and this was completed in 1914. This appeared to be an odd move, but although an extension to Roxburgh had been agreed on by the government during the construction to Beaumont, the shortages of men and materials during World War I halted construction. Like the Otago Central Railway to the north, the Lawrence to Roxburgh line had a relatively short lifespan, and all transport in and out of Roxburgh is now by road.

The last big move to affect Roxburgh was the building of the Roxburgh Dam at Coal Creek in the 1950s, (see chapter 25).

Today, Roxburgh is still the centre of the Teviot District. Today it is an attractive town, laid out around the Clutha River, with extensive orchards. In spite of its gifts, however, Roxburgh has over the years seen a declining population in favour of other towns in Central Otago, such as Alexandra, Wanaka and Queenstown.

Large elaborate hats, ankle-length gowns, layers of petticoats and tight corsets were what well dressed women wore at the beginning of the twentieth century.

HOCKEN COLLECTIONS S05-044C,
UNIVERSITY OF OTAGO, DUNEDIN

# 16
# LIFE IN MACETOWN
# 1862–1900

In 1862 prospectors from all over the world were roaming Central Otago looking to strike gold or, failing that, rushing to the latest strike in the hope of establishing a claim on the coat-tails of another person's find. That same year the Mace brothers, John, Charles and Harry, in the company of two other men, John and Joe Beale, discovered gold in the Arrow River, some 19 km inland from present-day Arrowtown. The Beales faded into obscurity, but the settlement that sprang up as a result of the discovery was named Macetown, and within a few months boasted a population of 3000 people. The location was very remote and difficult to access because of the lack of a decent track. Even today the site of Macetown is only accessible by four-wheel-drive vehicle and involves 23 crossings of the Arrow River on the journey. At 600 m above sea level, Macetown is very cold in winter and mild in summer.

## THE BEGINNINGS OF THE SETTLEMENT

When the gold strike of the Maces and Beales was made public, men poured in from all over Central Otago. They lived in tents with makeshift mudbrick or stone chimneys. Those who had already spent a winter in Central Otago knew how cold it could be and built themselves huts using local stone or mudbricks. Others built huts of corrugated iron, a building material that was light and easy to transport, but an unlined hut of iron was not a warm dwelling in winter. There were no trees that could be felled for timber to use in building huts or as precious firewood. The only firewood that was available locally was stunted matagouri. New arrivals who wanted timber for building, or coal to keep themselves warm, had to have it hauled in by dray from Arrowtown over a muddy track. In winter the Arrow River often froze

Living conditions of the early miners were basic. There are no buildings of any substance left in Macetown today, but the recreated structures shown here give an idea of what living conditions were like. Miners initially lived in tents and cooked over small open fires, using a makeshift stone fireplace with a corrugated iron chimney. This tent is quite luxurious as it has a wooden floor. Corrugated iron was another building material used extensively in Macetown, but most of this was scavenged in the 1940s.

over and the track used to access Macetown became very dangerous. The track was the scene of several fatal accidents when a combination of ice and steep terrain led to people and animals falling over the edge to their deaths. These access problems and the harsh weather led to most mining coming to a halt in winter.

Miners would return in summer, and those who had families would often leave them in Arrowtown while they worked their Macetown claims during these warmer months. This decision to mine only in summer appears to have been a sensible one, but it was risky for two reasons. Being unable to work a claim in winter usually meant that husbands and fathers had no income during those months, while quitting a claim in winter left it wide open to poaching and claim jumping by those tough or stubborn enough to brave the cold and spend winter in Macetown.

## WOMEN AND CHILDREN

Once huts and other semi-permanent accommodation had been built, men began to bring their families to live in Macetown. The women brought goats and cows with them to provide milk. Local businesses began to be established in the settlement to cater for these new arrivals. By 1870 Macetown had two grocery stores, two hotels, a drapery store and a post office, but it had changed. The easy alluvial gold was gone and many of the

ABOVE Macetown in 1900, looking in the direction of Arrowtown. The houses have gone now, leaving only the main street and trees planted by the early settlers.

HOCKEN COLLECTIONS S05-064G,
UNIVERSITY OF OTAGO, DUNEDIN

RIGHT Men going on shift at the Premier Mine in Macetown pose for a photograph.

HOCKEN COLLECTIONS S05-0656,
UNIVERSITY OF OTAGO, DUNEDIN

LIFE IN MACETOWN 1862–1900

miners had left to try their luck elsewhere. The population had dropped from a peak of 3000 to a permanent and racially mixed 400, as Chinese miners had moved into the settlement to rework the old tailings left behind by the Europeans. Following this decline, many of the married men began to work for wages in the quartz mines that were opened to exploit the gold seams lying underground.

Most women in Macetown in 1870 were fresh from the United Kingdom and had come to New Zealand to start a new life. Ending up in remote Macetown, in a valley that was barely accessible, miles from the nearest excuse for civilisation, often in the middle of a Central Otago winter, must have been a huge culture shock for them. It is a wonder that they survived the experience both physically and emotionally. That they did is testament to their strength of character and is also an indication of how desperate living conditions must have been in the country that they had willingly left behind to seek a better future. Life in Macetown could involve enduring months of intense cold, loneliness, uninteresting food and drudgery. In the homes of Macetown, cooking was done over open fires or in a camp oven. Water had to be collected by hand from the Arrow River and stored in buckets. Damper, a baked mixture of flour, salt and water, was the basis of a family's diet, supplemented by any meat that might be available. The meat was usually of birds or rabbit, until families began to raise their own chickens and sheep. Fruit trees were planted, as were gooseberries and blackcurrants, while some of the women made wine from cherries. They also began gardens for food and planted sycamore, willow and poplar trees as shelter.

The remains of this old, abandoned stamper battery can still be seen in Macetown today. It was powered by a waterwheel attached to the metal bar protruding from the right-hand side. This in turn drove the stamper heads in the middle of the battery, at the base of the wooden platform. Gold-bearing rock was fed into the stamper from the back and pulverised by the heads into dust which, when mixed with water, flowed out across the wooden platform shown. It was then collected and put through another process involving mercury to separate out the gold. Mercury poisoning was a danger that the early miners were exposed to, as was hearing loss, a result of the terrific noise made by the stamper when operating.

Large numbers of Chinese lived and worked in Macetown during the latter half of the nineteenth century. As in other mining areas of Central Otago, they were obliged to live in their own settlement. The hut shown here has the luxury of a corrugated iron roof covered in rice sacks, which were added in an attempt to provide some insulation against the cold. The photograph was taken by the Reverend Alexander Don, the Presbyterian missionary who walked all over Central Otago in his attempts to convert the Chinese miners to Christianity.

019150, ALEXANDER TURNBULL LIBRARY, NATIONAL LIBRARY OF NEW ZEALAND

In 1870 there was no doctor in Macetown, and very little medicine. When people became sick, old-fashioned remedies were used. If these failed, the invalid was packed up and taken out to Arrowtown. The lack of a doctor made childbirth risky, but most of the local women still gave birth at home, with the help of midwives. If complications arose during labour, it was usually too late to head for Arrowtown, and a number of women died in childbirth. Infants and young children also died of infectious diseases such as diphtheria. The Chinese miners in Macetown often doubled as herbalists and were able to prepare remedies from plants that grew locally. These often worked better than European medicines, and for that reason became popular among the local population.

## EDUCATION

In 1870 the first school, a one-roomed building, was opened in Macetown, with a roll of 21 pupils. Until that year local children either went uneducated or, if they were lucky, were tutored by their mothers, creating an added responsibility for the women. Often, however, mothers couldn't provide lessons as they had no education themselves. School attendance was not compulsory in 1870. All the pupils were young boys. There were two reasons for this: the families needed the income of the older boys who went to work in the mines as soon as they were able; and girls were victims of that blind spot of the nineteenth century which dictated that females did not need an education.

Macetown School in 1870. The building doubled as a hall and a church. From the clothes some of the children are wearing it is obvious that they were sewn on a machine at home, as the style and cloth are identical.

HOCKEN COLLECTIONS S05-064N, UNIVERSITY OF OTAGO, DUNEDIN

When the conditions in winter became too cold the school was closed and the pupils were given an impromptu holiday. The school was heated, but getting to and from the building was a problem, even though the school was within easy reach of the children's homes. Snow would lie a metre deep on the ground, and if frost followed snow, which it often did, everything would be frozen solid. Children exposed to these conditions often became prone to chilblains on their hands and feet. Schoolwork was done using a cold, hard slate with a slate pencil, and those whose hands were cracked and sore from the effects of their chilblains struggled to complete their lessons.

## SOCIAL LIFE

Macetown was so remote that there was nothing available in the way of formal entertainment. People had to make their own fun and became very skilled at amusing themselves, regularly putting on balls, dances and concerts in the hotels or the school house. Social life was more formal in the nineteenth century, and young people needed an excuse to declare their feelings. A popular way of doing this was with what was called the

Basket Auction. Young ladies took a basket of food along to a dance, where it was then auctioned. The young man who purchased a lady's basket also purchased the right to share its contents with her at supper and the right to escort her if she was unattached.

There were always plenty of local musicians to play at these dances, which often went on until dawn. The dances themselves had colourful names like Mazurka, La Rinka, Quadrilles, Maxina, Polka, First Set, Alberts and Lancers — sadly now mostly unknown in the twenty-first century. Balls in Macetown were more formal than the dances. Much more preparation went into organising them, and the ladies would wear their best gowns and have their hair crimped, while the men wore their dress suits, white gloves and dancing pumps.

Card evenings were held, with euchre and cribbage being people's favourite games. Another game called forty-five was restricted to mining towns of Otago, the West Coast and the North Island. It was supposed to be a fascinating game with obscure origins and is thought to have been brought to Otago from the Californian goldfields. Race meetings were held on the cemetery reserve, which was several hectares put aside by the people of Macetown for burials. This ground was never used as a cemetery and was ideal as a racetrack. The fact that the cemetery was never used is an oddity of Macetown. Most old goldmining towns in Central Otago have a historic cemetery, but not Macetown. Instead, bodies were shipped to Arrowtown and buried in the cemetery there.

Macetown was also out of step with the rest of Central Otago in that it had only two hotels, an unusually low number. Often hotels were the first buildings to be constructed and the last to close, but for some obscure reason Macetown settled for only two, the Alpine and the Macetown. The Alpine was demolished when the population of the settlement faded to almost nil, while the Macetown was destroyed by fire in 1906.

The lack of hotels did not discourage certain men who came to be known as the Twelve Apostles because of their heavy drinking. Possibly remittance men, a name given to black sheep sent out to the colonies by wealthy families and given an allowance to stay away, they lived at the end of the main street of Macetown. They would work in the mines until they had enough money to go on a drinking binge. When the money ran out, they would go back to work in order to repeat the performance. Other than their excessive drinking and gambling habits, most lived ordinary lives, taking pride in their flower and vegetable gardens and working hard when they were required to. In spite of their heavy drinking, the Twelve Apostles were described as being in very good health and lived to respectable ages. Some died in Macetown, while others ended their days in Arrowtown. All that remains today to mark their time spent in Macetown are the flowers from their long-forgotten gardens, which still bloom at the end of the main street in spring.

## RELIGIOUS LIFE

Macetown was one of the few settlements in early Central Otago that did not have a church. No church was ever built in the village. Church services were held in the school because it had an organ. The Catholics were the first to hold church services when a Father O'Donnell rode up from Queenstown in his buggy. Later, a Presbyterian minister used to ride in from Arrowtown. When the weather was bad, delaying the ministers, services were taken by

Macetown children drinking beer from bottles in 1902. It was not uncommon for children of this era to drink alcohol, which was regarded as having medicinal qualities.

F-31880, ALEXANDER TURNBULL LIBRARY, NATIONAL LIBRARY OF NEW ZEALAND elders of the Macetown Presbyterian community. The Salvation Army also featured, with meetings led by a Dane called Polsen.

## THE END OF THE SETTLEMENT

The boom years in Macetown were from 1862 to 1900. By that time the mines had either run down when the gold reefs were lost or had become too difficult to mine. People drifted away and the buildings they had erected were left to the elements. The settlement enjoyed a brief revival during the depression of the 1930s, when the government introduced a goldmining subsidy scheme to try and alleviate some of the unemployment that existed during those difficult years. A small wage was paid to those who wanted to try their luck at goldmining, with the added bonus of being able to keep any gold that was found. Several of the unemployed and their families moved out to Macetown and began living in the abandoned homes that still existed there. Some were moderately successful in their search for gold but most were not. Because of the isolation and lack of education opportunities for the children, these families moved out as soon as the depression ended and better employment opportunities became available elsewhere.

By the end of World War II, Macetown had one citizen, a man by the name of Billy Jenkins. Many of the houses that remained were sold to people from Arrowtown for the price of the materials they contained. People also made foraging trips looking for corrugated iron, which was scarce in the late 1940s.

Today, only two buildings remain in Macetown, a stone building that was once used as a bakery and a wooden building that is better described as a large shed. The legacy of the miners and their wives are the beautiful, mature English trees they left behind, making the area where the town was once located very attractive and peaceful.

# 17
# THE RISE AND FALL OF ST BATHANS

St Bathans is a small village with a goldmining history that is a reminder of the huge effort that went into the search for gold in Central Otago in the nineteenth and early twentieth centuries. Located at the base of the St Bathans Range at the northern end of the Manuherikia Valley, St Bathans was the site of a hill 120 m in height that was sluiced and elevated by goldmining equipment into a 68 m deep gash in the ground. Over time this hole filled with rainwater and seepage and is now an attractive sheet of water known as the Blue Lake.

For many years after its glory days had ended, St Bathans lay off the beaten track, and as a result the small township remained untouched and unaltered. Today, it is accessed by an excellent bitumen road and is home to a handful of permanent residents and a smattering of part-time residents who own holiday homes there. The main street contains one of Central Otago's best known and most photographed hotels, the mudbrick Vulcan Hotel, which still functions as a going concern. Within the town are two historic cemeteries, one Protestant and the other Catholic, which contain headstones of an early inhabitant who froze to death and another who was killed when a cliff in the diggings that formed the Blue Lake collapsed on him. The policeman's house, the small jail, the stone ruins of the school, the wooden post office and the teacher's house still stand, as does the mudbrick hospital and the small Anglican church donated to the town by one of early New Zealand's largest sheep farmers, Frederick Dalgety.

Bleached cliffs, shaped by the sluicing and elevating that took place in St Bathans for several decades under the guidance of goldmining entrepreneur John Ewing, now enclose the Blue Lake.

**ABOVE LEFT** Two historic cemeteries exist in St Bathans — a Catholic cemetery in the township and a Protestant one on the outskirts. Many of the early miners and settlers of St Bathans and the neighbouring village of Cambrians were Welsh. Reflecting this ancestry, a number of the headstones in the Protestant cemetery are written partly in Welsh.

**ABOVE RIGHT** The Church of St Alban the Martyr was gifted to the citizens of St Bathans by Frederick Dalgety, the owner of several runs in the area and the founder of the stock and station company Dalgety & Co. Ltd. Prefabricated in England, the church was erected in 1883. The first service was taken on 27 November 1883 by the vicar of Maniototo, the Reverend J. Davis. In 1947 the title passed from Dalgety & Co. to the Dunedin Diocesan Trust Board, which gave the church its current name.

## THE DISCOVERY OF GOLD IN 1864

Unlike many of the other small settlements in Central Otago, Naseby for example, which were established to cater for the early runholders and those who worked for them, St Bathans did not exist before gold was discovered there in 1864. In that year St Bathans began life as Dunstan Creek and by the middle of 1864 was a canvas town that sported 13 hotels, two canvas banks and seven canvas shops all catering to a population of 2000. The rough canvas settlement nearly came to an abrupt end in the same year when a violent nor'wester gale destroyed all these canvas structures in one night. The town was renamed St Bathans and rebuilt using more permanent materials. By 1865 it had several new hotels, the most popular of which were the Montezuma, Colonial, Vulcan, Ballarat and Smiths. The new town also contained churches, schools, police barracks, butchers' shops, bakers' shops, stables, banks, a smithy, a cottage hospital and even its own newspaper. In spite of these symbols of civilisation, early St Bathans was not for those who preferred the quiet life. In a letter to the editor of the *Otago Witness Newspaper* in 1864, a citizen of the town complained that 'drunk and disorderly seems to be the rule with us, night after night', behaviour that resulted in 'a large number of black eyes, smashed heads and a good number of other crimes'.

What St Bathans lacked in law and order it made up for in gold as it was the site of the richest auriferous quartz drift in Otago. The main gold-bearing seam was one of the richest leads in the world, producing an average of 16,000 oz of gold annually for several decades. There were three locations around St Bathans where gold was taken: St Bathans itself, Vinegar Hill and Cambrians. Vinegar Hill was so named on account of the many fights that took place between the miners in this location. This led to a comparison with the Battle of Vinegar Hill in Wexford, Ireland, in the 1700s.

Sluicing commenced in the 1860s but quickly began to fade because there was inadequate slope for the gold tailings to clear the sluicing sites, which became choked. This changed in 1879 when hydraulic sluicing and elevating were developed, and the mines around St Bathans were given a new lease of life.

## 1879–1904

In 1879 John Ewing was one of the first to take advantage of the new hydraulic technology, and within a few years he came to dominate the mining scene at St Bathans, Vinegar Hill and Cambrians. He was prepared to invest large sums of money in his mining ventures, and by 1884 he employed 100 men. He finetuned the process of hydraulic elevating and, using this method, was able to lift gold-bearing spoil a massive 33 m, to start the pit that would become the Blue Lake. Expansion was his downfall. His success in St Bathans led him to invest in mines as far away as Roxburgh, but he was unable to personally supervise them all. Without his leadership, these later investments began to fail, and in 1904 John Ewing was declared bankrupt. However, during his time as the leading employer at St Bathans and Cambrians, he was the driving force and brains that developed the area and brought it through difficult times, in particular the depression of the 1880s.

## 1904–1935

In 1904 John Ewing's role as leading citizen and employer was taken over by Neil Nicholson. Unlike Ewing, Nicholson was an academic who had studied at the Otago School of Mines and had an extensive knowledge of the ins and outs of operating a complex goldmining operation. In 1906, the Scandinavian Water Race Company, a public company managed by Nicholson, began work where John Ewing had left off. It was this company,

A funeral procession under the supervision of Jack Wilkinson, the St Bathans undertaker, in 1900, on the road that leads to the Protestant cemetery on the outskirts of the town. Oddly, the pallbearers are all children, many of whom are wearing armbands, which probably indicates that the deceased was one of their own age group. It was unusual for females to take part in funeral processions at the turn of the century, but here the young women are part of the procession, although segregated behind the young men.

HOCKEN COLLECTIONS S05-045J, UNIVERSITY OF OTAGO, DUNEDIN

operating in what was known as the Nicholson Mine, which completed the excavation that became the lake. Later, in 1926, the St Bathans Goldmining Company was formed to excavate the pit left by the Nicholson Mine by sinking shafts and tunnels. For the first time in St Bathans, poppet heads to access these shafts appeared on hills around the town. The venture, however, was a failure as quicksand and the collapse of shafts led to the project being quickly abandoned.

A return to hydraulic elevating by a newly formed public company, the Kildare Consolidated Mining Company, began in 1926. In 1934 operations had opened up such a large hole, moving ever closer to the township of St Bathans itself, that the Maniototo County Council became concerned that the diggings would undermine the buildings in the main street of the town. To prevent this happening, all mining work in this area ceased in 1934. Today, only one building remains on the mine side of the main street in St Bathans, the others having been shifted or demolished because of the possibility of subsidence.

During most of the 1930s a seam of coal close to the Blue Lake smoldered out of control after catching fire accidentally. A column of smoke rose from the fire for many years and often affected the living conditions in St

Bathans. When the weather was fine this smoke did not cause pollution, but if conditions were wet or foggy the town smelt badly of sulphur. At other times the fire would break into flame and scatter hot cinders, which were a fire hazard during a hot, dry Central Otago summer. After burning for many years the fire suddenly stopped, and it was assumed that the coal seam had burnt itself out because it never reignited.

By 1935 St Bathans was a shell of its former self. From a peak of 2000 people, the township had only a handful of permanent residents and there were many deserted and unoccupied buildings. In that same year there was a short revival when work began on the construction of the Falls Dam on the Manuherikia River to provide a more reliable water supply for irrigation that was required downstream. To provide access to the dam site, a new road that ran north off the Oturehua–St Bathans road was constructed. The country was in the middle of a depression and it was deliberate government policy that the majority of those workers employed on the dam site were to be taken from the ranks of the unemployed. A large number of men accompanied by their wives and families moved into the area. The population of St Bathans surged when many of these families took up residence in the abandoned houses of the town. This boost was shortlived, however, as most of these people moved out when the dam was completed. By 1939 St Bathans had again reverted to the status of a ghost town.

An early photograph of the main street of St Bathans. Sluicing threatened to undermine many of these buildings, and the two-storied building at middle left is the only one that remains on that side of the street today.
ALEXANDRA MUSEUM

## TROUBLES WITH THE SCHOOL COMMITTEE

In the early days St Bathans had two schools, one a state school and the other a private Catholic school. The first state school was built in 1866, some distance from where the earthquake-damaged stone school, which remains today, was constructed. From the very beginning the relationship between the school committee and the teachers was not a happy one. The first teacher, a Mr Dodds, was no sooner employed than he was in trouble, real or imagined, when he was charged by the committee with excessive discipline of a pupil. By July 1869 he was gone and replaced by a Mr McDiarmid, who in turn ran foul of the committee when he was accused of drunkenness and neglect of duty. By April 1870 he was also out. Next came a Mr Yorston, who lasted until 1873 but resigned when accused of not disciplining his pupils. He was replaced by his wife, who taught until early 1876, when she too had had enough and resigned.

In 1876 the attractive school and teacher's house were built in stone on their present sites. The new school opened with a new teacher, Mr Darling, who was soon in trouble with the committee for supposedly taking an extra two weeks' holiday. His departure was followed by the appointments and

Ruins of the St Bathans school, built of stone in 1876. The building had to be abandoned in 1948 after suffering severe damage during an earthquake in that year.

resignations of Messrs Morris, Coutts and Cowan, until the committee's ranks were decimated by age and school life began to settle down.

In 1948 the school was damaged in an earthquake and lessons were transferred to the ground floor of the post office. On 1 February 1949 it was shut down completely and the ruins, along with the useful teacher's house, were sold to private owners. The loss of the school was a serious blow to the future of St Bathans.

## THE BUILDINGS IN THE MAIN STREET

The people of St Bathans were staunch supporters of the Liberal Party and its leader Sir Joseph Ward. This loyalty was rewarded in 1907 when construction began on the attractive, two-storied wooden post office that still stands in the town. When it was built, the post office was located on the ground floor, while the postmaster lived upstairs. The builder was a J. Drummey of Alexandra and the cost was 685 pounds. The new post office contained valuable interior fittings, such as coach lamps, stairway lanterns, night lampions and copper braziers, which were removed and placed in museums throughout Otago when the building was sold to private ownership. Today, the building is a postal agency and gift shop called Dispatches.

The St Bathans police station and jail were opened in 1887. The first policeman to work there was Constable James Kennedy, who remained in the position for 25 years and is described as the ideal country policeman, which can be taken to mean he was friendly to, but not familiar with, the locals. Kennedy was replaced by Constable Robert Young in 1912, to be followed in turn by Constables Hood, Sugrue and King, until the station was closed in 1940. Today, the building still stands and is operated as an upmarket bed and breakfast.

The Bank of New South Wales is the only bank with a presence in the town. However, it is a building only and no longer operates as a going concern. The banking facilities were another casualty of the fall of St Bathans, which once had three commercial banks: the Bank of New Zealand (BNZ), the Bank of New South Wales and the Colonial Bank. The BNZ and the Bank of New South Wales opened for business in St Bathans in 1864, while the Colonial opened in 1887. After the initial rush of gold, when people began to leave St Bathans, the BNZ followed, quitting the town in 1869. In 1895 it bought the Colonial Bank when the latter was on the verge of bankruptcy. It was through this takeover that BNZ returned to the town, until it quit again in

The citizens of St Bathans' staunch support for the Liberal Party and its prime minister, Sir Joseph Ward, reaped dividends when the government built this handsome wooden post office in the town in 1907. Constructed with a post office on the ground floor and living quarters for the postmaster upstairs, the building cost 685 pounds to erect. When the local school was damaged during an earthquake in 1948, the ground floor of the post office served as a temporary school. The building has not been used as a post office for many years; it is now a postal agency and gift shop.

1901, which left only the Bank of New South Wales to offer banking facilities to the citizens of St Bathans. Today, there are no local banking facilities. The old wooden Bank of New South Wales building was shifted to Oturehua in 1975, where it was restored by the Oturehua Historical Society. Several years ago the restored building was shifted back to St Bathans and is now located in the main street between the post office and the Vulcan Hotel.

The Vulcan began life as the Ballarat Hotel in 1869. It is believed to be one of the oldest mudbrick buildings in Central Otago and was built by two men, Thomas Griffiths and John Gallagher. The original Vulcan was located further down the street, but that building was twice destroyed by fire. After the second fire, the Vulcan's liquor licence was transferred to the Ballarat and the name changed to Vulcan. Today's Vulcan stands mostly unchanged from the original. It has had its ups and downs and was threatened with closure a few years ago, until a consortium of local investors was put together to purchase it and keep it open. Losing the Vulcan would probably be the final nail in the coffin of St Bathans as the hotel is now the heart of this small settlement.

# 18
# FROM BLACKS TO OPHIR

Ophir began life as Blacks in 1857 when a Melbourne doctor, Thomas Black, took up the lease of two runs that extended from the top of the Dunstan Range to the Manuherikia River, the Lauder and Dunstan Creeks and over to Poolburn, and settled his sons William and Charles there to manage them. This was not an act of paternal kindness, but was instead a business investment by a shrewd medical man living in Australia, who was not in a position to personally manage some 36,000 hectares of unfenced land with no facilities in another country. When the leases of the big runs were being handed out in Central Otago in the late 1850s and early 1860s, the authorities were not inclined to lease more than one run per individual. Thus, Black's decision to put a run in the name of each son made good sense if the rules were to be bent. For a Melbourne-based doctor there would have been a certain prestige in being able to claim that he was the owner of a lease of thousands of hectares and was running several thousand sheep in another country. The fact that those two properties were really in the middle of nowhere at the time, and his sons had to begin from scratch to develop them, would probably not have been mentioned. Subsequent events were to prove that the investment was not a sound one.

William and Charles Black were the first settlers to reside in the Manuherikia Valley and chose to live on Run 244, which extended from the Manuherikia River over the Raggedy Range to the area that would become known as Poolburn. With their father's money they were able to build a three-bedroom stone homestead on the property. The house still exists today, fronting what is now Booth Road, a few hundred metres to the north of the township of Ophir. Once the homestead was complete the first thing the brothers did was employ an African American named William Williams to cook and keep house for them — probably the only African American ever to have lived in Ophir.

The two brothers had very different personalities. Charles was portly and cheerful, and was fond of drinking, gambling and playing cards. William was the opposite: slim, religious and quiet. William mostly worked the run, while Charles owned a house in Dunedin and spent most of his time in that city, following the lifestyle he preferred.

In common with most of the runholders in Central Otago at the time, the Blacks' world was invaded by goldminers when gold was discovered on their run in April 1863. Like many of the runholders, the brothers were also quick to profit from supplying meat to the would-be miners and by allowing them to camp in the shelter of the rock outcrops located behind their homestead.

In spite of their best efforts and their father's financial backing, the brothers were unable to make the two runs profitable, and in 1866 the leases were sold to neighbours. Before this happened, however, the brothers made the mistake of setting fire to their run, which burnt down as far as Galloway, near Alexandra. The land was irrevocably damaged and the way was opened for later infestation by rabbits and erosion by the strong north-west winds that blow in the summer when the ground is dry and vulnerable. With the lease of the Blacks' run being taken up by neighbours there was no need to use the homestead they had built on Booth Road, and for this reason it remained in its original form for 130 years. In 1922, it was leased by two locals, William and Charles Pitches, but within a year was purchased along with 4 hectares by Kathleen Stafford for 43 pounds. It remained in the Stafford family, being used as a hay barn, until it was purchased in 1998 and completely renovated.

*The Blacks homestead in Booth Road, Ophir. Built of stone in 1857 to house William and Charles Black, it was originally the headquarters of a huge run totalling 36,000 hectares. When it was completed, the two bachelor brothers employed William Willams to keep house for them. When gold was found in Central Otago the brothers allowed miners to camp in the shelter of the rocks, behind and to the right of the homestead. This was always a popular spot, out of the full force of the strong nor'westers. The property is under private ownership today and has been extensively and tastefully renovated, to convert it from the haybarn it had become.*

## A CHANGE OF NAME TO OPHIR

Blacks township was surveyed in 1866, and the locals requested at that time that the name be changed to Blackton. This was turned down by the Otago Superintendent, James Macandrew, who named the town Ophir, after the fabulous land where the Queen of Sheba brought gold to Solomon. This upset those who wanted the alternative name, and in retaliation many of the facilities that were later built in Ophir were named Blacks. The Blacks Hotel, a name that persists to the present day, was one example, and Blacks School, which was built in 1867 and closed in 1975, was another.

In spite of the fact that Ophir was never a particularly rich goldfield, high hopes were held for the town's future, and several buildings were constructed that now seem far in excess of what was required. Today, however, it is these same buildings that add character to Ophir. The stone courthouse is one example of this extravagance. Built to the same specifications as the old courthouse in Centennial Avenue, Alexandra, the Ophir courthouse has not been used for the purpose for which it was built for many years and is now a holiday home. The stone post office is another example of the optimism held for the town. Built in 1886 for 323 pounds, it is now owned by the Historic Places Trust and still operates as a part-time post office, opening for 15 hours a week. Other original buildings still in the town that date from this period include the stone church located at the southern end of the main street, the policeman's house, the cottage hospital, a bank, a dress shop, St Andrews church and the hall. Apart from the hall and the church, which are still used by the community, these buildings are now all privately owned and occupied. Far from being a ghost town, Ophir is thriving, with new buildings being constructed as the population increases.

Both the stone school and teacher's residence were once located in the middle of Ophir. Demolished in the twentieth century, the removal of these two historic buildings is now regretted.

ALEXANDRA MUSEUM

RIGHT ABOVE McKnight Brothers, farriers and blacksmiths of Alexandra, also had a branch in Ophir, which did business from these premises. The building still exists in Ophir. The patriarch of the family, Jimmy McKnight, is the man standing on the left. He was the forefather of the McKnight family, which is well represented in modern-day Central Otago. In addition to this business, he was the builder who constructed the Ophir Union Church and the Ophir Hall. He was also one of the partners in the Golden Progress Mine near Oturehua; and he was the local undertaker.

ALEXANDRA MUSEUM

RIGHT CENTRE The main street of Ophir, photographed at the end of the nineteenth century. The old stone Catholic church is at extreme lower right, the current post office is the building on the right with the horse tethered outside.

ALEXANDRA MUSEUM

RIGHT BELOW Ophir has always had a Blacks Hotel. The first, pictured here, was a wooden building owned by J.W. Macintosh, which catered for the needs of both man and horse.

ALEXANDRA MUSEUM

## MURDER AND SUICIDE

For all its short history and small population, Ophir has over the years been the scene of one attempted murder–suicide and a second, successful murder–suicide, with three out of the four people involved dying as a result. The first happened in January 1879 when John Waldron shot and wounded his wife, Honora, with a shotgun at close range, on a quiet road just outside Ophir. Following this confrontation, John's body was found later the same day in a gully not far from the road where he had attacked his wife. He had discharged the shotgun into his side, using a ramrod to force the trigger. His body was buried in an unmarked grave in the Blacks cemetery, and the coroner's verdict was that he had taken his own life while labouring under temporary insanity. Honora was badly wounded in her right arm and shoulder during the confrontation and was hospitalised for several weeks. John Waldron was from Wiltshire in England and had left England in his late teens for Victoria, following the discovery of gold in Australia. While in Melbourne he met the young Irish-born widow Honora McLaughlin, who was his senior by nine years and who had been forced out of her native country by the first potato famine when she was 12 years old. The couple married in Melbourne in 1862. In 1866 they and their three children emigrated to New Zealand and arrived in Ophir by wagon. Not long afterwards the marriage deteriorated to the point where both led separate lives. John eventually left for the goldfields on the West Coast but returned to Ophir on the fateful day the tragedy took place.

The second incident took place in Ophir over 100 years later in the 1990s, when the middle-aged publican of the Blacks Hotel left Ophir on a pretence and then returned unexpectedly, as he suspected that his young wife was having an affair. His suspicions were confirmed, and blinded by

The Ophir courthouse in session in 1926. Built of stone, it still stands today. The other stone building on the left is the policeman's house, which is now privately owned. Gone are the trees, which, when they reached their use-by date, were cut down and never replaced.

ALEXANDRA MUSEUM

RIGHT The second Blacks Hotel, shown here, was a more substantial building than the first. The former was demolished to make way for the third and final Blacks Hotel in Ophir, which today stands on the corner of Swindon Street and the Omakau–Ida Valley Road.

ALEXANDRA MUSEUM

BELOW A fine suspension bridge, the Daniel O'Connell Bridge, still spans the Manuherikia River at the southern end of Ophir. Built in 1880 it was named in memory of the nineteenth-century political leader, in recognition of the large number of Irish miners working and living in Ophir at the time.

jealousy he took a gun, killed his wife and then committed suicide. The police cordoned off the hotel and carried out an investigation, but no third party was ever charged with any crime.

## TEDDY RYAN AND NED KEARNEY

As discussed elsewhere in this book, many of the young men who were conscripted from Central Otago in the two world wars were damaged psychologically when they returned. Edward (Teddy) Ryan and Ned Kearney were two of these men, and both lived in Ophir for the greater part of their lives, trying to exist as best they could. Teddy Ryan lived alone in a rudimentary one-room hut in Booth Road, Ophir, and eked out a living rabbiting and waiting for the next pension day. He was a veteran of a machine-gun squadron in World War I and had been a bricklayer before he left for the trenches. On his return he was initially able to look after himself, but as time went on his standards slipped so badly that when the chimney of his hut collapsed he did not replace it. He continued to use the fireplace, minus the chimney, and as a result would always have red eyes and appear partly

Matakanui is a tiny village a few kilometres from Ophir. Now, supporting a resident population of only a handful of people, it was once a thriving gold town. The wall on the left is that of the mudbrick building that served in the latter half of the nineteenth century as headquarters of the Mount Morgan Sluicing Company, an offshoot of the mighty Mount Morgan gold, copper and silver mine in Mt Morgan, Queensland, Australia. The latter, which closed in 1982, is regarded as the richest single goldmine in the world, with an ore to gold ratio that often topped 20 per cent. When the gold ran out at Matakanui, the building shown to the left was taken over by Teddy Duggan, who operated it for many years as a general store. It is now a Historic Places site. The Newtown Tavern, as shown, was the last hotel in Matakanui. Its final owners were the Donnelly family, who quit when the hotel lost its licence in the shake-up of licences that took place during the 1970s. It is now used as a holiday home, complete with original mudbrick stables at the rear.

covered in soot. It was also quite common to see fleas crawl up from his collar and then disappear back down under his shirt. Teddy ended up living with the Little Sisters of the Poor until he died in 1960 at the age of 80.

Ned Kearney lived alone in a small hut in the middle of Ophir and suffered from the same problem as Teddy Ryan. The only difference between the two men was that Ned was a veteran of World War II. He also received a war pension but boosted his income by labouring on farms in the district. Pension day was blowout day when he spent most of the money given to him by the government in the local hotels. Some of the men who had served with him during the war knew what he was suffering from and kept an eye on him, making sure he did not starve after he had been on a bender and spent all his money.

These men were only two of a larger group of ex-servicemen who had fought, often unwillingly, for their country and had been scarred by the experience. They were often looked upon as alcoholic deadbeats, but their problems went much deeper than that. They were very much a part of Central Otago during the first half of the twentieth century, and for that reason deserve to be included in the history of the area.

# 19
# WANAKA AND HAWEA — LAKES AND MOUNTAINS

Millions of years ago the material that today forms the mountains, plains, valleys and lake beds of Wanaka and Hawea was silt, laid down on what was once the sea floor. During the ice age, glaciers formed and gouged out the shape of the lakes to depths well below sea level. When the world's temperature warmed, these glaciers melted and much of the debris that they were carrying became natural dams at the southern ends of two of the new valleys, creating lakes Wanaka and Hawea in the process. The terraces and escarpments that remain today are the flood remains of the rivers that swept away much of the surplus rocks and shingle from the melted glaciers.

Maori legend tells a different story. Lakes Wanaka and Hawea, along with the other South Island lakes, were dug out by the Maori chief Te Rakaihautu. When he had excavated the lakes he used the spoil to create the mountains that surround them.

*Makarora*, one of the early steamers that carried cargo and passengers on Lake Wanaka, shown tied up at the wharf at the head of the lake in 1908.
HOCKEN COLLECTIONS S05-065F, UNIVERSITY OF OTAGO, DUNEDIN

Maori who travelled to this area before European settlement lived in small villages near lakes Wanaka and Hawea, but used these more as camps when hunting moa or travelling to the West Coast to collect greenstone, rather than as permanent settlements. However, Maori knew the area well and were familiar with all the rivers and passes long before European contact was made. Today, the main pass to the West Coast is named after the early European explorer who drew the first map of the Southern Alps, Julius von Haast. James McKerrow, a young Scotsman, also carried out a number of exploration trips in the Wanaka and Hawea district between 1861 and 1863, while acting under instructions from John Turnbull (Mr Surveyor) Thomson. As an assistant surveyor, it was McKerrow who in 1862 made the first survey of Wanaka and Hawea.

## ABEL FERRIS DOMINI

The patriarch of the first family to settle at Wanaka itself was Abel Ferris Domini, who in spite of having such an elaborate name was better known as Henry Norman. The reason why is unknown. In 1860 the Domini family travelled down from Wellington to Oamaru by sailing boat and made their way to Wanaka. They built the first homestead on the shores of the lake, at the south side of the present-day road to Glendhu Bay. Abel Domini had come to Lake Wanaka to manage a run established by a John Roy in 1859. In March 1861 his son, Robert Domini, was the first European child to be born in the area. Roy's run was the second to be established near Wanaka; the lease of the first run was taken up in 1858 by Robert Wilkin and his brother-in-law Archibald Thomson. Thomson died two years later, but Wilkin went on to become one of the largest landholders in the area. When these first runs were settled the population of Otago was a mere 2400, of which 1200 lived in Dunedin, so Wanaka and Hawea were very remote. Absentee owners were also a feature of the first Wanaka–Hawea runs, and this trend continues in the area to the present day, with several large properties owned by expatriates.

Lakes Wanaka and Hawea, showing the locations of the townships of Wanaka and Hawea Flat, plus several other names that featured in the early history of the area. The Clutha River begins its journey to the sea at the outlet of Lake Wanaka and is joined a short distance downstream by the Hawea River, the small stretch of river that drains Lake Hawea.

ALEXANDRA MUSEUM

## GOLD IN THE LINDIS RIVER

Gold was found in the Lindis River in 1860, a year before Gabriel Read's discovery at Gabriels Gully. The difference between the two strikes was that Gabriels Gully proved to be a hugely profitable goldfield, while the Lindis did not. In 1860 hopeful prospectors rushed to the Lindis River, and by April that same year there were 300 miners camped along its banks. Like many of the prospectors who would follow them to Central Otago, these first arrivals came unprepared, and had little in the way of food and equipment. Their position was not helped by the local runholders, who were anti-goldmining because of the disruption it caused to their way of life and who hoped to discourage the prospectors by not supplying them with food. This was done in a subtle way by making food available but only at very high prices.

The hungry miners were as reluctant to leave their claims as the Lindis River was to give up its gold. Today, this first strike is regarded as a failure, but there were important lessons learnt by the Lindis miners that they were able to put to good use in later goldrushes. They had learnt how to prospect for gold and they now knew how cold and often dangerous the Central Otago winters could be, but most importantly they realised the importance of heading to any new goldfield with sufficient food and equipment, if their efforts were to be successful.

A feature of the Lindis that made it unique in Central Otago was the miners' attempts to bring some semblance of law and order to these diggings. This was most unusual as later settlements were infamous for their lawlessness.

When Gabriel Read finally made his discovery in 1861, the majority of the miners on the Lindis River headed for Gabriels Gully. The ones who stayed put, however, were in a handy position to stake alluvial claims when gold was discovered in the Clutha River near Cromwell in 1862.

## GEORGE MAGNUS HASSING AND CHARCOAL JOE HEBDEN

Early in 1861 when the owners of West Wanaka station advertised for labour to cut and supply timber for the station, George Hassing, a Dane who was living in Wellington at the time, responded. His arrival in Wanaka marked the beginning of his influence on the future of Wanaka and Central Otago.

After completing the timber contract for West Wanaka Station, Hassing and a partner began felling and cutting timber for all the local runs. The timber used came from local native forests of totara, black pine and beech.

This was pit sawn into planks and then towed across Lake Wanaka to its outlet. Once this point was reached, Hassing either supplied the local runs or rafted the timber down the Clutha River to Cromwell, a distance of some 80 km. Over time, some of this timber became jammed on rocks in the river, where it was abandoned. Most of it made it through, however, and was used to build many of the towns downstream, in the wood-starved interior of treeless Central Otago. It was the abandoned timber that Charcoal Joe Hebden, a man who would become the fourth partner in the wealthy Cromwell Quartz Mining Company's mine at Bendigo, would use to manufacture charcoal

George Hassing had the ability and foresight to supply building timber where it was required in early Central Otago. Others would follow, in particular John Ewing and Theodore Russell, who operated a mill for many years on the north side of the Matukituki River. Today, their mill is remembered by the name Mill Creek, a small tributary stream that runs into the Matukituki. Their competition was a mill owned by Yankee Dan Colville and Alfred Nees that was sited beside the Wilkin River opposite Makarora, and a mill owned by a J.D. Ross located on the western side of Lake Hawea. In 1871 three men, Farquhar, Ross and Isbell, built a new sawmill at Makarora and began to manufacture tongue and groove flooring, a very important building material at the time. All these sawmills were powered by water, which was used to drive a waterwheel designed to operate a circular saw. Hassing was the first, however, and without Wanaka timber and his ability to deliver it to Cromwell, the early development of Central Otago would have been much more difficult.

## ALBERT TOWN, PEMBROKE AND HAWEA FLAT

In the 1860s Albert Town, now a small settlement on the Clutha River, became the hub of the Wanaka and Hawea districts, a position it gradually acceded to Pembroke, the first name given to the township of Wanaka. The mail service operated from Albert Town until 1873 and the first area school opened there in 1870, but more importantly it was where the punts that ferried people, provisions and livestock over the Clutha River were located.

Theodore Russell and Charles (Captain) Hedditch were the first permanent residents of Pembroke, where streets had been surveyed for a town as early as 1863. Russell built a hotel there in 1867 using timber from the mill he owned in partnership with John Ewing, while Hedditch owned and operated the *Surprise*, the first vessel on Lake Wanaka.

The Drake brothers were the first settlers at Hawea Flat. Sons of Reverend

D.A. Jolly was a Scot who came to New Zealand as a seaman on the *Aboukir* in 1862 and jumped ship at Port Chalmers to join the goldrush. Not faring well as a miner he began a general merchant business in Cromwell, which he expanded in 1869 with a branch in Pembroke (now Wanaka). The Pembroke store was very successful and remained open until 1930, when it became a victim of the depression.

HOCKEN COLLECTIONS S05-037M,
UNIVERSITY OF OTAGO, DUNEDIN

Drake of Cromwell, their name remained there for 100 years, carried on until the 1960s by Murdoch Drake, a bachelor who owned a station at the top of Lake Wanaka where he lived with his sister before retiring to Hawea Flat.

The whole region suffered in September 1878 when three floods came in rapid succession. The level of Lake Wanaka rose 4 m above normal, causing severe damage as far down river as Albert Town, where guests staying at the hotel were forced to run for their lives. The small village of Cardrona was also badly affected when the swollen Cardrona River swept through it. Goldmining at Cardrona never fully recovered as the damage caused by the flood convinced the majority of miners that there were easier and safer places to invest and work in.

In March 1881 the newspaper the *Cromwell Argus* predicted that, as Pembroke was by then the centre of some 18,000 hectares of grazing land, it was destined to become the wealthiest township in Central Otago, but the reality proved to be very different. Two factors — a depression and rabbits—combined in the 1880s to bring Pembroke and the wealthy runholders to their financial knees. In 1883 the prices for primary products plunged, sending many runholders, sawmill owners and other business people bankrupt. Most of the runholders who survived the depression were in turn finished off by the rabbit plague and overgrazing of the land. In the space of only 30 years large areas of open country around the two lakes, which had been described by John Turnbull Thomson as 'magnificent sheep country, clothed in luxuriant grasses and native herbs', had been reduced to a pastoral desert and abandoned. The only positive at this time was that tourism was beginning to develop on lakes Wanaka and Hawea. This began when the redundant boats, once used to transport timber, began to take tourists out on regular trips.

The attractiveness of lakes Wanaka and Hawea and the adjoining mountains was such that tourists first began to arrive in the area as early as the 1870s, via the mail coach from Cromwell. By 1881 the legendary coach operators Cobb & Co. had taken over the run, and this company provided reliable transport until the turn of the century, when horse and coach became redundant. However, times were different and the early development of Pembroke was definitely not tourist-oriented. In 1878 a slaughterhouse was built on the banks of Bullock Creek a few hundred metres from Pembroke. Bullock Creek ran through the new township and was used as an open drain for both the slaughterhouse and an adjacent piggery. The extensive and attractive beech forests in the Matukituki Valley were also being devastated by the sawmilling that was taking place there.

With the decline in the fortunes of the runholders and with tourism only just beginning, it was the opportune discovery of gold at Long Valley in 1880, on the western side of Lake Hawea, that kept the small settlements

The wharf at Pembroke (Wanaka) in 1902. On the right is the propeller-driven steamer *Makarora*, and at left is the paddle steamer *Theodore*. One sports the Union Jack at the tip of its mast while the other displays the naval ensign.

HOCKEN COLLECTIONS S05-065H, UNIVERSITY OF OTAGO, DUNEDIN

alive. This find was further boosted in 1885 when a field called Criffel was discovered between the Cardrona River and Luggate. This field would be hampered by a lack of water, with wash dirt having to be moved to water by sledges, which was both time-consuming and expensive. Neither field was a bonanza as the gold was fine and discoloured. The banks were suspicious of its quality, paying well below market rates for it. In spite of these drawbacks, Pembroke and Hawea Flat did benefit from the advantages of having a goldfield nearby.

In 1881 tourism had a real boost when the paddle steamer *Theodore*, named after sawmill owner Theodore Russell, was built and launched by Asher Smith. It was a wood-burning vessel that made good use of the driftwood around the edges of the lake and was specially designed to accommodate tourists. It toured around Lake Wanaka every week, carrying cargo as well as passengers, and was advertised outside the area to attract customers. The cost of a round trip was 2 pounds per person, and a brass band was often taken along to entertain the passengers.

## THE TWENTIETH CENTURY

Coupled with the beginnings of tourism, the economy of the area receive a large boost in 1910 when Morven Hills Station was subdivided into 23 smaller runs supporting several dozen families. This was followed in turn by subdivision of other large runs, which again increased the population dramatically. Irrigation began to be developed to increase production and soften the effects of regular droughts. A leader in this field was Sir Percy Sargood, a Dunedin merchant and lessee of Wanaka Station. He introduced ideas that were far ahead of their time, planting 8000 fruit trees to begin a successful orchard and developing other areas of trees for timber, in a decade when the culture was to cut down existing forest. He was also responsible for beginning a farm cadet scheme, which employed and trained young men from underprivileged backgrounds. In 1917 Sargood showed further capacity for progressive ideas when he introduced electric light to Wanaka Station.

Tourism was given a boost in 1910 when, at the request of the Government Tourist Department, Mrs Ewing, the wife of sawmill owner John Ewing, opened a guest house at Makarora. The milling of timber had begun to decline at the turn of the century to be replaced by the harvesting of flax for its fibre. After a shaky start, the flax industry took off and by 1910 was employing 25 people.

Milk supplied in cartons or bottles was a long way off when this photograph was taken. Early runholders and farmers in Wanaka and Central Otago had to provide their own milk. Most kept one or more house cows which were milked twice a day, morning and evening. Apart from milk for the kitchen, butter was also made from cream, while the skim milk was fed to the pigs. This practice carried on throughout Central Otago into the 1950s.

HOCKEN COLLECTIONS S05-037G,
UNIVERSITY OF OTAGO, DUNEDIN

These early years of the new century also saw the development of gold dredging in the Clutha and Cardrona rivers. The dredge master of one of these dredges, the *Rolling Stone*, was Julius von Haast, the well known explorer. Sir Percy Sargood also became involved in dredging, but by 1910 most of the dredges were gone from the Wanaka and Hawea region. One dredge, the *Lowburn*, later began operations in 1938 under the control of the Austral-New Zealand Mining Company and dredged the Clutha in the surrounding area until 1953. By that time the locals, who were more conservation-minded than their parents, were pleased to see the end of the ruin of good land by the *Lowburn*.

By 1910 Pembroke had grown to a township that contained a wardens court, magistrates court, a golf club, a cricket club and a tennis club. Along with Hawea Flat, it also boasted a jockey club and held regular race meetings. In the same year tourism received another boost when deer stalkers began to visit the area in large numbers to shoot deer, mainly in the valleys around Lake Hawea. Deer, which had been imported from the estate of the Earl of Dalhousie at Forfar in Scotland in 1871, had thrived and by 1910 numbered in the thousands. By 1919 deer numbers had got completely out of hand and culling was introduced.

The shooting of game birds was another sport that attracted tourists; but the most important move for tourism was the introduction of brown trout to Lake Wanaka in 1876 and rainbow trout to Lake Hawea in 1911. From the very beginning these species thrived, and trophy fish quickly became the norm, with fish over 10 kg being caught regularly in the two lakes. To

ABOVE The Lake House at Hawea was a hunting lodge for those interested in stalking red deer in the hills that surround the lake. Antlers of several stags adorn the posts on the verandah of the lodge.

HOCKEN COLLECTIONS S05-065C, UNIVERSITY OF OTAGO, DUNEDIN

BELOW Red deer stags in the high country around Lake Hawea were renowned for their trophy heads. The desire to shoot one of these stags brought large numbers of deerstalkers to Lake Hawea and aided the early development of the local tourism industry.

maintain fish stocks a trout hatchery was established in Pembroke in 1917 and, several years later, a further 122,000 rainbow and 7000 brown trout were released into Lake Hawea. Quinnat salmon had also naturally established in the lakes from 1900, having made their way up the Clutha River from the Waitaki River, via the ocean.

In the twentieth century mountaineering also became a popular sport. The mountains that had been a barrier to movement through to the West Coast now became an asset. Mt Aspiring was not climbed until November 1910, when Captain Bernard Head, Alex Graham and Jack Clarke made the first successful ascent. Today, the desire to climb Mt Aspiring and other mountains in the Southern Alps brings large numbers of tourists to Wanaka and Hawea, as do the ski fields that have been established on the foothills.

During the first years of the new century the wood-burning paddle steamer *Theodore* was replaced on Lake Wanaka by the steamer *Makarora*. The latter was purchased in 1906 by the Wanaka Shipping Company, which also owned the first oil-driven boat on the lake, the *Tilikum*. Both vessels were used to transport tourists, sheep, timber and wool, until the *Makarora* was wrecked in 1909. To fill the gap, the *Tilikum* was upgraded to carry more passengers, while another, larger boat, the *Kura*, was built and launched to carry cargo. A third, the *Elswick*, was built by two Dunedin businessmen, and with a surplus of boats on Lake Wanaka the *Kura* was transferred for use on Lake Hawea. Unlike Lake Wakatipu, where the refitted *Earnslaw* still operates today as a tourist boat, no steam-powered vessel now exists on lakes Wanaka or Hawea.

The road through the Lindis Pass in 1926. Today the same road is a modern highway, minus the gate.

HOCKEN COLLECTIONS S05-065G,
UNIVERSITY OF OTAGO, DUNEDIN

World War I left the residents of Pembroke and Hawea Flat bewildered by the changes it brought, along with deaths caused by the Spanish Flu that the returning soldiers carried home with them. During the 1920s Pembroke underwent many changes, with some of the original buildings being torn down and new ones built. The depression of the 1930s brought government works to the area, along with construction camps to house the people employed. These years saw the construction of the Haast Road, the connecting road to the West Coast, started and continued through the decade. The construction was halted many times, and it was not until the 1960s that the road was completed.

In the 1950s Lake Hawea underwent a huge change when the level of the lake was raised by 18 m as part of a scheme along the Clutha River to generate electricity. Large camps were set up to house those working on the scheme. The raising of the lake resulted in thousands of hectares of farmland, houses, woolsheds, fences and even established roads being lost to the water.

One final and lasting change was made to Pembroke on 1 September 1940 when its name was changed to Wanaka. Today, Wanaka is a thriving, sophisticated town that contains a mixture of permanent residents and those who visit only during holidays. It has recently undergone a huge boom in property prices, caused in part by North Island and overseas buyers moving into the area. Hawea has not undergone the same commercial development as Wanaka, but has seen considerable growth in the twentieth century.

# 20
# NASEBY AND KYEBURN

Naseby began life as a small settlement called Parkers, named after a party of miners who panned for gold there, led by B.R. and W.C. Parker, sons of the Victorian protector of Aborigines in Australia. This name was changed to Hogburn shortly afterwards and finally to Naseby, to reflect the birthplace in England of Otago Provincial Superintendent John Hyde Harris.

Located at the foot of the Hawkdun Range, Naseby was originally established to cater for the large runs that had taken up most of the land in the Maniototo by 1858, but boomed when gold was discovered there in 1863. As with all the areas where gold was mined in Central Otago, Naseby's supply of the precious metal eventually ran out. When that happened, Naseby was in the fortunate position of being the administrative centre of the Maniototo Plain and prospered in that role until Ranfurly was built at the beginning of the twentieth century. Ranfurly had the advantage of the railway running through it, and Naseby, some 15 km away, never really recovered its importance.

As the century progressed the town struggled to survive, especially with the closing of its hospital, school and post office. For a time it appeared it would become a ghost town, but Naseby revived when its attractive and historic cottages began to be bought up for use as holiday homes. Conifer trees that were planted to hide the scars left by the sluicing carried out around the town eventually led to the establishment of an important commercial forest. Today, the permanent population of Naseby hovers at around 150, with those numbers swelled to some 2000 during long weekends and holidays. It has two hotels and several shops, plus an art gallery, a café, an all-seasons skating and curling rink and a large holiday park. The historic appearance of the settlement has been maintained and enhanced by the foresight of the early settlers, who planted a large number of English trees which have now reached maturity.

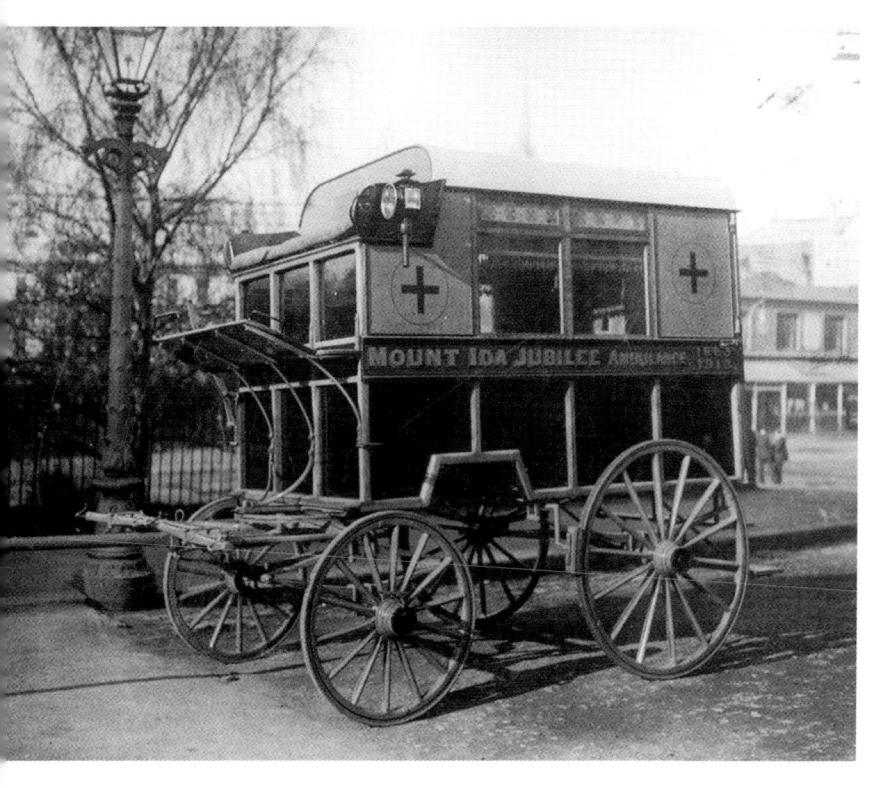

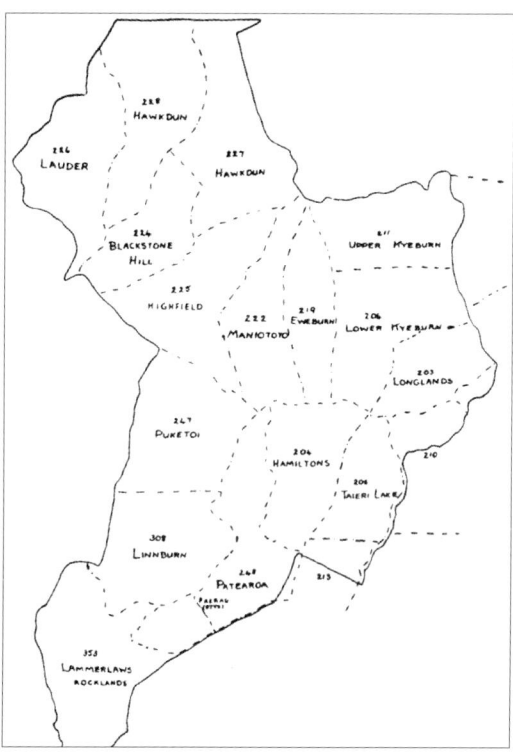

## A SLUDGE CHANNEL FROM NASEBY TO THE TAIERI RIVER

The sluicing for gold in Naseby had a dramatic effect on the surrounding countryside. In 1877 a sludge channel was built from Naseby to the Taieri River to help remove the overburden that was being created by sluicing. At that time there was a large, beautiful lake on the Taieri River near Waipiata, supporting a varied range of wildfowl, but over the years this was filled in by the sludge flushed down the channel and it has now disappeared completely.

Along with sluicing came gold dredging, and the two combined to produce enough gold to make Naseby an important service centre. Fortunes were not made easily in the Naseby area, as the district was always regarded as a poor man's diggings. In the 1800s, this description meant the gold claims were payable but none were rich. In spite of that, by 1880 the settlement had a courthouse, a warden's office, three banks, council chambers, a town hall, an athenaeum, a hospital and a newspaper, plus several churches and hotels. The hospital began in the Ancient Briton Hotel when miners paid

**ABOVE LEFT** As part of the celebrations for the Mount Ida Jubilee, which included the village of Naseby, this early ambulance was renovated and put on display.

HOCKEN COLLECTIONS S05-037E, UNIVERSITY OF OTAGO, DUNEDIN

**ABOVE RIGHT** The early runs of the Maniototo, which were quickly taken up after the area was explored and surveyed by John Turnbull Thomson and his team. The town of Naseby was established to service these runs and was strategically located on Run 219, Eweburn. Many of the names remain today, but the runs themselves were broken up into much smaller properties during the land reforms of the early 1900s.

ALEXANDRA MUSEUM

Naseby was isolated by the big snowfall of 1908 that also affected other parts of Central Otago. The roofs of houses threatened to collapse under the weight of the huge falls of snow. These two men have removed as much snow from the roof as they can, to prevent its collapse.

MANIOTOTO EARLY SETTLERS MUSEUM

for a room in that hotel to house an injured companion. From that humble beginning, subscriptions were later raised to maintain a hospital room at the hotel, until a permanent hospital was built in 1871. This wooden building was later replaced with a grander one and was used until the 1930s, when it in turn was made redundant by a new hospital constructed in Ranfurly.

One of Naseby's problems, which probably figured in the decision not to take the new railway through it, was the fact that it was at a higher elevation than Ranfurly and as a result suffered heavy snowfalls. The heaviest fall occurred in 1908, when 2 m of snow fell, killing most of the runholders' sheep and cutting Naseby off from the outside world for two months, before melting and causing severe flooding.

## MT BURSTER

When the goldrush hit Naseby in 1863 a field was soon found in an area which would initially be named Mt Burster, possibly because it was at a high altitude, steep and difficult to get at. The Mt Burster field was located in the Hawkdun Range between Naseby and Danseys Pass, at an altitude of 1200 m above sea level. It was particularly rich, but due to its high altitude could only be worked in the late spring and summer as the water races froze solid during the colder months. When the miners returned to their claims in the spring they often had to plough through a metre of snow to get to their huts and then drive snow tunnels to open their doors; one miner lost his life in

1879 when a tunnel collapsed and smothered him. Getting water to the field was also difficult and required the construction of 103 km of races. In spite of all these difficulties, by 1869 the Mt Burster field supported the claims of 25 European and 100 Chinese miners, spread over three gullies, which gives an indication of the richness of the field.

Before the end of World War I most of the mining had faded out on Mt Burster. By then it was referred to as Mt Buster, the name which remains today. In 1901 local runholders saw the potential of Mt Buster and all that area of quite steep land in the Hawkdun Range as ideal summer sheep country and signed a lease with the government to graze it in the same year. This lease ran until 1918, when it was renewed by several of the returned servicemen who had taken up the smaller properties that had been created in the area when the big runs were subdivided. The land they leased was not fenced into separate areas, so the new lessees formed a syndicate to graze their sheep in one large flock of several thousand animals over the summer months. As most of them were returned servicemen they called themselves the soldiers' syndicate under an arrangement that would last 100 years, being passed from father to son.

## MUSTER ON THE BUSTER

Under the rules of the soldiers' syndicate each member was allowed to put a set number of sheep on the leased land. These sheep were earmarked for identification and then allowed to roam free until the approaching winter and the threat of snow made it wise to bring them down to lower altitudes. The round-up that took place at the end of each summer came to be referred to as the Muster on the Buster. This muster took several days, was men-only and became a tradition in the area. It seemed that nearly every local farmer took part at one time or another, often just for the fun of it and the exhilaration of being out among the hills with their teams of dogs. Young boys who are now middle-aged farmers could not wait until they were old enough to join their first muster and still talk about those times with a wistful look in their eyes.

In the beginning there were no roads on the syndicate's lease. To cope with the steep terrain, mules were specially bred by syndicate members to carry all the gear required for a successful muster. Because mules live a long time, often 40 years, some of these animals became characters in their own right. Once in the hills, the musterers lived in tents in the early years and were often snowed in for several days at a time. Later, they graduated to tin sheds with roofs held up by a centre pole. The men slept on tussock cut for the purpose, with their feet facing inwards to this pole, and it was not unusual to wake in the morning covered in a dusting of snow if the wind had been strong enough to blow it through the cracks in the walls.

Living conditions on the muster improved when a road was bulldozed through the area in 1969 and later when two huts were used as living quarters instead of tents. When the New Zealand Railways closed the Otago Central Railway line in the 1990s, most of the small station buildings were sold. Syndicate members purchased the Kokonga and Ida Valley stations and shifted them into the hills to be used during the Muster on the Buster. The Ida Valley station was taken in over what must be one of the steepest and most winding private roads in New Zealand, on a huge trailer with a bulldozer at each end to provide power. The move took a week, and it is an indication of the skills of the men involved that when the building was finally placed on piles in its new location it had suffered only a broken window. Both station buildings remain in use today in their remote locations.

## KYEBURN DIGGINGS AND KYEBURN

Much of the locality that is referred to as Kyeburn is based on the Kye Burn river, which flows out of the Hawkdun Range and disappears into the Taieri River at Waipiata. The area encompassed is large and can be confusing as there is no settlement of any significance today to evidence the hectic activity that took place there in the nineteenth and early twentieth century. Kyeburn does, however, have an interesting history, which is brought to life by the reminders of the past that have made it into the twenty-first century. The locality is roughly divided into three areas: Kyeburn Diggings, the old Kyeburn village site and the area south of the Kyeburn Bridge on State Highway 89, south to Kokonga, which includes the Swinburn cemetery.

Kyeburn Diggings is at the northernmost end of the Kye Burn river, 20 km east of Naseby, and begins where the Danseys Pass Hotel is located today. Danseys Pass was and still is a strategic location as it is one of only two major exits into the Waitaki Valley and the north, from Central Otago. The pass was named after W.H. Dansey, a partner in the large Otekaieke Run in North Otago. In 1855, he and three other young men, who were also runholders, along with a donkey and a mule to carry their gear, entered Central Otago from the north by way of this pass. They were looking for suitable sheep grazing country but were not impressed by what they saw, and all four chose to remain in North Otago and Canterbury. In spite of the fact that the pass was at high altitude and was dangerous for early travellers, who could be caught out in winter snows, it became an important route. By 1869 snow poles had been laid out to indicate the route, and the following year a horse track was developed as far as the Maerewhenua Diggings, near Livingston. The first Danseys Pass Hotel was opened in 1863 by Edwin George and his wife. Today, the pass is still in use as quick access to North Otago and Oamaru, but is not a favoured route as the road is winding and dusty.

Gold was found in the Upper Kye Burn river in 1861, close to where the present-day Danseys Pass Hotel is located, but serious prospecting did not take place until the search for gold gathered momentum with the Naseby rush in 1863. Coal was also found and became an important local industry. The immediate area became known as Kyeburn Diggings, while a town of the same name sprang up a few kilometres south of the Danseys Pass Hotel. By 1880 this area also supported a population of some 600 Chinese miners. The last Chinese miner to live in Kyeburn Diggings was a man by the name of Joe Shum, whose life was suddenly ended when he was murdered for his gold in 1928 by a visiting European named Hardie. As was usual for the times, Hardie was tried and sentenced to life imprisonment but was released after serving only a few years. Extensive sluicing was carried out along the Kyeburn River and its surrounds, and there are serious scars left as evidence of this today. Dredging was also tried when two small dredges were put on the river in 1890, but these were not successful as there was inadequate water flow for them to operate properly.

Little is left of the settlement of Kyeburn Diggings today. There are hedges and trees but no early buildings, with the only reminder of the population that once lived there being the well kept cemetery, which is still in use. Buried there is one of Central Otago's best known citizens,

Maisey's Kyeburn Hotel, pictured in the 1890s. This building no longer exists.
MANIOTOTO EARLY SETTLERS MUSEUM

**RIGHT ABOVE** Kyeburn Diggings was a popular location for Chinese miners, whose numbers reached 600 there during the 1880s. Part of their preference for the area was the fact that they became involved in sluicing for gold by combining their claims and pooling their resources to secure the necessary supply of water. Sluicing by Chinese was not always possible in others parts of Central Otago, as prejudice demanded that they rework old claims turned over previously by Europeans.

019158, ALEXANDER TURNBULL LIBRARY, NATIONAL LIBRARY OF NEW ZEALAND

**RIGHT BELOW** The large stone building, photographed here in the 1920s, began life as the Kyeburn Hotel. With some later additions it became the historic Danseys Pass Hotel, a smart hotel that occupies the same site today. The road running between the car and the man in this photograph is the present-day road over the Danseys Pass to the Waitaki Valley.

HOCKEN COLLECTIONS S05-044A, UNIVERSITY OF OTAGO, DUNEDIN

Eden Hore, an eccentric man who loved all things beautiful. Eden owned a farm at the edge of the Kyeburn Diggings but is better known for the large collection of women's ball gowns that he amassed during his lifetime. Today, this collection is the main feature of a museum display at Glenshee Park, his former property on the road between Danseys Pass Hotel and Naseby, and several of the dresses are also on display at the Museum of New Zealand Te Papa Tongarewa in Wellington. He was also an original thinker; and he is probably the only Central Otago farmer to have been involved in the administration of the Miss New Zealand beauty contest, popular in the 1950s and 1960s. Another of his interests was the introduction of the yak to New Zealand, with the intention of breeding these exotic animals for their hair. Their introduction was not successful as it was found that the yak was prone to tuberculosis in the Central Otago climate. The last crossbreed animal bred from Eden Hore's yaks still exists in Central Otago today, grazing nonchalantly in a roadside paddock.

The area that was simply named Kyeburn was located a few kilometres further south, downriver from Kyeburn Diggings. This settlement was more modern than the Diggings, as it grew up at the junction where State Highway 85 crossed the Kye Burn river and carried on into the Pigroot to the east coast, or turned south onto State Highway 87 to travel through to Dunedin via Middlemarch. Kyeburn School opened at the Ranfurly end of this junction in 1882. It served the children of local runholders, miners and farmers for 104 years, before it was closed in 1986. The farmers who sent their children to the school had taken up the 200-acre (80-hectare) farms

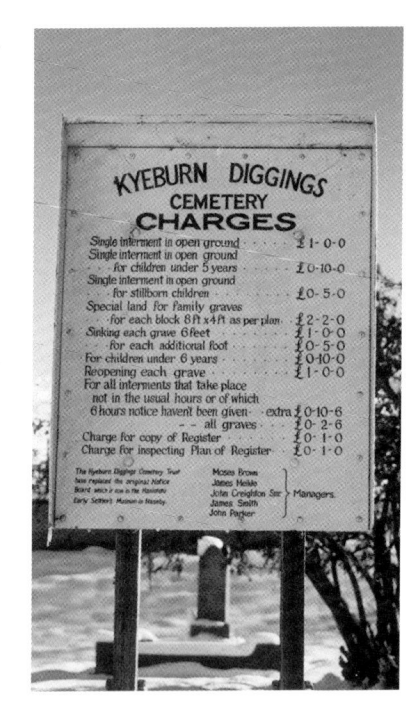

ABOVE Once a thriving settlement supporting those involved in the search for gold, all that remains of Kyeburn Diggings today, apart from some mature trees, is the original cemetery. This sign has been replicated from the original in the Maniototo Early Settlers Museum in Naseby and erected at the cemetery gates. Burial prices are very definite and wide-ranging, but expensive, when compared with the average weekly wage of one pound at the time the charges applied.

LEFT Kyeburn School opened in 1882 and educated local children for 104 years before it closed in 1986. Located in Kyeburn Village, beside State Highway 85, it exists today as a private holiday home.

MANIOTOTO EARLY SETTLERS MUSEUM

that were cut off the large runs in 1875 and called the Kyeburn 200. The Kyeburn 200 were located between Kyeburn and the Kakanui Mountains, but as the years progressed these smallholdings became uneconomic and were bought up by neighbours, a move which resulted in a shrinking population and aided the eventual demise of the school.

The Kyeburn cemetery is located on State Highway 87, about halfway between Kyeburn and Kokonga. To avoid confusion with the Kyeburn Diggings cemetery it was called the Swinburn cemetery. It was used by the people of both Kyeburn and Kokonga. The area produced two prominent early politicians, who are both interred there. One, Scobie McKenzie, was the local MP from 1884 to 1894 and a Dunedin MP from 1896 to 1899. He was a popular and gifted politician who at one time also owned most of the farming land around Kyeburn. The other is Sir Robert Scott, a dapper man with a goatee beard who was the MP for Tuapeka and Central Otago from 1905 to 1919. He was appointed to the legislative council in 1920, while also serving on the boards of several local institutions, before dying in 1944 at the age of 90.

In its natural position as a crossroads and river crossing, Kyeburn once supported a large population with all the attendant facilities. As times

Stone was an important building material in early Central Otago. The remote Serpentine Church shown here was built in the 1860s. Local miners contributed towards its cost. Abandoned after the gold ran out, it was renovated by the Department of Conservation and is currently regarded as the highest church, by altitude, in New Zealand.

Stone was used to build the facilities required on the early runs. These are the original sheepyards and woolshed of Puketoi Station, near Patearoa. Apart from some later additions in timber, they were built entirely of local schist.

changed, communication improved and populations shrank, it became like its more northerly relation, Kyeburn Diggings. Kyeburn cannot today be regarded as a town or, for that matter, even a village.

## KOKONGA

Located at the extreme southern end of the Kyeburn area, Kokonga was once an important railway town. The location was one of the earliest farming settlements in Central Otago, which came into its own when it was decided that the Otago Central Railway would be built through Kokonga and given a station of the same name. The first farming families prospered in the 1890s when they supplied food to the large railway camp that was established at Daisybank, a few kilometres to the south of Kokonga. The flat land close to the Taieri River at Kokonga was prone to flooding, which restricted the growth of the village and resulted in the railway station being built on higher ground behind the present-day buildings. When the railway was closed in the 1990s, Kokonga had no reason for being, and like Kyeburn and Kyeburn Diggings, it faded into obscurity, surrounded by prosperous farms whose attentions, as a result of improved communications, were now diverted elsewhere in order to secure the services they required.

# 21
# RANFURLY — ART DECO ON THE MANIOTOTO PLAIN

Ranfurly was different from most of the other towns in Central Otago in that it did not start life to cater for the needs of farmers or goldminers. Instead, it began as a tree nursery, spent its teenage years as a railway town and entered middle age as the business centre of the Maniototo Plain. The journey was not without its trauma, but the town survived and today it prospers.

## IN THE BEGINNING

When John Turnbull Thomson crossed the Maniototo Plain in 1857, his comments regarding the farming potential of the area were so favourable that by 1858 all the land on the Maniototo had been taken up by runholders. Gold was discovered at Naseby and Hamiltons in 1863, with both finds being a short distance in opposite directions from where Ranfurly would be developed many years later. As a result of these discoveries, Naseby became the first business centre of the Maniototo, a position it held for more than 30 years.

Hamiltons was a typical gold settlement that started off with a flurry, but as the gold ran out the population drifted away, until the diggings were finally abandoned. Today, very little evidence of Hamiltons remains, other than a historic cemetery and the damage done to the environment by sluicing. The location is important, however, as the area would become the site where the Waipiata Tuberculosis Sanatorium was established, running at near to full capacity until the development of antibiotics made it redundant in the 1940s. From there it became a correctional facility for boys and is now privately owned by a religious group. As a sanatorium and correctional facility, both employing and caring for a large number of people, its existence was very important to the early economy of Ranfurly.

When the Otago Central Railway was routed directly across the Maniototo Plain it was inevitable that Naseby would decline as its location was too far from the new line. Another town, closer to the tracks, was required to service the railway, and the Eweburn Township reserve of 300 hectares was where the new settlement would be built. At that time, 8 hectares of this reserve were being used as a tree nursery under the management of New Zealand's first state forester, Henry Mathews. Eweburn was the name proposed for the new town, but in 1897 the then governor of New Zealand, the Fifth Earl of Ranfurly, was asked whether his name could be used to identify a new town on the Maniototo Plain in Central Otago. The governor was also asked whether he would like to name the 18 newly surveyed streets of Ranfurly. This he did, giving them all titles that related to his family tree. The most significant of these is Charlemont Street, the main street of Ranfurly, named after a relative, the Seventh Viscount Charlemont.

When Ranfurly had been surveyed and named, an auction of 75 sections was held at Naseby in June 1898. On the day, 65 sections sold to local people, at an average price of 9 pounds, while 10 were passed in.

## THE DEVELOPMENT OF RANFURLY

In spite of the sale of the sections and the beginnings of local businesses, it would be another six months before the first train finally arrived in Ranfurly, on 1 December 1898. A fortnight later a public meeting was held in the new town to push for the establishment of essential services such as a post office, a telephone exchange and a school, as these facilities were all based in Naseby. Once they were established in Ranfurly, Naseby's days as a town of any significance were numbered.

By 1899 Ranfurly had its first post office, located in the corner of a building used by the local ironmonger, where it would stay until shifted to the new railway station in 1904. A hotel was soon established, but it was not immediately successful and had a series of owners before it burnt down in 1933. A new hotel was built in 1934 by a consortium of Dunedin business people, who leased it out until it was sold in 1965. The buyer was the local Maniototo council which then leased the hotel back to local residents as shareholders in a company set up for the sole purpose of owning the hotel. This move was a first for New Zealand, and objections to a local council purchasing a hotel resulted in 10 years of legal threats, until the sale was finally ratified by the Supreme Court in Dunedin.

Ranfurly's first school was built in 1901, and the town was on its way.

An old telephone of the type used in Ranfurly in the 1930s. Shared telephone lines, called party lines, were used by several different households on a first come, first served basis. No telephone calls were private — they could be listened to at any time by others who shared the party line, simply by picking up their own telephone. All calls were connected by an operator working at the local telephone exchange who was contacted by lifting the black earpiece with cord attached, at left. Once connected, the person making the call listened via the same earpiece and spoke into the round mouthpiece protruding from the front of the wooden box.

The years that followed the arrival of the first train saw several businesses established in the town. A blacksmith was one of the first. When horses became redundant as everyday transport, the blacksmith showed his ability to adapt by converting his business to a garage with a Ford and Buick agency. A second blacksmith moved to Ranfurly from Naseby. He also displayed adaptability when he diversified into hardware and undertaking. A third man, a saddler, which was also a dying trade, set himself up as a dealer in farm implements.

In spite of the development that was taking place, Ranfurly maintained the appearance of a wild-west town for some 20 years after it was established. The streets were unpaved, there were no footpaths and local businesses were all housed in plain, single-storied wooden buildings. The only thing that appears to be lacking in early photographs of Ranfurly to qualify it as a frontier town of the type seen in a Hollywood set is a tumbleweed blowing down the main street in the wind.

In the 1920s the image of the town began to smarten up. During this time many of the art deco buildings that would become a feature of Ranfurly were built. A large post office was opened in 1922, complete with a telephone exchange that had 30 subscribers. In 1923 the Bank of New South Wales shifted its Naseby premises to Ranfurly in two pieces, towed by a traction engine. A new school to replace the original was opened in 1926. The red brick, art deco Catholic church was also built in 1926, on the outskirts of town, with a wooden presbytery opposite. In 1927 another art deco building, still in use today as a garage, was built in the main street, and the red brick hospital was constructed in 1930.

Cars parked at the rear of the red brick, art deco Catholic church in Ranfurly in 1926.

MANIOTOTO EARLY SETTLERS MUSEUM

RANFURLY — ART DECO ON THE MANIOTOTO PLAIN | 169

The Central Otago headquarters of the railway were also becoming more established in Ranfurly. Because of its location, the town became the ideal place for train crews to change over from the northbound train to the southbound. Crew who stayed over between trains did so in Ranfurly. It also became a lunch stop when timetables were adjusted to ensure arrival at the appropriate time. This arrangement was spoilt somewhat when the decision-makers in the Railways deemed that seven minutes was long enough for the passengers to compete with each other for something to eat at the Centennial Refreshment Rooms, opposite the station, before the train continued its journey.

## A DEPRESSION, ARSON AND A TRAIN WRECK

The 1930s and 1940s were not good years for Ranfurly or the Otago Central Railway. The depression of the 1930s had the same serious effect on the economic life of the town and the general wellbeing of its citizens as it did in the rest of New Zealand. In and around Ranfurly, as noted previously, many of the farming families would not have survived the depression without the sympathy of the stock firms and the credit extended by the Gilchrist family, who were the local grocers. It was not unusual in those years for farmers to shop weekly but pay their account only once or twice a year. Some did not pay at all, and the Gilchrists carried them as long as they could, regarding it as their civic duty.

To add to the misery of the depression, during this time it seemed that most of the buildings in the business area of the town burnt down, some by accident but others as a result of arson by Harold Black, a local man who was eventually caught and convicted of his crimes. The fact that these buildings were constructed of timber contributed to the problem. First to

Maniototo Hospital was both the maternity and emergency hospital of the Maniototo for several decades, but was abandoned by the government in the 1980s, when the town's population was in decline. Set in pleasant grounds, it still operates today as a community hospital, with some modifications to help boost income. The second storey with the verandah, on the right, is open to the public as motel-type accommodation, while a resthome has been established at the opposite side of the building.

The Dental Centre in Ranfurly is an example of classic art deco architecture, with the addition of a modern ramp to allow disabled access.

go was the teacher's house in 1930, followed by the town hall, the hotel, the tobacconist shop and premises called Clancy's dining rooms. After a gap, the grocery shop and the bakery followed in 1938. The situation was not helped by the fact that no fire brigade existed until 1948. Before it was established, fires were fought by volunteers using buckets. So many fires among so few buildings was a calamity for a town the size of Ranfurly. The fires were another reason for the art deco architecture that exists there today as this reflects the period in which much of the damaged business area was rebuilt.

The 1940s saw the town involved in what was then the most serious railway accident in New Zealand. The accident occurred a short distance south of Hyde, at a bend called Straw Cutting, on 4 June 1943. Ranfurly became involved in the aftermath, in its role as the Central Otago headquarters of the railway. The driver of the train had spent the previous night at the hotel in Ranfurly and the town had the nearest hospital, where many of the casualties were treated.

On the day of the accident, the train heading for Dunedin jumped the rails at Straw Cutting, causing the deaths of 21 passengers and injuring a further 41. The accident was close to the main highway and the rescue effort was coordinated from Ranfurly, with many of the local population taking part, providing all types of vehicles, including the butcher's van, for the bodies. After it was all over, a formal investigation was held. It was found that the train had crashed because the driver and the guard failed to slow it down, as they were both asleep. The driver, John Corcoran, was tried and convicted of manslaughter when evidence was given that he had been seen drinking in the bar of the Ranfurly Hotel on the morning of the accident. He was sentenced to three years' hard labour and died a broken man, shortly after his release. Today there is a memorial, close to the site of the accident, to those who were killed on that fateful day in 1943.

## THE 1950S TO THE 1980S — BOOM AND BUST

In the early 1950s the United States' involvement in the Korean War caused the greatest boom in wool prices ever seen in New Zealand. The Americans were not faring well as their troops were badly affected by, and poorly equipped for, the freezing Korean winters. This created a huge demand for raw wool to manufacture warm clothing and other necessities of life. Mills in the United States competed against each other at the wool sales, and this

This fine art deco building was paid for by a legacy bequeathed to Ranfurly by a local, to build a library. Its days as a library were numbered, however, in line with the decline in the town's population. The building now serves as the headquarters of the local radio station, Classic Gold.

pushed prices skyward. The result for New Zealand farmers was a situation known at the time as a pound for a pound: one pound for one pound (500 g) of wool. Sheep farmers suddenly had more money than they had ever dreamt of and many, if they were smart, were able to pay off their mortgages in one season.

Ranfurly was in the middle of a wool producing area and enjoyed the benefits of this new prosperity. The population of the town doubled in 10 years, and anyone who wanted to work did not need to look far for a job. Married couples employed to help out on the farms lived in a house provided onsite for them. The arrival of these people boosted the rural population and increased the need for services such as education. The Ranfurly council took advantage of this prosperity and during the 1950s and 1960s put in a new water supply reservoir, a sewage treatment works and pensioner flats, while the government built a new area school to cope with the increase in population.

Art deco is the theme that played a major part in the revival of Ranfurly as a town. An art deco weekend is held in February each year and attracts visitors from all over New Zealand. The weekend begins with a ball on the Friday night, which is attended by revellers dressed in 1920s fashions. A street festival is held on the Saturday, where again people are encouraged to dress for the occasion, view the line-up of vintage cars, or bet on the pig races. In the background is the art deco Centennial Refreshment Rooms a Central Otago icon. Built to serve hordes of railway passengers, it now functions as a museum and art gallery.

EDNA MCATAMNEY

RANFURLY — ART DECO ON THE MANIOTOTO PLAIN | 173

Local businesses also expanded during this period of prosperity. In the 1960s many of the retailers shifted premises from the western side of the railway lines to their present-day locations on the eastern side. Changes were also afoot that would affect the rail connection with the town. A railcar service was introduced in 1956, doing away with the mixed passenger/freight trains that had operated from the very beginning of the rail service.

The 1970s was also a decade of prosperity and growth for Ranfurly. Many new houses were built in the town, and the Maniototo irrigation scheme was developed. This scheme brought money into the tills of local businesses, led to extra staff being employed at the post office and put pressure on the availability of rental accommodation. Tennis courts, four hockey fields, two rugby grounds and an ice-skating dam were all built during the 1970s, as were the stadium and new business premises. There was even talk that the population of Ranfurly would reach 2000. But the good times were not to last.

The 1980s saw the beginning of a decline that started slowly but gathered momentum as the decade progressed. Ranfurly, like many other rural centres in New Zealand, suffered during the 1980s from rural depopulation. Between 1984 and 1990 no new houses were built in the town, down from an average of 12 new houses per year between 1980 and 1984. The post office was closed, the hospital ceased to exist as a public hospital with government funding, the manual telephone exchange went with the loss of 15 jobs, and local government was reorganised and centred in Alexandra. Other factors also contributed to the decline. Farm returns were such that it was no longer economic to employ married couples, which meant a large reduction in population and the need for services. Farms had to increase in size to remain economic. To stay in business, established farmers bought out their neighbours when the latter sold up, retired or simply died, and then amalgamated the property into one larger farm. This in turn led to a further decline in rural population. The final nail in the coffin was driven on 15 December 1989 when the government announced that the railway, the very reason why Ranfurly existed in the first place, was to close.

A pipe band leader in the main street of Ranfurly. A large portion of the population of Central Otago is of Scottish ancestry, and pipe bands are very popular and perform when and wherever possible.

EDNA MCATAMNEY

## RECOVERY

With the imminent departure of the railway and a declining population, the end of the town seemed near; but the opposite became the reality. A group of local people got together and decided that Ranfurly was worth saving. With their enthusiasm and hard work, the hospital was kept running under the auspices of a community trust and the Chalet Home for the Aged, located next to the hospital, was put under the management of another local organisation, the Chalet Community Trust.

When the railway tracks were removed, the station threatened to become an embarrassing empty building in the middle of the main street. Instead, it was renovated by local people and organisations and now houses an information centre and a museum that contains a large display of railway memorabilia. One of the best known buildings in Central Otago, the art deco Centennial Refreshment Rooms, faced demolition when most of its customers disappeared with the railway. Again, locals got together and renovated the building, which is now an art deco museum that also houses an invited artist in residence for part of each year. When the line closed, the Otago Central Rail Trail was developed for walkers, cyclists and horse riders. This has brought an influx of visitors to Ranfurly, and locals have been quick to capitalise. The old post office is now a backpackers. Myola, a plain red brick house in the main street that once served as the Presbyterian manse, has been beautifully and tastefully renovated as an upmarket homestay, while many local people have developed other amenities catering for the Rail Trail.

Ranfurly has made good use of its art deco buildings and has marketed its modern image along those lines. The town now features shops that sell art deco merchandise. An art deco weekend, which is becoming more and more popular, is held every year, with appropriate festivities based on an art deco theme.

# 22
# CROMWELL AND BANNOCKBURN

As the town in New Zealand most distant from the sea, Cromwell experiences an average of one frost every two days. It is a town that has been changed almost beyond recognition since it started life as The Junction in 1862, when gold was discovered a kilometre downstream from where two rivers combined to form the mighty Clutha. As a result of the flooding caused by the construction of the Clyde Dam in the 1980s, Cromwell lost its original business area and bridge to the floodwaters and is now located on the shores of an attractive lake. Nearby is Bannockburn, a village named by the Scottish immigrants who founded it, in memory of the location where, in 1314, an army of 5000 Scots, led by Robert the Bruce, defeated the 25,000 strong English Army, a victory that secured the future of Scotland as an independent nation for the next several hundred years. With large areas of Bannockburn sluiced almost out of existence by the goldminers, it survived and today is one of the recognised grape-growing areas of Central Otago, producing high-quality pinot noir for sale worldwide.

### THE AUSTRALIAN & NEW ZEALAND LAND COMPANY

The Australian & New Zealand Land Company was set up in the early 1800s by a group of wealthy Scotsmen whose interest was in acquiring tracts of land in Australia and New Zealand where they could run large numbers of sheep. They were not interested in living in these countries, but simply wished to operate as absentee landlords. In 1858 two men named Alderson and Douglas took up the lease of 84,000 hectares of land, on behalf of the company, that was centred where Cromwell would be built. Their holding extended south over the Carrick Range into the Nevis Valley and took in part of the Cairnmuir Range. The property was named Kawarau Station, and

With the discovery of gold on the far side of the Carrick Range in 1863, the small village of Nevis was built to cater for the miners there. It was, and still is, very remote; located on the south side of the Remarkables from Queenstown, its only road access today is via Bannockburn or Kingston. None of the buildings shown here remain. The access road is still unsealed and has several fords.

CROMWELL MUSEUM

it remained in the hands of the company for the next 52 years, until the big runs were broken up by the government in the 1900s for closer settlement. The station supplied the necessities of life to the goldminers who arrived in 1862, and that material support contributed to the successful establishment of Cromwell and Bannockburn. James Cowan was appointed manager of Kawarau Station in 1867, and his influence in local affairs also contributed to the success of the two settlements.

The first prospectors in the area, Hartley and Reilly, took 1400 oz of gold out of the Clutha River in July 1862, but this amount was insignificant when compared to the 16,000 oz taken from the river in the two months that followed the announcement of the discovery. In such rich gold-bearing country it was usual for a settlement to spring up nearby. The town that sprang up around this discovery, instead of becoming one of the abandoned gold towns that simply faded into history, survived to become Cromwell.

By 1863, miners had fanned out to Bannockburn and over the Carrick Range to establish the now-defunct villages in the Nevis Valley. In the same year The Junction was renamed Cromwell, while the new town survived a mass exodus of population resulting from a later discovery on the Arrow River near Arrowtown. By 1865 the alluvial gold was gone and sluicing started at Bannockburn and Cornish Point, opposite Cromwell, with water brought in by race from the top of the Mt Pisa Range and Bannockburn Creek. This kept Cromwell and Bannockburn alive and prosperous, with the annual take of gold from Cromwell in 1873, which included gold from Nevis, amounting to 19,947 ounces. In 1873 the price paid for gold was 3 pounds 2 shillings and sixpence an ounce, which ensured that Cromwell maintained a healthy annual income of 74,800 pounds, in an era when people earned wages of 50 pounds a year. This figure was boosted in 1875 when sluicing became widespread on the Bannockburn terraces.

## THE RISE OF CROMWELL

Cromwell was surveyed in 1863 by a man named Connell, who came to New Zealand from Northern Ireland. His heritage is evident today in the names he gave to the town and many of its first streets. His survey covered only three blocks located close to the river as those in power were not confident of Cromwell surviving. A larger survey was done in 1875 by James McKay, who added street names drawn from the south of Ireland.

Cromwell's lack of timber was the biggest obstacle to its early development, although this problem was overcome, in part, by planks rafted down the Clutha by George Hassing, who owned a mill at Makarora on Lake Wanaka. By 1864 the town was starting to take shape with the construction of two banks, the establishment of a permanent, if small, police force and the opening of a branch store by the Queenstown businessman Bendix Hallenstein, who would eventually become one of New Zealand's wealthiest citizens.

In 1869 the first auction of sections in Cromwell was held, with prices of 2 pounds being paid for a residential section and 4 shillings per foot of business frontage. In that same year the first mayor was elected and Cromwell gained its own resident doctor and eight substantial hotels, plus all the retailers required to help make life more civilised. During these years, until 1899, Cromwell was regularly covered in sand when the nor'wester blew from the Lowburn Terrace some 5 km away and blotted out the town. This problem was alleviated in 1899 when marram grass was planted to hold and permanently stabilise the sand.

By 1878 Cromwell had 100 dwellings, six hotels, two drapers, three butchers, two blacksmiths, a tinsmith, a wheelwright, a painter, a printing office, a registrar of births, deaths and marriages, a telegraphist and a postmaster. Two of its leading citizens at this time were D.A. Jolly and George Goodger. The story of one of these men is of a happy life, while the other is tragic.

Jolly came to Port Chalmers as a seaman on the ship *Aboukir* in 1862, just in time to desert and join the goldrush. Mildly successful, he invested his gold takings in a general store, which he built in Cromwell in 1869. This stone building still stands today in a corner of old Cromwell that was not flooded

RIGHT ABOVE Looking down Melmore Terrace in early Cromwell in the direction of the Clutha River and bridge. This was once the business area and main street of Cromwell, until flooded by the building of the Clutha Dam and the creation of Lake Dunstan. Today a tiny part of it has been reconstructed in a location at the edge of the lake.
CROMWELL MUSEUM

RIGHT BELOW A boarding house in early Cromwell photographed with its proud owners.
HOCKEN COLLECTIONS S05-044B, UNIVERSITY OF OTAGO, DUNEDIN

by Lake Dunstan. Jolly was very successful as a merchant and expanded his business throughout the district, while at the same time serving for a number of years as mayor. He was also a member of the borough council, the Vincent County Council, the Masonic Lodge, all the local sporting clubs and the hospital trust. In 1906 he retired to Dunedin, where he lived until his death in 1916.

George Goodger was not so lucky. An American, he began his business

CROMWELL AND BANNOCKBURN | 179

life in Cromwell in 1863 with a timber yard, but his nature was such that he was prepared to invest in anything that looked likely to make a profit. It was this personality trait that led him to invest as the fourth partner in the Cromwell Quartz Mining Company mine at Bendigo, then being developed by Thomas Logan, an investment that proved to be a bonanza as the richest quartz mine in Central Otago. He invested his share of the profits in property and farmland in or near Cromwell. These went badly for him when a flood destroyed his farm property in 1878 and his property investments went sour. Technically bankrupt, he set up business in Cromwell as an engineer and a machinist, but his health failed and he was forced to see others make a success of the property he had once owned. In 1883 he took his own life by jumping off the Cromwell Bridge at the age of 54. Today, that would be impossible as the bridge he jumped from is permanently under the waters of Lake Dunstan.

Cromwell was always interested in newspapers and was one of the first towns to publish a weekly paper, the *Cromwell Guardian,* first published on 1 November 1869. Two days later its rival, the *Cromwell Argus,* also appeared

A photograph taken of early Cromwell shows the town's layout before it was flooded, with the Kawarau River on the left and the Clutha in the foreground. The bridge, which was the approach to Melmore Terrace, is now some 15 m underwater and most of the business area as far as the bend in the road on the left has gone. A new bridge has been built off the photograph at right, to connect with the new shopping and business area, again off the photograph at top right.

HOCKEN COLLECTIONS S05-044D,
UNIVERSITY OF OTAGO, DUNEDIN

for the first time. The latter, owned by William Matthews and George Fenwick, carried in its first edition its own prospectus seeking investors in the new venture. The *Cromwell Guardian* lasted only three months, while the *Argus* went on to fame and fortune under the guidance of several owners, until it finally closed in 1948, an amazing length of time for a small-town newspaper to survive. Today, the original building which once housed the early *Argus* has been rebuilt in old Cromwell, beside the building owned by D.A. Jolly, and is now a museum and memorial to this tenacious little newspaper.

## THE CHINESE IN CROMWELL

It is well documented that Chinese miners were invited by the Otago Provincial Government to take up claims in Otago as early as 1864. By 1866 they were well established in Cromwell, living in their own camp at Gibraltar Rock, 3 km down river, and a year later they were spread as far afield as Nevis and Bannockburn. Chinese made up a large portion of the local population, often accounting for as much as 50 percent of residents, but in spite of that they were often badly treated, and if anything went wrong it became the norm to 'grab the nearest chow' (James Parcell, *Heart of the Desert*).

In 1868 the government issued a proclamation extending to the Chinese some limited civil rights. In the Nevis the number of Chinese was double that of Europeans, a situation that alarmed the latter. Chinese were also living in Bannockburn, where public opinion against them was particularly hostile. The European miners at Bannockburn had strong racial beliefs and were determined to enforce them. By 1885, Cromwell had its own Chinatown on Melmore Terrace that accommodated Chinese businessmen with names such as Won Kee and Cum Goon Wah & Co. A squalid canton, or living area, also existed along the riverbank in front of the terrace. This area was not settled from choice, but was the only place the Chinese were allowed to occupy in Cromwell. These tense situations and obvious differences could well have given rise to violence between the Chinese and European residents, but, in fact, little in the way of real trouble arose. The European population was not overwhelmed by an influx of Chinese, and the beginning of the twentieth century saw Chinese numbers shrink to a representation only. The area beside Melmore Terrace where they lived in Cromwell is gone now, drowned by Lake Dunstan, but a faithful replica of the village has been recreated at the modern-day Goldfields Mining Centre in the Kawarau Gorge.

*The Halfway House Hotel was strategically placed in the Cromwell Gorge, to cater for customers travelling on the rough road between Clyde and Cromwell.*
CROMWELL MUSEUM

## THE RAILWAY

The Otago Central Railway took decades to build between Dunedin and Clyde. Before the line reached Clyde, residents of Cromwell and points further afield were not sure how far it would be extended as there was talk of running trains through from Dunedin to the West Coast. Locals formed the Upper Clutha Railway League to agitate for the line to be built to Cromwell. This was not to be, however, as the government of the day decided that the line would terminate at Clyde, and all work stopped in 1909. The agitation by the league picked up speed in 1912, and by 1914 a reluctant government had authorised an extension from Clyde to Cromwell. By 1917 the line reached Cromwell, and in 1918 the railway station was built, but this new section did not become operative until 1921. Still not content, the league then began to lobby for an extension to Luggate, but Cromwell was where the Otago Central Railway finally terminated. A special fruit train was started from Cromwell to Dunedin in 1925, and this rapid transit to a large market helped the development of orcharding in the Cromwell area enormously over the years that followed.

The railway link with Cromwell only lasted until the 1980s. By then roads had improved communications in Central Otago to such an extent that the Railways could not compete. At the same time the line through the Cromwell Gorge was earmarked to become another victim of the waters of Lake Dunstan.

## BANNOCKBURN AND THE CARRICK RANGE

Bannockburn came to life in 1862, as did most of the easily accessible areas where gold was found in Central Otago. The town was initially located upon the flat at the mouth of the Bannockburn Creek nearly a kilometre from the Kawarau River rather than at its present-day site. The town was not large as the sluicing site at Bannockburn was never a bonanza, while further up the Carrick Range gold had to be extracted using expensive quartz mining.

Although close to Cromwell, Bannockburn had the disadvantage of the Kawarau River flowing between the two towns, and it found itself on the wrong side of the river. This caused problems when freight and supplies had to be brought in over a pack track from Clyde at huge expense, restricting the early development of foundling Bannockburn. It was 1867 before a ferry operated over the Kawarau, some 180 m below where the bridge now crosses the river.

In the years that followed, the miners moved out in the direction of Nevis, and Bannockburn moved with them, strung out along the track that led over the Carrick Range. By 1871 the small goldmining villages of Quartzville and Carricktown, on the lower reaches of the range, were all part of the Bannockburn settlement. The population was mainly Scottish with some English and Irish. The township of Bannockburn started to take permanent shape in 1872 when a school and a teacher's house were built. By 1888 pupil

This building was the first school in Bannockburn.

CROMWELL MUSEUM

numbers had reached 108, but as the population dwindled from lack of opportunity, so did the roll, which was down to 36 by 1918.

The first bridge over the Kawarau at Bannockburn was built in 1874 and was swept away during a flood in 1878. It was rebuilt, then destroyed again in 1896 by what was described as a successful fire, as by then it had fallen into disrepair. A new bridge was built and opened a year later at a ceremony attended by 1200 people.

Although development had taken place there, Bannockburn was not surveyed until 1880, the same year an auction of sections was held. Very few of the new sections sold, as locals were already living on them under the conditions set down by the Mining Act of the day and could not be convinced to pay for what they already occupied.

Many of the local miners were socialists and were interested in setting up cooperative businesses. During 1880 several of them issued a prospectus to raise 2000 pounds capital to establish an experimental store, butchery and bakery based on cooperative lines. The issue was soon fully subscribed and the business established. Enthusiasm was such that a hotel was also bought in Cromwell in 1882 with the intention of converting it to a branch store. Unfortunately, their efforts ended in shambles, and the cooperative folded in 1883, swamped by debt.

Much of the land around Bannockburn was sluiced almost out of existence by the early miners. Water brought in by race from the Nevis River was used as a tool in this destruction. The top of the cliffs shown here is the original level of the land before sluicing began, with the disturbed soil disappearing off down the tailrace and into the Kawarau River. All that remains today are rock tailings and weeds, which have in parts been softened by the development of surrounding vineyards.

James Horn was the local storekeeper in Bannockburn at the turn of the nineteenth century.

HOCKEN COLLECTIONS 505-0371, UNIVERSITY OF OTAGO, DUNEDIN

Other problems were caused by the fact that the land that the miners were tearing to pieces with their sluicing actually belonged to Kawarau Station under a pastoral lease. It is obviously very difficult to establish a permanent town when the land where it is located belongs to another owner. This obstacle was overcome when the management of Kawarau Station set aside 800 hectares around Bannockburn as common ground to be used by both parties. When the station was subdivided in 1910, the citizens of Bannockburn were able to take up most of the lower part of the Carrick Range under terms of Crown lease. The land was dry and the holdings were small. To make the land productive the new farmers realised they had to irrigate if they wanted to hold on to their properties. An arrangement was made with the county whereby a 5000-pound mortgage was raised using the settlers' properties as collateral, and work started in 1922 to extend the water races that had originally been built during the sluicing era to bring water in from the Nevis.

An odd-looking line-up of Bannockburn Volunteers for the New Zealand Contingent that fought the Boer War in South Africa at the end of the nineteenth century. It is not known whether these volunteers actually went to war, or even if they made it back, as the Boers were reputed to be crack shots who could kill a man from horseback at 300 m. Two of the volunteers are carrying rifles that were well out of date, while a third has only a shotgun. The volunteer on the left makes do with his whisky flask.

CROMWELL MUSEUM

## A SENSE OF COMMUNITY

Whenever early Bannockburn is mentioned, one thing that always comes through is the community spirit that existed there. The attempt at co-operative business is an example of this, but the residents also clubbed together to raise money and provide voluntary labour for various projects that were considered necessary for the town. Over the years, funds have been raised to build a hall, a library, two stone churches, a war memorial, a bowling green, tennis courts and a sports field. This spirit carried over into sports, and Bannockburn regularly fielded championship teams in cricket, rugby, athletics, bowls, tennis and, oddly, rifle shooting.

Today, Bannockburn has changed so dramatically that the early miners would not recognise it as the area in which they once lived. This change has been for the good and has been brought about mainly by the growing of grapes. Land that was once almost useless has been rejuvenated and supports smart vineyards and elegant houses. A backwater for much of the first half of the twentieth century, Bannockburn is now a thriving corner of Central Otago.

# 23
# CLYDE AND THE DUNSTAN — THE FIRST 10 YEARS

Clyde and Dunstan are two names that are nearly always mentioned in the same sentence or statement when writing or talking about early Clyde. The former was the town that came into being with the discovery of gold there in 1862, while the latter was the name given to an area of some 100 square kilometres surrounding it. Clyde was called Hartley's Township for the first few years of its existence after Horatio Hartley, one the two men to discover gold in the Clutha River, until it officially became known as Clyde on New Year's Eve 1864.

As in other parts of Central Otago, gold led to the establishment of towns along the Clutha River from 1862, but interest had already been shown in the surrounding area that would become known as the Dunstan several years before that date.

## ALEXANDER SHENNAN, WATSON SHENNAN AND WILLIAM FRASER

No history of Central Otago would be complete without the mention of three men: Alexander Shennan, Watson Shennan and William Fraser. They were the first runholders to settle the land that included the area which would become known as the Dunstan.

The Shennan brothers made an initial foray into the Manuherikia Valley in 1857 where, along with the ample grassland they were looking for to feed the stock they were hoping to graze, they saw wild pigs, native ducks, wild dogs and, oddly, a wild white horse. The two men had big ambitions and applied for the lease of 40,000 hectares of this land when they returned to Dunedin. Once granted, it was split into two runs, an arrangement designed to comply with the conditions set down by the authorities who, as stated previously, were not keen to grant more than one run per applicant. One of the properties they named Galloway, after their home in Scotland. The other they called Moutere, a Maori name used to describe land almost surrounded by water; in this case, river water.

Both runs were stocked with sheep purchased in Balclutha and driven overland, but in the first years life was not easy as the animals were harassed by wild dogs that had been brought to New Zealand by the early sealers and whalers. These dogs remained a problem until they were exterminated using the kangaroo hound — a large dog that was a cross between a Scottish deerhound and an Irish wolfhound specially bred for the purpose of chasing down and killing other dogs.

Transport was another early problem. After the brothers' sheep had been shorn under a canvas shelter in what is now Mutton Town Gully, a few kilometres south of present-day Clyde, the wool had to be taken out to Waikouaiti by packhorse and from there to Dunedin by sea. The runs also had to be supplied in the same arduous and expensive manner until proper wagon routes were put in place.

The remoteness and conditions would eventually take their toll, resulting in the early death of Alexander Shennan. He returned to Europe in early 1862 and purchased the first merino sheep seen in New Zealand, from the King of Prussia's Potsdam Stud. These arrived in Central Otago safely

The second Clyde Bridge, shown here, was built in 1879 after the first was swept away when the Clutha River flooded some years earlier. Constructed on schist stone foundations, it is a suspension bridge that is very similar to the first bridge at Alexandra and the Daniel O'Connell Bridge at Ophir. It was common practice to build low stone walls at the entrance to early Central Otago bridges to enable stock to be funnelled onto the bridge and to restrict their ability to escape at either side.

HOCKEN COLLECTIONS S05-065D,
UNIVERSITY OF OTAGO, DUNEDIN

With a parrot for company and a glass of beer in his hand, an old goldminer spends his days on a seat outside one of the hotels in Clyde in the 1940s. This was a not unusual scenario for those men who had spent a lifetime in the search for gold, many of whom had never married or raised a family.

HOCKEN COLLECTIONS S05-045J, UNIVERSITY OF OTAGO, DUNEDIN

and formed the basis of a merino stud on the Moutere run, a stud that still operates today. Alexander would never return to his runs as he died the following year in Edinburgh from rheumatic fever. His brother, Watson, sold both properties soon after and settled Puketoi Station on the Maniototo Plain. He eventually retired to Dunedin and died there in 1920 at the age of 85.

Another large Dunstan run, this time located on the south bank of the Clutha River from Clyde, was settled by William Fraser and A.C. Strode and given the name Earnscleugh. Although the run began with great hopes, it became overrun with rabbits and was eventually abandoned. Before this happened, however, Earnscleugh made William Fraser a wealthy man and enabled him to enter politics in 1893. He was a member of Parliament for 16 years and became Sir William, before his death in 1923. Today, with clever management and the ability to control rabbits with poison, Earnscleugh Station has been returned to its former glory and is known for its large, red brick homestead whose architecture resembles a castle.

## CLYDE

Following the discovery of gold in 1862, the first alluvial miners were more interested in prospecting than building a town and were content to live on the banks or near to the Clutha River, close to where the towns would eventually be built. They lived in tents, rock caves or mud huts, or just scooped out shelters in the soft earth of the riverbanks. The township of Clyde began to be established the same year when others, looking to profit by catering for the miners' needs, started building more permanent shelter. The winter of 1863 hastened the process when the Clutha flooded, killing nearly 100 miners camping on the river banks and giving a sharp lesson of the need to establish better living quarters.

One of the first signs that a new, more permanent town was being built at Clyde was the publication of a newspaper, the *Dunstan News*, in December 1862. The name would eventually be changed to the *Dunstan Times*, but the newspaper remained until it was sold in 1948 and replaced by the *Central Otago News*. A few days later, on 31 December 1862, the first race meeting was held in Clyde, with several thousand miners present. These two events give some idea of the speed of the development of Clyde as both took place only a few months after the discovery of gold in the Clutha was made public by Hartley and Reilly in Dunedin, in the winter of 1862. The bonanza had been found by these two men in a part of Central Otago that was then so isolated

A supply of good clean water was, and still is, a problem in Clyde. Today there are often restrictions on water use during a dry summer. Early Clyde was well established before a respectable water supply was installed. This photograph was taken on the day the first water supply came on line. The location is the main street of Clyde and the gothic columns of the building originally constructed to house the local council can be seen in the background. This building exists today as a Freemasons' Lodge. The elegance of the clothes worn by the women of the era is in sharp contrast to the practical boots worn by the children.

HOCKEN COLLECTIONS S05-0451, UNIVERSITY OF OTAGO, DUNEDIN

and underpopulated that they had had no problem in keeping their find a secret for several months, until ready to make it public.

The chaos and deaths that had been caused by the floods and snow of 1863 meant that Clyde became the choice of location for an early hospital to be built in response to the disaster. By 1865 it had a hospital that could treat 24 patients in two wards, with all the hospital trappings of matron, house surgeon and, most important of all, access to government money. The township would continue to provide hospital facilities for the surrounding areas from the 1860s to the present day.

In 1863, Clyde's first armed robbery took place when the local bank manager, a Mr Skinner, was accosted by two masked men while on his way to buy gold. The robbers tied him up and made off with the large amount of cash he was carrying, but made a mess of tying the knots that held him. The bank manager was able to struggle free, return to Clyde and identify the two men, who were arrested, tried and sentenced to 10 and six years' hard labour. Only 24 hours elapsed between the time of the robbery and the arrests, giving the robbers little if any opportunity to spend their winnings.

On 23 December 1863 a public meeting was held in Clyde, attended by two representatives of the Otago Provincial Council, who agreed to requests to spend a huge sum of money, for the times, to build roads and bridges in and around Clyde. At this meeting it was also announced that 485 hectares would be set aside to enable settlers to buy sections and set up house in Clyde. This was the impetus that Clyde needed. By 1864, houses of stone or wood were being built to replace tents. Shops were constructed, corrugated iron shanties were demolished and replaced with proper hotels and the first Anglican church began to take shape. The Catholics were quick to follow in 1864 when St Mary's Church was completed, but this building disintegrated in a gale in 1869. In the 34 years that followed its destruction, the local Catholics used the Clyde school for their services, until St Dunstan's, the stone, Gothic-style church that would replace St Mary's, was built. One of the staunchest Catholics in early Clyde was the Irish-born wife of Jean Desire Feraud, the winemaker and owner of Monte Cristo.

Clyde was proclaimed a municipality in April 1866 and remained so for 10 years until 1876, when the town was merged with the County of Vincent, but the new entity's offices remained in Clyde. This was in the future, however. Elections to select the town's first municipal representatives were held in July 1866. The town was divided into three sections called wards, each with four candidates contesting the election. After the votes were counted, Jean Desire Feraud was declared the first mayor of Clyde by a majority of only seven votes. He would hold this office until he resigned to pursue the use of water rights, which he considered were held illegally by the council, in order to irrigate his own property of Monte Cristo.

In May that same year the new town saw the installation of telegraph contact with the outside world, and the following month, the arrival of the first Chinese. These new immigrants were not sure of the reception they would receive and were careful at first to work only claims that had been turned over previously by Europeans. They built small huts using stone or earth, with roofs thatched from all types of materials, including their empty rice sacks. Like the rest of the Chinese in Central Otago, whose numbers would reach 1000 by the end of 1866, they lived in the less desirable part of town, where in the winter months the sun rarely shone. There was rapid growth in Clyde in 1866; several new businesses were established, a lodge was built for the Ancient Order of Foresters and the Dunstan Jockey Club was formed.

An advertising poster dated 1874 announcing a change of landlord at the Bendigo, one of the early hotels in Clyde. Horses were the main form of transport, and good stabling was obviously a requirement for a hotel if it was to attract travellers.

HOCKEN COLLECTIONS S05-045K, UNIVERSITY OF OTAGO, DUNEDIN

In spite of these advances, life in Clyde remained a little precarious. During the winter of 1870 a second gold robbery occurred that resulted in one of the local policemen being accused of acting on the wrong side of the law. On the night in question, 1300 pounds worth of gold was stolen from the Clyde jail, where it was being held pending removal to Dunedin by gold escort the next day. The plan was to bury the stolen gold in the Clyde cemetery, but one of the robbers in his nervous state took off in the wrong direction, while the other went home. The former's horse was laden down with gold and quickly became exhausted, meaning that much of the stolen gold was unloaded and hidden at different intervals between Clyde and Gentle Annie Stream, to ease the animal's burden. Both men were arrested, tried and found guilty. A policeman, newly arrived in Clyde, was prosecuted as a third accomplice. Although he was eventually found not guilty, he was sacked from the police force.

A photograph of the partly constructed Clyde Dam in the 1980s provides a clear picture of the location of Clyde and the changes brought about by the dam. The remnants of the original highway that traversed the town can be seen as the road exiting Clyde. The line of the present-day highway that replaced it is at the top left-hand corner.

CLYDE HISTORICAL MUSEUM

One of the features of the history of Clyde's early years was the large number of stone buildings constructed in the town. Many of these were built by John Holloway, a talented stonemason and builder. Today, these stone buildings still exist in Clyde and include the old post office, which is now the Post Office Café, the attractive Dunstan Hotel, Oliver's Restaurant and Lodge plus a large number of houses and cottages.

Since the 1860s Clyde has gone through several changes. Beginning as the administrative centre of the Dunstan, it has conceded that position to the larger town of Alexandra. At the same time it was also a gold town but, inevitably, the gold ran out. Clyde then became the centre of a district that was heavily involved in orcharding and was also a stopping point on the main route to the Queenstown Lakes District from the east coast and the city of Dunedin. This last description ended when the go-ahead was finally given to build the Clyde Dam in the 1970s. For a time Clyde became a dam town, but in the process lost its position on the main highway, which today only skirts the edge.

Clyde's final hat is one of part holiday destination and part retirement town. Today, it sits right in front of the Clyde Dam, which holds back countless millions of litres of water in a storage lake that stretches up through the once gold-rich gorge, as far as Bendigo. Once level with Bendigo, Lake Dunstan then reverts back to the Clutha River that has drained Lake Wanaka and its partner, Lake Hawea, for thousands of years.

# 24
# THE ROAD TO SKIPPERS

There are few roads in Central Otago today that are as well known as the Skippers Road, a reputation that these 22 km have gained for all the wrong reasons. Tourists are made aware of the road from the moment they arrive at any airport in New Zealand and approach a rental car counter to hire a car. Written into the hire agreement is a clause which states that if the car is taken over the narrow, winding and unsealed Skippers Road it will not be covered by insurance, making it one of only two roads in the country where such a provision applies. The Skippers Road has seen many accidents over the years and is not a road that should be driven over by inexperienced drivers, hence the rental car owners' caution. It does have another side, however, as a historic route, skilfully constructed through high-country New Zealand in the nineteenth century as a route to the gold-rich Shotover River, the goldmining village of Skippers and the quartz mining settlement of Bullendale. Today, the twisting road is used by rafting companies to give their clients access to the Shotover River, and by bungy jumpers who seek the ultimate thrill of launching themselves off the historic Skippers Bridge.

## GOLD IN THE SHOTOVER RIVER

In November 1862 two men, Thomas Arthur and Harry Redfern, both hopelessly broke, arrived on Williams Rees's property looking for work. Rees employed them as shearers, but they only lasted in the job for a week as they had better things to do with their time than shear sheep. The two had wandered down to a place now called Arthurs Point on the Shotover River in their off-duty hours, and found more gold than they had ever dreamt of. Working as full-time goldminers, they took 4000 pounds worth of gold, a fortune in 1862, out of the river in two months.

Within six months there were 4000 miners swarming all over the river. The Shotover River was difficult to access as it had steep banks and flowed

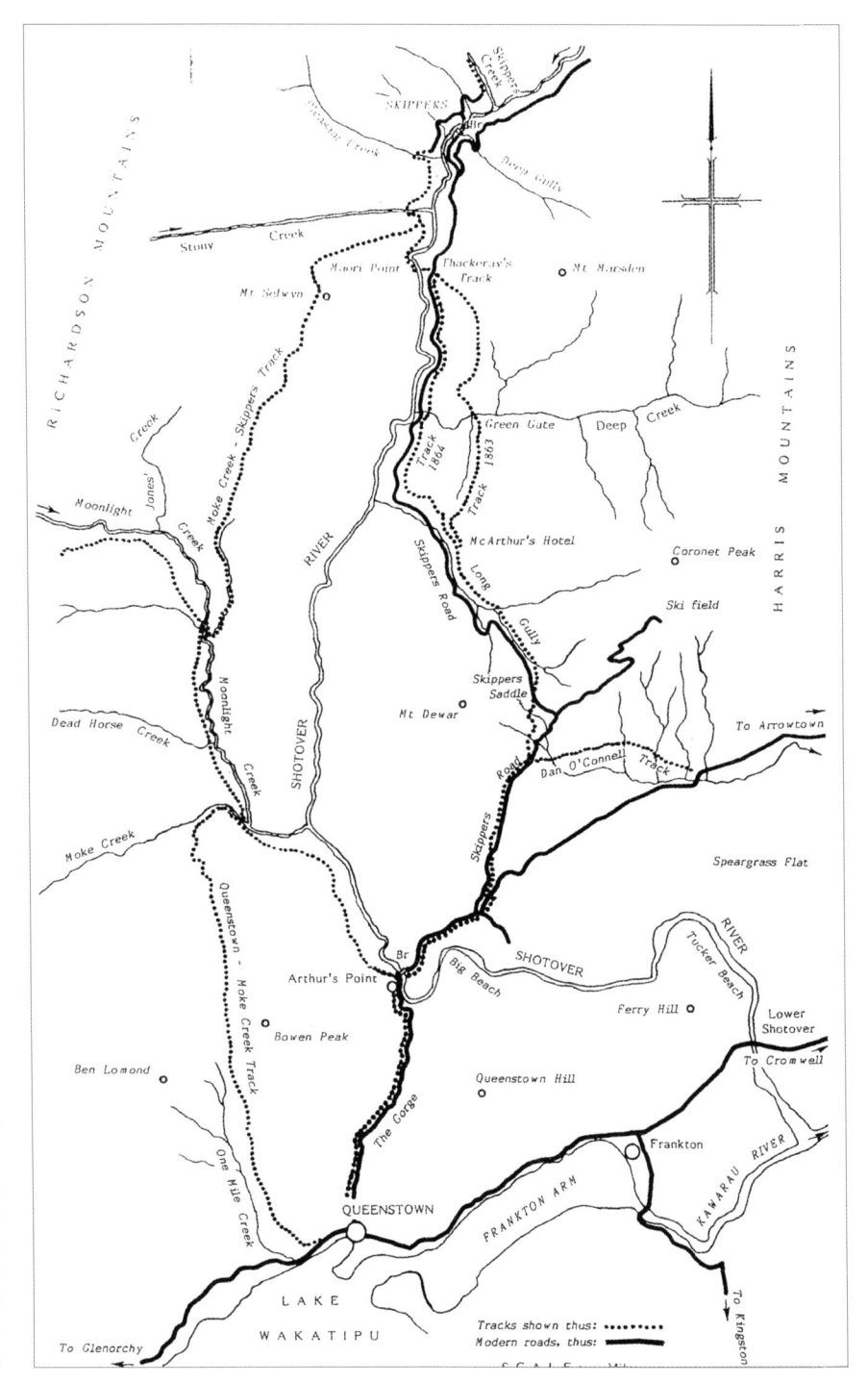

A map showing the general location of the Skippers Road and the Shotover River. The Skippers Road begins at the Skippers Saddle to the north-east of Arthurs Point, on the main road up to the skifield at Coronet Peak. Where the road forks at this point on the map is the beginning of the winding, gravel Skippers Road that travels north as far as Skippers Village, shown at the very top.

LAND INFORMATION NEW ZEALAND

THE ROAD TO SKIPPERS | 195

through precipitous country. Miners often had to be lowered down the cliffs by rope to work it, and supplying them was almost impossible as initially there was no track up the Shotover. Provisions were taken into the area by packhorse, led by a French Canadian named Julien Bourdeau, a man whose name would become synonymous with the Skippers Road. Described as a vision of Santa Claus, an old man with long white whiskers, rosy red cheeks and blue eyes that sparkled, he would continue to move freight in and out of Skippers Gorge for 54 years, until his death in 1916. He was so involved with the area that today a memorial in his honour is located at the side of the Skippers Road. On his last trip into the gorge at the age of 80, when he reached his destination, he simply lay down for a rest and quietly passed away.

In winter, access was gained across snowfields, with the route marked by red poles set in the ground and connected by wire. As time passed a track was formed, with horse-drawn sledges and narrow wagons being used instead of packhorses, but communication with the miners working the river were still far from satisfactory. In the winter months the track often became a sea of mud or dangerously icy, and Bourdeau was required to fit his horses with spiked iron shoes to prevent them from slipping.

Skippers Gorge became a major goldfield. The Shotover is often described as the richest river in the world, which is an overstatement as there were failures as well as successes, but huge amounts of gold were taken out of the immediate area. When the alluvial gold began to run out, the miners' attention turned to sluicing, dredging and quartz mining. To do this successfully major equipment was required, as was contact with the outside world. The need for a road to the settlement of Skippers was recognised, and the route was constructed.

## THE SKIPPERS ROAD

The route that the road would take was surveyed in 1883 by a man named Morrison. The road was a major feat of engineering and by the time it was completed in 1888, four contractors had been involved in its construction. The entire road was paid for by a tax imposed on Shotover gold, and Chinese labourers were brought in from Canton to work on it, with their wages being paid in gold sovereigns or raw gold. Working conditions were not as stringently supervised as they are today and several Chinese were killed during the construction. It was not unusual for workers to be lowered down a cliff face by rope, armed with a hammer and chisel to fashion holes,

*Exhausted horses carrying firewood on the Skippers Road late last century show the difficulties experienced while negotiating what was then only a glorified track.*

HOCKEN COLLECTIONS S05-064B, UNIVERSITY OF OTAGO, DUNEDIN

into which explosives would be placed. This would be repeated over and over until enough of the cliff had been blasted away to form a flat surface on which to build the road. The result was a road that often had almost vertical cliffs on both sides.

Today, the Skippers Road is reached by turning left about halfway up the access road to Coronet Peak ski field. Over the crest of the first hill the road enters Long Gully where two of its most photographed features, The Lighthouse and Castle Rock, are located. In geological terms, both are shaft tors. These develop in Central Otago wherever quartz foliation and schistosity are horizontal and therefore erode less than the surrounding rock, which over the millennia weathers at a much faster rate, leaving the tor exposed. There are several corners on the Long Gully section of the road which are completely blind and must be negotiated with extreme care. If two vehicles meet on the corners, one must be backed up to give the other room to pass. What follows between Long Gully and the settlement of Skippers are features called Devils Elbow, Corners, the Staircase, Hells Gate, Heavens Gate and Pinchers Bluff; descriptive titles which give some idea of the topography of the road.

Deep Creek is the first point where the road touches river level and also

**ABOVE** The Welcome Home Hotel once catered to those using the Skippers Road. Located at one of the more easy-going and level parts of the road, all that remains today is the hotel's chimney.

HOCKEN COLLECTIONS S05-064A, UNIVERSITY OF OTAGO, DUNEDIN

**LEFT** Pinchers Bluff was one of those sections of the Skippers Road that was blasted out of sheer rock by labourers lowered on ropes. The bluff gives an indication of just how difficult the construction of the road was. Very little has changed since this early photograph was taken, and anybody venturing over the road today can expect the same tortuous bends and sheer drops.

HOCKEN COLLECTIONS S05-064D, UNIVERSITY OF OTAGO, DUNEDIN

The Shotover River was so rich at Maori Point that gold was still being taken from it in the 1930s. The Maori Point dredge shown worked the river during that decade with moderate success. After the claim had been worked out, the dredge was just abandoned and parts of it can be seen today at the same location.

1265MNZ, ALEXANDER TURNBULL LIBRARY, NATIONAL LIBRARY OF NEW ZEALAND

where many of the rafting companies today assemble their clients to start the run down the Shotover River. Several hotels existed along the road in years gone by, but now evidence of only one remains, in the form of a chimney that was once part of the Welcome Home Hotel. Pinchers Bluff and the Devils Elbow must then be negotiated, the former being named in honour of the contractor who cut this very difficult section with picks, shovels, hand drills and explosives. Next is Maori Point, one of the few places where Maori were involved in goldmining in Central Otago. This section of the river was particularly rich in gold and has been worked over many times during the past 140 years, by miners using everything from gold pans to a dredge. From here the road crosses a small saddle, and the area known as the Golden Canyon, which is distinguished by the sluiced cliffs fronting the river, comes into view. The next man-made feature is the Skippers Bridge, but before this is crossed, the Blue Slip, a hazard that has existed since the road was first built, must be negotiated. The ground here is a slip face, on which very little in the way of vegetation grows. It moves constantly, particularly after heavy rain, and must be repaired regularly to keep the road open.

## SKIPPERS VILLAGE AND THE SKIPPERS BRIDGE

The best known feature on the road, before it terminates at Skippers, is the Skippers Bridge. The first Skippers Bridge was built in 1866, downstream from the present one, and was designed by the surveyor John Turnbull Thomson. Much nearer the waters of the Shotover River, at only 6 m high, it was 24 m long and less of a landmark than the present bridge. The new bridge that replaced it in 1901 was opened in March that year by the then prime minister, Richard Seddon. It is a suspension bridge, 90 m above the river and 96 m in length, supported by 14 wire cables each weighing 7 tonnes. With a total breaking strain of 75 tonnes, it was a bridge built to carry the heaviest traffic, but unfortunately was constructed at a time when the wealth of the Shotover River was beginning to fade.

Over the bridge is the village of Skippers. Once a thriving settlement supporting several families, its own school, a store owned by Julien Bourdeau and the Mt Arum Station homestead, it is now a ghost town. Given all the Chinese working in the area and the recorded deaths of many of them, it would be expected that the cemetery at Skippers would contain a number of Chinese graves. This is not the case as most of the Chinese, if buried locally, were later dug up and their bones shipped to their homeland. Only two Chinese graves now remain, that of Hoy Yow Ku, which is marked with a headstone, and an unmarked grave that is the last resting place of Ah Quay, who starved to death in his hut at Skippers in 1904. Life was dangerous in this remote location. Twelve miners, also buried in the cemetery, were killed by a slip one night in 1863, the year of the great snow and floods in Central Otago that claimed hundreds of lives through drowning and exposure.

Prime Minister Richard Seddon opened the new Skippers Bridge in 1901. Built to carry heavy traffic, it is 90 m in height, 96 m long and supported by 14 wire cables, each weighing 7 tonnes. Unfortunately, the bridge was built too late to be of much use, as by 1901, gold production in the area was beginning to fade. Today, while still part of the Skippers Road, it is also used as a bungy-jumping site.

HOCKEN COLLECTIONS S05-064C, UNIVERSITY OF OTAGO, DUNEDIN

## BULLENDALE

Further into the hills, past the end of the Skippers Road, are the remains of the township called Bullendale. This was a settlement that grew up around a quartz mine that operated for 38 years until 1901. The owner was George Bullen, and his manager was Fred Evans, the latter a man who possessed a keen mechanical mind. It was Fred Evans who placed Bullendale on the historical map as the first location in New Zealand where electricity was generated. Today, nobody lives in Bullendale and no signs remain to indicate the important activity that was pioneered there.

# 25
# ELECTRICITY — FROM BULLENDALE TO THE CLYDE DAM

The first hydroelectric generation of electricity in New Zealand took place in Central Otago. The year was 1886 and the site was a remote goldmining settlement at the far end of the Skippers Road named Bullendale.

## FRED EVANS AND BULLENDALE

In 1884, Fred Evans, the manager of the Phoenix Mine at Bullendale, read of the progress that was being made in other countries with the use of a new form of energy, electricity. He was impressed and decided to try and harness it to drive the machinery being used in the mine because, once the establishment costs had been met, electricity provided a much more advanced form of energy than the coal-fired steam or raw water power available at the time.

The Phoenix Mine was a quartz mine which required large amounts of energy to drive the stamping battery that crushed the gold-bearing ore to a gritty powder and prepared it for a process that used mercury to extract the final gold. In common with many other mines in Central Otago, it was located in a remote spot where there was plenty of water but little in the way of coal, thus the more efficient use of the water resource at hand made good sense. The mine was also experiencing problems with its machinery, which was being driven at the time by water taken from the right branch of Skippers Creek. Other users had first option on the supply, and the flow was insufficient for eight months of the year as it was low in summer and frozen solid in winter. Fred Evans calculated that he could build a powerhouse beside the left branch of Skippers Creek, which had a greater flow than the

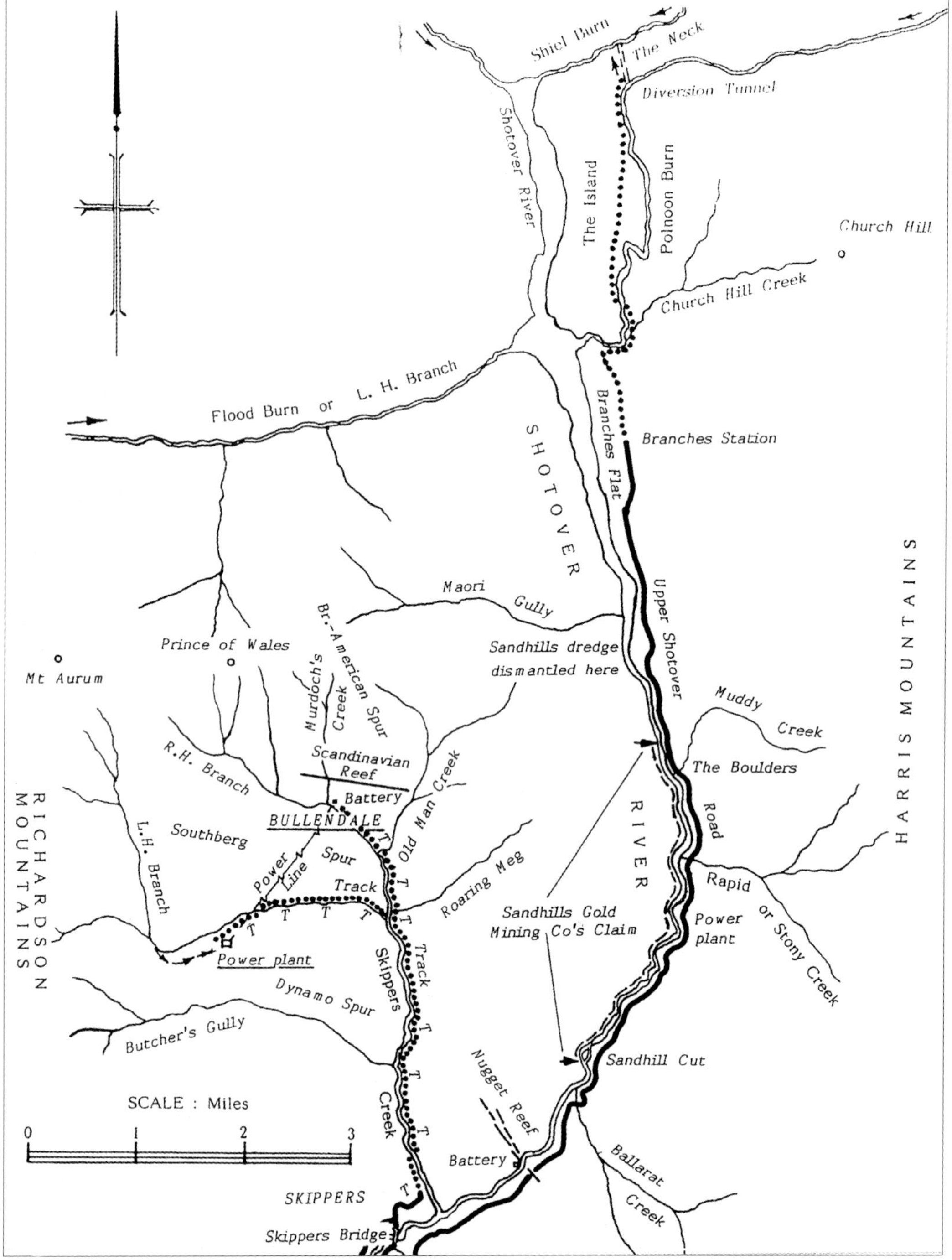
Shiel Burn
The Neck
Diversion Tunnel
Shotover River
The Island
Polnoon Burn
Church Hill
Church Hill Creek
Flood Burn or L. H. Branch
SHOTOVER
Branches Flat
Branches Station
HARRIS MOUNTAINS
Upper Shotover
Maori Gully
Sandhills dredge
dismantled here
Prince of Wales
Mt Aurum
Br.-American Spur
Murdoch's Creek
Muddy Creek
The Boulders
Scandinavian Reef
Battery
R.H. Branch
Old Man Creek
BULLENDALE
RICHARDSON MOUNTAINS
RIVER
Road
Southberg
L.H. Branch
Power Line
Spur
Track
Roaring Meg
Rapid
or Stony Creek
Sandhills Gold
Mining Co's Claim
Power plant
Power plant
Track
Skippers
Dynamo Spur
Butcher's Gully
Sandhill Cut
Nugget Reef
SCALE : Miles
0
1
2
3
Creek
Battery
Ballarat
Creek
SKIPPERS
Skippers Bridge

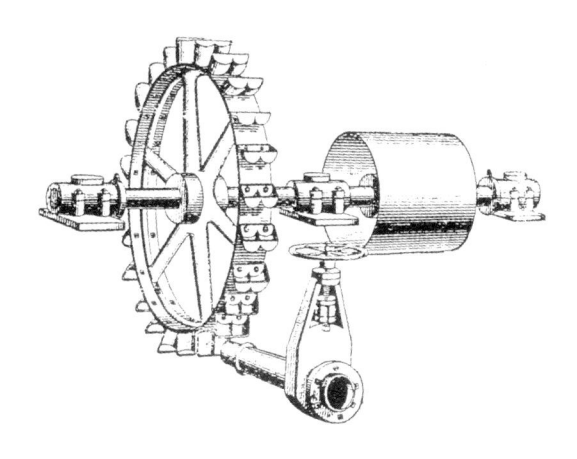

**OPPOSITE** A map showing the location of Bullendale in relation to Skippers Village, the Shotover River and the left- and right-hand branches of Skippers Creek. It was the water from the left branch of Skippers Creek that was harnessed here in 1886, to generate the first electricity used on an industrial site in New Zealand.

LAND INFORMATION NEW ZEALAND

**ABOVE** A diagram of an early Pelton wheel used to harness water for the generation of electricity. The wheel is such a clever and simple design that larger and more sophisticated versions are still in use today. Water from a river or stream is gathered via the pipe at the bottom middle of the picture and then forced out under pressure through the nozzle, onto the series of blades mounted on the large wheel. This creates a momentum that turns the wheel, which in turn drives the arm at middle picture to power a generator, which is not shown.

AUCKLAND MUSEUM

right, and then transmit the electricity generated back over the hill to the mine. As it eventuated, this is exactly what took place.

In October 1884 plans were drawn up to build a powerhouse capable of generating enough electricity to drive the mine's machinery for the eight months of the year it would not normally operate. Water was carried to the new powerhouse by an open race and then directed at high velocity through nozzles onto two Pelton wheels that had been installed. The movement of the Pelton wheels was the point where electricity was generated as they in turn drove DC Brush Arc dynamos. Power lines made of Number 8 copper wire were then strung to carry this power over the ridge to the mine, a distance of 3 km, where it was picked up by a Brush Victoria motor.

Twenty-five men were employed to build the powerhouse, which was the easy part. Getting the equipment required to generate the power was much more difficult. It must be remembered that all this was happening at the end of one of the most notorious, winding roads in New Zealand. The dynamos were imported from England and weighed more than a tonne each. One of them was almost lost over a bluff during its journey over the Skippers Road. Two hundred metres of iron pipe also had to be transported in, as did the heavy Pelton wheels that were manufactured in Thames in the North Island by A. & G. Price Ltd. Added to all this was another smaller generator purchased by Fred Evans' son in Dunedin, which was installed in the new powerhouse and attached to one of the Pelton wheels to generate a separate source of electricity to provide electric light.

The project was supervised by a Dunedin man called Fletcher, who was a pioneer in the supply and installation of electrical equipment. Working for Fletcher was a man named Walter Prince, who not only had considerable technical expertise but was an intelligent and flamboyant marketer of the concept of electricity.

New Zealand's first major use of electricity was not without its problems, however. A setback to the project occurred when Walter Prince was badly injured after falling from his horse on the Skippers Road. Then it was discovered that the two generators had not been installed correctly and were producing very little electricity. As a result, Fletcher's contract was terminated in July 1886, and he was declared bankrupt shortly afterwards. Fred Evans and his son carried on until, by a process of trial and error, they were able to produce enough electricity to power a 30-stamper battery, a stone breaker, a pair of air compressors, rock drills and electric light. This was a major achievement and emphasises the capability of the two men. The Phoenix Mine, with its named changed to Achilles, continued operating until 1907, when the gold ran out. The electrical plant, which was still in good order when the mine closed, was scrapped in 1916.

This was not the end of the involvement of Bullendale in the pioneering use of electricity. In 1890 a company called the Sand Hills Gold Mining Company began to operate the first electrically powered dredge in the world, working the Shotover River not far from Bullendale. Initially powered by steam generated through the burning of coal, the dredge was converted to electricity when its owners witnessed the success at the Phoenix Mine, and coal had become too expensive to haul in over the Skippers Road. The water to generate the electricity for the dredge was taken from Rapid Creek, and generation was based on the same principle as the Phoenix mine, using Pelton wheels. The electricity was fed to the dredge by flexible cables from drums, which allowed it to move freely up and down the Shotover River in its search for gold.

## AFTER BULLENDALE AND BEFORE ROXBURGH

With the success in Bullendale, other goldmining entrepreneurs began looking seriously at electricity by the mid 1890s. In 1895 another remote mine, the Premier in Macetown, followed Bullendale, and by the turn of the century gold dredges on the Clutha River also began to convert to electricity. The *Fourteen-mile Beach* dredge was the first, when a powerhouse was built in 1900, 27 km downstream from Alexandra. The next year the No. 3 Dredging and Electric Power Company built an electric dredge driven by three-phase AC electric power, generated in a specially built power station on the Fraser River near Alexandra. This latter dredge was so successful that it operated in and around the Clutha River for another 20 years.

For much of the first three decades of the twentieth century, electricity was generated and paid for locally rather than on the basis of a national grid paid for by the taxpayer. Local power boards were established, and these then set out to buy or build a source of supply. In 1904 a report prepared by the Public Works Department named the Teviot River as a likely source of electricity. Nothing was done until 1920, when three Roxburgh residents initiated a meeting to discuss ways of irrigating drought-prone East Roxburgh by diverting the Teviot River through a tunnel. At this meeting it was suggested that the water to be diverted could also be harnessed to

Another local scheme for the generation of power in Central Otago was built on the Fraser River near Alexandra.

HOCKEN COLLECTIONS S05-044K, UNIVERSITY OF OTAGO, DUNEDIN

generate electricity for Roxburgh, using the generating plant owned by the nearly bankrupt Ladysmith Gold Dredging Company. A committee was formed with the grand name of Teviot District Electric Lighting, Power & Irrigation Board, which would be followed by the formation of the Teviot Electric Power Board in the same year. The first moves for a public supply of electricity in Central Otago had been initiated. The Teviot scheme was officially opened in March 1924 to supply electricity to 321 consumers at Coal Creek, Roxburgh and Roxburgh East and a short time later to Dumbarton, Ettrick and Millers Flat. In 1925 the Otago Central Electric Power Board (OCEPB) was given the right to purchase power in bulk from the Teviot scheme by the Teviot Electric Power Board under a ten-year agreement of supply, and these two boards remained closely linked until they were amalgamated in 1960.

Queenstown was the second area in Central Otago to be supplied with power when the Queenstown Borough Council built an arched concrete dam and installed a completely automatic generating plant at One-mile

Creek. The opening on 18 September 1924 was a memorable occasion when people in fancy dress joined in a procession led by the mayor of Queenstown up to the generating plant. As demand increased and Queenstown grew, supply became a problem. A diesel generator that ran during peak demand was purchased, but this was noisy and could be heard all over town. In 1945 Queenstown arranged a supply agreement with the OCEPB. The One-mile Creek scheme remained in use until 1966, when its generating capacity was shut down. Local power generation ceased at Queenstown, but the scheme remained in use to supply water for irrigation.

As mentioned, the OCEPB's first supply of electricity came about through an agreement to purchase power from the Teviot scheme in 1925. This was made possible by the construction of a transmission line from Roxburgh to Earnscleugh during 1924, and the first power came to the Borough of Alexandra on 31 March 1925. In 1926 the supply was extended to Cromwell, Bannockburn and Lowburn with the erection of a transmission line between Clyde and Cromwell. Power was also extended up the Manuherikia Valley as far as the Lauder district in 1930. However, by that year the power available from Teviot was diminishing, as a result of Teviot's local needs. To solve this problem a loose partnership, involving payment for power in advance, was formed between two gold dredging companies and the OCEPB to build a power station on the Roaring Meg Stream in the Kawarau Gorge. Construction of the Roaring Meg Power Station began in 1935, and the station was opened by Minister of Public Works Bob Semple in March 1936. The cost of the scheme was 42,000 pounds, financed by a payment of 15,000 pounds from the Clutha Dredging Company, 12,000 pounds from the Molyneux Dredging Company and another 15,000 pounds from the OCEPB. Once opened, Roaring Meg was able to carry the OCEPB's load unaided and the Teviot supply was terminated. Extra capacity was generated when the OCEPB purchased the Wye Creek generating plant in 1941. Wye Creek is sited on the eastern shores of Lake Wakatipu, 13 km south of Frankton, adjacent to the highway leading to Invercargill. Further capacity was added when the Upper Roaring Meg Power Station was completed in 1947 and the Fraser River station near Alexandra was finished in 1954.

When the Teviot Power Scheme was completed in 1924, two days were put aside for locals to attend the opening ceremonies that were planned.

ALEXANDRA MUSEUM

The Roaring Meg Power Station was built at the junction of the Kawarau River and Roaring Meg stream, adjacent to the main road between Cromwell and Queenstown. What the architect had not planned for was an unprecedented flood in the Kawarau River that nearly put an end to the scheme. The waters of the Kawarau River rose by 10 m and threatened to sweep the powerhouse downstream. The building survived and power is still being generated there today, using the waters of the Roaring Meg Stream to drive Pelton wheels, which in turn spin the generators. Originally built for use by the local power board and two gold dredges, the power that is generated here is now fed into the national grid.

HOCKEN COLLECTIONS S05-044F, UNIVERSITY OF OTAGO, DUNEDIN

## THE ROXBURGH DAM

When it was built in the 1950s, the dam on the Clutha River at Roxburgh was New Zealand's largest hydro scheme. After World War II the need for electricity took off and supply barely kept pace with the government's ability to provide it. The dam at Roxburgh was part of the attempt to satisfy this demand, particularly in the South Island. A dam on a large South Island river had been approved by the government as early as 1946, but a suitable site could not be found. One location considered was near the future Benmore Dam on the Waitaki River, but the final decision was to build at Roxburgh. Labour and materials were in short supply at the time and the fact that a dam at Roxburgh would require only half the materials required to build a dam on the Waitaki was the deciding factor.

In 1949 construction started at Roxburgh on a concrete gravity dam 365 m long and 76 m high, with three large spillways, each weighing 135 tonnes. When it was completed in 1956, eight welded-steel penstocks over 5 m in diameter led the water to turbines that in turn generated 320 megawatts of electricity.

The project was a major undertaking for Central Otago. At the beginning it was proposed that the levels of the three Queenstown lakes would be raised to provide adequate storage. Proceeding with this plan would have flooded Queenstown out of existence and the level of Lake Wanaka would also have been altered dramatically. A public outcry caused the plan to raise these three lakes to be changed, with less populated Lake Hawea being the loser. That lake would eventually be raised by 18 m in the late 1950s.

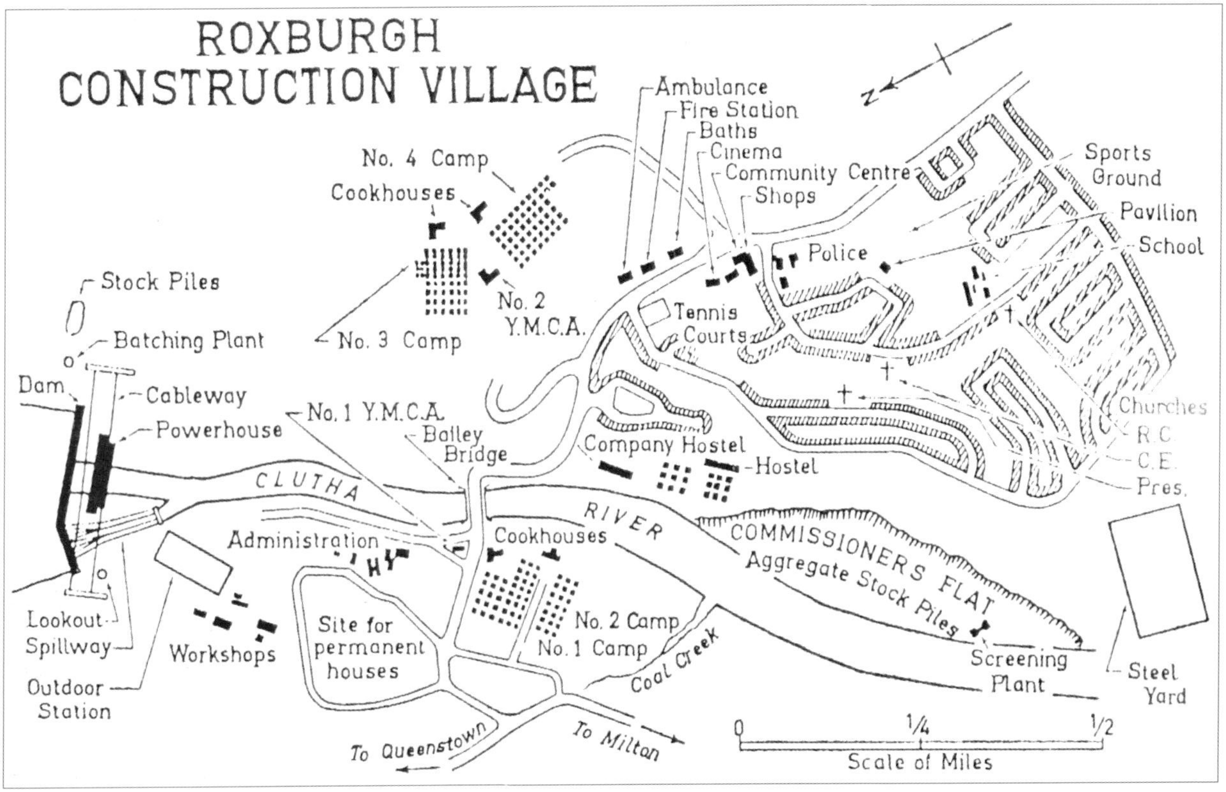
ROXBURGH
CONSTRUCTION VILLAGE
Ambulance
Fire Station
Baths
Cinema
Community Centre
Shops
Police
Sports Ground
Pavilion
School
No. 4 Camp
Cookhouses
No. 2 Y.M.C.A.
No. 3 Camp
Stock Piles
Batching Plant
Dam
Cableway
Powerhouse
No. 1 Y.M.C.A.
Bailey Bridge
Tennis Courts
Company Hostel
Hostel
Churches
R.C.
C.E.
Pres.
CLUTHA
RIVER
COMMISSIONERS FLAT
Aggregate Stock Piles
Administration
Cookhouses
Lookout
Spillway
Outdoor Station
Workshops
Site for permanent houses
No. 2 Camp
No. 1 Camp
Coal Creek
Screening Plant
Steel Yard
To Queenstown
To Milton
0
1/4
1/2
Scale of Miles

**OPPOSITE ABOVE** Roxburgh Village at Commissioners Flat was purpose-built in the 1950s to house the people engaged in building the Roxburgh Dam. When the dam was complete a large portion of the village was sold off or shifted to other sites. Parts of it remain at Coal Creek today, mostly as tourist accommodation.

AUCKLAND MUSEUM

**OPPOSITE BELOW** Roxburgh Dam under construction in the 1950s. The Clutha River had to be diverted, as shown at the top of the photograph, before work could start. This diversion left the original bed of the Clutha River high and dry and resulted in an influx of gold seekers to work it over. Little gold was found, as it is thought that the river was too swift at this point to encourage gold to settle in its bed over the millennia.

AUCKLAND MUSEUM

A large construction village complete with everything from a police station to a cinema was purpose-built at Commissioners Flat, below the proposed dam site, to house a population that would peak at 3000. In July 1949 a start was made on the diversion channel, requiring the removal of 450,000 cubic metres of spoil, but a critical shortage of qualified staff, labour and materials slowed progress considerably. Moves were made to look overseas to solve these problems, and in July 1952 a construction contract was awarded to a British consortium named Holland and Hannen, which duly arrived in Roxburgh with 400 overseas staff. A Johnson concrete batcher that had originally been used in the reconstruction of Pearl Harbor was imported from the United States to produce the huge amounts of concrete required. Progress was slow, target dates and costs were disorganised and there were labour disputes over the living conditions provided in the village. The British consortium appeared to be inexperienced and out of their depth, with a general manager who knew little about building a dam. Termination of the contract was discussed but avoided when a local firm called Downers joined forces with the American firm Morrison-Knudsen, which in turn linked with the original British consortium and appointed a new project manager.

A revised schedule of wage rates was agreed upon and a new target of February 1957 was set for completion of the dam. Good progress was made in the years 1954–1955, the diversion channel was completed and on 1 July 1954 the Clutha was finally diverted. By 1956 the powerhouse was half finished and the dam three quarters complete. Lake filling behind the dam began on 15 July 1956 and the first electricity was generated eight days later. The completed scheme was officially opened on 3 November 1956. Once the powerhouse in the dam was running at full capacity, instead of facing power cuts, the South Island was assured of surplus power for several years. It was not long, however, before that surplus threatened to turn to a deficit and the government was looking for suitable sites on the Clutha River on which to build a second dam.

## THE CLYDE DAM

As early as 1962 Roxburgh had reached its full capacity and the government was forced to put in motion the preliminaries required to construct another dam. There was unused generating capacity on the Clutha River, as close monitoring of the Roxburgh Dam showed that 20 percent of the river's flow went over its spillway rather than through the turbines in the powerhouse.

From hard lessons learnt during the selection of the site for the Roxburgh

Dam, the government knew it was politically unacceptable to tamper with the level of lakes Wakatipu and Wanaka. The choices were a series of five low-level dams between Luggate and Tuapeka or a high dam at Cromwell, which would flood that town completely. Both proposals were very unpopular, and in 1968 a storm of protest erupted in Otago and spread throughout New Zealand. Since the Roxburgh Dam had been first mooted, people's attitudes had become more conservation-conscious and although the electricity was needed, they were not prepared to settle for the environmental damage the two proposals would cause. This protest went on for several years, and the election of 1972 saw the National government of the day lose its once-safe Central Otago seat, a factor that contributed to a change of government. National won back power in 1975, and the matter of the dam on the Clutha was partly settled on 20 December 1976 when the cabinet gave their approval for a high dam to be built at Clyde.

In spite of that decision, controversy still raged, and in July 1977 the Supreme Court began hearing the first of 17 appeals lodged with the Planning Tribunal on the matter of water rights. The government then began to prepare legislation to override water rights. On 30 September 1982 it passed the Clutha Development (Clyde Dam) Empowering Bill when two Social Credit MPs crossed the floor of the house to support it, and the way was opened for the Clyde Dam to be built.

The old and the new. A 1970s Euclid truck passes the stone remnants of a 1860s miners hut on the banks of the Clutha River, while preparing the ground to begin construction of the Clyde Dam.

HOCKEN COLLECTIONS S05-037L, UNIVERSITY OF OTAGO, DUNEDIN

ABOVE TOP A huge turbine is lowered into one of the four machine bays in the powerhouse of the completed Clyde Dam.

CLYDE MUSEUM

ABOVE BOTTOM In the foreground is a 280-tonne rotor. At left rear is a 240-tonne stator and right rear, a 55-tonne turbine runner. All equipment installed in the Clyde Dam powerhouse.

CLYDE MUSEUM

RIGHT ABOVE Early blasting at the base of what would become the Clyde Dam.

HOCKEN COLLECTIONS S05-045C,
UNIVERSITY OF OTAGO, DUNEDIN

RIGHT BELOW A cross-section drawing of the layout of the Clyde Dam.

CLYDE MUSEUM

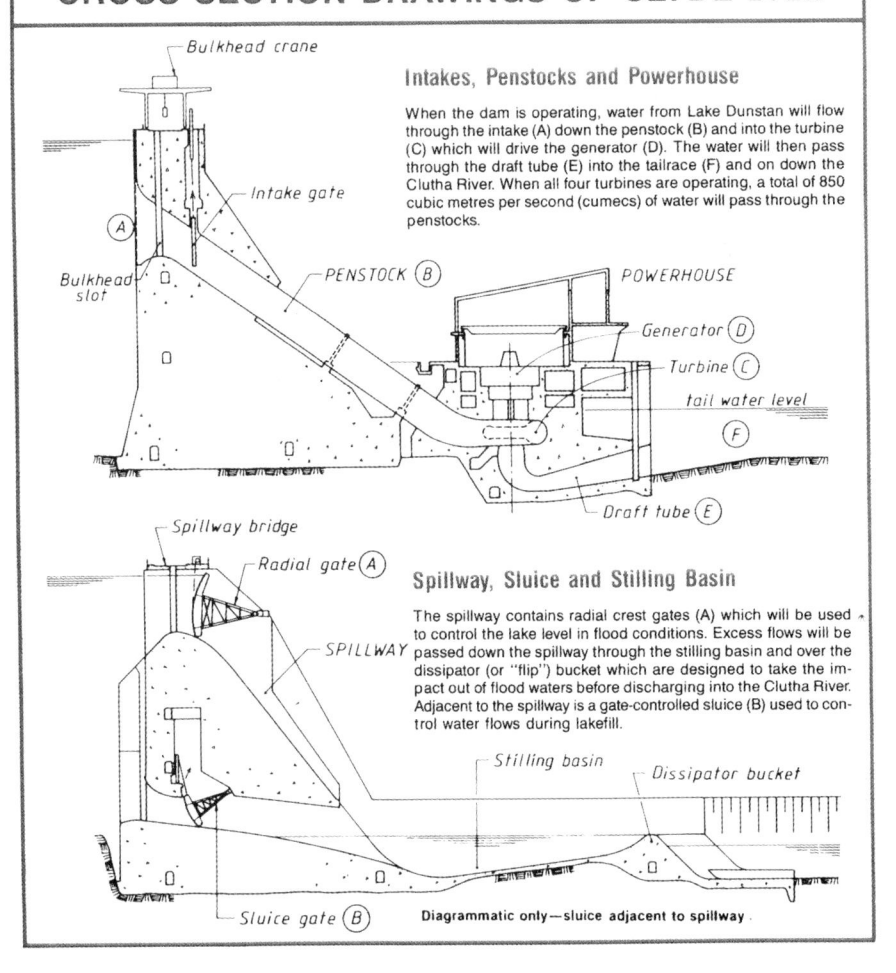

## CROSS SECTION DRAWINGS OF CLYDE DAM

### Intakes, Penstocks and Powerhouse

When the dam is operating, water from Lake Dunstan will flow through the intake (A) down the penstock (B) and into the turbine (C) which will drive the generator (D). The water will then pass through the draft tube (E) into the tailrace (F) and on down the Clutha River. When all four turbines are operating, a total of 850 cubic metres per second (cumecs) of water will pass through the penstocks.

### Spillway, Sluice and Stilling Basin

The spillway contains radial crest gates (A) which will be used to control the lake level in flood conditions. Excess flows will be passed down the spillway through the stilling basin and over the dissipator (or "flip") bucket which are designed to take the impact out of flood waters before discharging into the Clutha River. Adjacent to the spillway is a gate-controlled sluice (B) used to control water flows during lakefill.

Diagrammatic only—sluice adjacent to spillway.

The spillway of the Clyde Dam as it appears today. In times of flood the gates are opened and a frightening wall of water spurts from it, dramatically changing the calm, quiet scene shown here.

Earthworks had started on the dam site at Clyde as early as 1978, and once the Empowering Bill was passed work began in earnest. Zublin-Williamson Consortium became the main contractor, while the contract to build the turbines and generators was granted to Hitachi of Japan. In 1983 a fault-line was discovered under the dam's foundations, which delayed progress considerably and required 250,000 cubic metres of additional excavation work, plus the building of tunnels filled with concrete. The last concrete for the dam was poured in mid 1989, and the turbines and generators were installed the same year. In theory the dam was now finished, but more problems were encountered with the stability of the land behind the dam. The worry was that if a landslip fell into the lake behind the dam, water could wash over the dam, causing damage and possible loss of life in the towns downstream. Remedying this required 2 million metres of buttressing, thousands of drain holes and several tunnels, which was a massive undertaking and delayed the filling of the lake by several years.

The Clyde Dam is now complete and fully operational. It is New Zealand's largest concrete gravity dam at 490 m in length, 102 m in height and 68 m wide at its base. Construction required 1.2 million cubic metres of concrete, and for safety reasons the dam contains a slip joint that allows 2 m of movement in the event of an earthquake. Four turbines drive 108 megawatt generators producing a total of 432 megawatts of power, enough to satisfy the demands of a medium-sized city.

# 26
# HAYES ENGINEERING WORKS — OTUREHUA

One couple who made a difference to the history of Central Otago were Eben Ernest and Hannah Hayes. From humble beginnings in Oturehua, drawing on a combination of Ernest's skills as an inventor and Hannah's business acumen, they would develop an engineering business that would ensure the name Hayes became known throughout New Zealand and the 20 countries where their products are sold.

Ernest Hayes was always called by his middle name. Born at Monks Kirby, Warwickshire, England, he was the oldest of 10 children of a father with the grand name of Ebenezer and the odd occupation of mole catcher. When Ernest left school he completed an apprenticeship as a millwright, which was a broad training in the nineteenth century that involved fitting and turning and dressing millstones. These were handy skills for the era as grain was still reduced to flour by millstones, driven either by a water-powered Pelton wheel or a windmill. When he had completed his apprenticeship, he spent several years practising his trade, and married Hannah in 1881.

In 1882 the couple emigrated to New Zealand with their first child, arriving at Port Chalmers aboard the *Taranaki* on 14 November 1882 and making their way to Central Otago. Unlike many early immigrants, Ernest was lucky enough to have the promise of a job before he arrived, working for an uncle, Josiah Jones, who owned the Vincent Flour Mill. For the first two years after their arrival the couple lived in Ophir but then moved to Oturehua, or Rough Ridge as it was then called. Ernest managed a flour mill there, while Hannah worked as a sewing teacher at the Rough Ridge School. The school has now gone, but the stone flour mill still exists in Oturehua, converted to a residential property, as does the small wooden cottage the family initially lived in.

Flour milling was a lucrative occupation in Central Otago until 1900,

Ernest Hayes, pictured here in 1896, was the inventor and engineer who, with the aid of the selling skills of his wife Hannah, developed the Hayes Engineering Works at Oturehua.

HISTORIC PLACES TRUST

when the local price was undercut by cheap flour being brought into the area from Dunedin via the recently constructed Otago Central Railway. Finding himself and the mill redundant when nobody wanted to purchase the more expensive Oturehua flour, Ernest turned to developing his 60-hectare farm that was located next door to the flour mill. He was never an enthusiastic farmer as his talents and interests lay in the mechanical side of life. After looking at his requirements as a farmer, he began to invent machinery and tools to make his job easier. His inventions were made by hand in the beginning and then on a hand-operated lathe that Ernest fashioned from a gatepost and an old chaffcutter wheel. His first invention was a cutter designed to make pellets from strips of rabbit poison, in an attempt to control the rabbits that infested his farm. It was never his intention to take his invention to the next level, but Hannah was able to see the potential in such a product, and she set out to sell the idea to other farmers in Central and North Otago who were also being overrun by rabbits. She left her growing family, which eventually numbered five sons and four daughters, in the care of her oldest daughter and set out on her bicycle to sell the poison cutter. Hannah and her bicycle became a familiar sight on Otago roads, winter and summer, and it was through her determined efforts that the product became a commercial success.

Encouraged by and enjoying the financial benefits of their move into

When Ernest and Hannah Hayes immigrated to New Zealand, they began their new life at Ophir before moving to Oturehua, where Ernest operated a flour mill. Both the mill and the house in which they lived are close to the site of the Hayes Engineering Works. The stone mill is in use as a private home and their first house, shown here, is now a holiday home.

ABOVE All the main buildings at the Hayes Engineering Works have been stripped back to the original mudbrick. This was an important building material in early, treeless Central Otago, but in most instances is not seen, as the bricks were usually plastered over to protect the walls. Constructed in 1914, this building is a stable with a stone floor and two stalls. The ladder leads to a second-storey loft where hay and oats for the horses were stored.

BELOW Hannah Hayes, wife of Ernest Hayes and partner in the Hayes Engineering Works at Oturehua. While her husband concentrated on the mechanical side of the business, Hannah was the company's sales representative, riding her bicycle throughout Otago in all seasons to secure orders.

engineering, the couple decided in 1902 to concentrate on production rather than farming. Ernest built a forge and began to invent and manufacture small farm implements. He invented and developed the Monkey brand wire-strainer, a jack for lifting a cart so that its wheel could be repaired, plus a wire-coiler. The latter was a simple device used to carry wire to where it was being used and then allow the user to unravel wire from it, as and when required. At the same time, Ernest was adding to the buildings and installing machinery at the site in Oturehua that today is known as the Hayes Engineering Works. Most of the buildings were constructed from mudbricks (adobe), a very successful and common building material in the dry Central Otago climate.

Ernest then began to look for ways to drive the machinery he had built on the site, as there was no electricity. His first attempt was a wind-driven cone windmill, but when this was unsuccessful he built a larger windmill with a 12-m tower and multi-bladed sails 2 m in diameter. The driving power it produced was then transferred into the workshops by a series of belts and shafts. The idea was a good one, but wind power is unreliable in Central Otago, especially in the winter months. Weary of the hold ups this caused, he switched to water power in 1927, harnessing this energy by the use of a water wheel.

By 1912 Ernest's dabble with the windmill had given him the experience to begin the manufacture of a farm windmill for use in pumping water from underground wells and bores. If the water was destined for use in the farmhouse, the windmill pumped it to a holding tank placed close to and higher than the house itself, where gravity took over to run the water inside the building when required. This windmill was one of the better known products of the Hayes Engineering Works and at one time was sported by most rural properties in Central Otago. Although the introduction of electricity would make water power obsolete, the Hayes windmill can still be seen in various locations throughout the region today.

By 1926 Hayes had invented, developed and marketed several other products that were all manufactured at the expanding site in Oturehua. A pulley block was one, a cattle-stop was another, as was a device for lifting subsided fence standards. He had also invented the hand-held Hayes Wire Strainer, which is still in widespread use, is exported to 20 countries and is the product Ernest and Hannah Hayes and their company are remembered for today. By this time their sons had also joined the business and a large, elegant villa, complete with fountains, had been built beside the works to house the expanding family.

Ill health forced Ernest to retire in 1926, and he died at home in

Oturehua in 1933. Hannah died in 1946. Both are buried in the small Hills Creek cemetery at the northern end of the Ida Valley.

The business continued to expand until 1952, when freight costs out of Oturehua were such that the company was required to relocate to Christchurch to stay competitive. Family members retained the historic Oturehua site until 1975, when it was sold to the Historic Places Trust, which still owns it. Many of the original buildings have been renovated and the power plant rebooted to run all the machinery left on the site, which is now open to the public at selected hours.

BELOW LEFT In the early twentieth century attempts were made to introduce some safety measures into the workplace to combat the many unnecessary deaths that resulted from industrial accidents. Hayes Engineering Works was one of these enlightened companies, as this sign suggests.

BELOW RIGHT A sign at the Hayes Engineering Works at Oturehua displays some of the products invented by Ernest Hayes. The Smooth Grip Wire Strainer, the Metal Top Motor Gate and the Permanent Wire Strainer are his best known inventions. All are still manufactured today.

HISTORIC PLACES TRUST

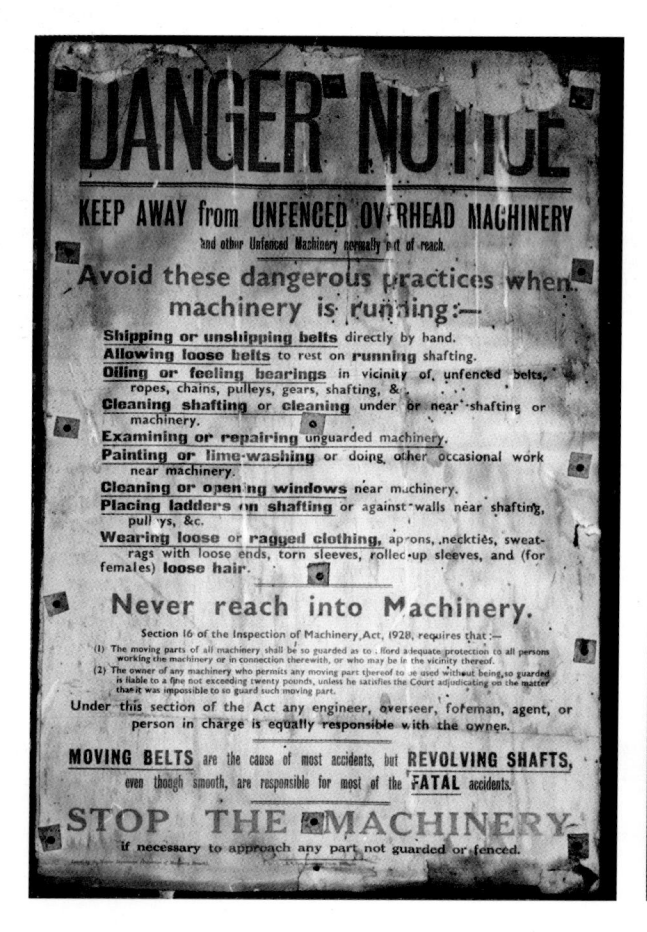

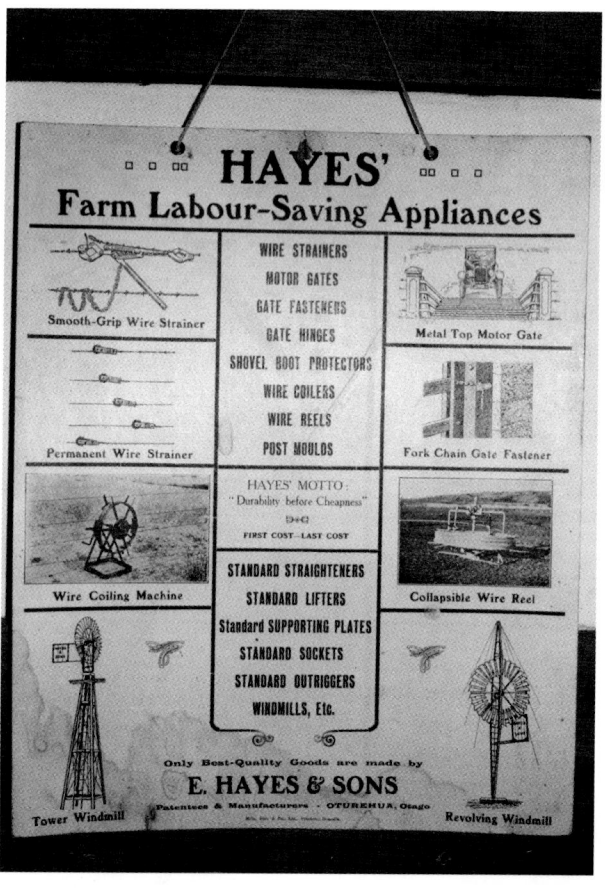

**RIGHT ABOVE** At the beginning of the twentieth century, Ernest and Hannah Hayes were the owners of a prosperous business. This enabled them to build this attractive double-fronted villa next door to the Hayes Engineering Works at Oturehua in 1919. It is constructed of mudbricks that were stored outside under a cover of tussock for several years before being used. After the bricks were made, World War I intervened, making labour almost impossible to get during the war years and thus putting a stop to any housebuilding plans. Once completed, the house had several fountains in its grounds — an unusual feature in water-starved Central Otago. The interior walls are also of mudbrick, smoothed over with a plaster made from mud slurry and dung and then painted or wallpapered.

**RIGHT BELOW** Tractors have come a long way in the twentieth century. This old tractor in the ground of the Hayes Engineering site was equipped with solid rubber wheels on the front, metal grips for traction at the rear and a seat that exposed the operator to all weathers. It would have been noisy and uncomfortable, but much more efficient than the horses it replaced.

HAYES ENGINEERING WORKS — OTUREHUA | 217

# 27
# FOLLY OF THE KAWARAU FALLS DAM

The promise of gold often makes wise people do odd things. At the point where the waters of Lake Wakatipu leave the lake and form the Kawarau River at Frankton Arm there is an example of gold fever that ran out of control. Perfectly rational people, many of whom lived locally and should have known better, became involved in a scheme to dam the Kawarau River at this point. The plan was so bizarre, so poorly thought out and such a monumental failure that it is difficult to believe today that it was not a confidence trick.

## THE KAWARAU GOLDMINING COMPANY

Winning gold from the two big rivers in Central Otago, the Kawarau and the Clutha, was never easy because they are both swift and deep. Experienced miners knew that the river beds were full of the precious metal in locations where conditions for accumulation were suitable as both rivers had acted as natural tailraces over the millennia, washing the gold eroded from the surrounding hills and depositing it along their beds and beaches. Both rivers were formed at the narrow outlets of lakes Wakatipu and Wanaka and were added to from Lake Hawea, and it seemed a perfectly rational idea to dam the rivers at those points to dry out their beds, making for easy access to the gold that supposedly lay there.

With this idea floating around for many years, it was only a matter of time before it was acted on. In 1922, an entrepreneur named Iles was able to convince a number of wealthy Dunedin individuals to invest in a scheme to construct a dam on the Kawarau River at the Kawarau Falls, in Frankton. The Kawarau Goldmining Company was formed for this purpose with a capital of 10,000 pounds, in shares of 5 pence each. At the same time, 128

**OPPOSITE LEFT** Building the dam at the Kawarau Falls near Queenstown to halt the flow of the Kawarau River was a huge undertaking for the Kawarau Gold Mining Company, a public company funded by the sale of shares. In 1924, the year construction started, tools were primitive. Wooden scaffolding was the norm, as was the wheelbarrow. Concrete was mixed by hand on the bank of the river, then tipped down the leather chute into the boxed foundation at the bottom of the photograph.
HOCKEN COLLECTIONS S05-044M, UNIVERSITY OF OTAGO, DUNEDIN

**OPPOSITE RIGHT** The design of the Kawarau Falls Dam was based on a series of concrete foundations, built in the bed of the river, to support iron gates that would eventually be lowered to halt the flow of the river. Foundations were dug by labourers using picks and shovels. Once at the required depth, concrete was poured via the chute shown at top left.
HOCKEN COLLECTIONS S05-044E, UNIVERSITY OF OTAGO, DUNEDIN

dredging claims were applied for and granted to the company, extending over the 50 km of the Kawarau River bed that would dry out when the dam was built. The directors of the company had no intention of financing the construction of the dam themselves. They amalgamated the 128 dredging claims into 84 claims of 590 m each in length and then sold these to investors at 1000 pounds a claim, with a share of any gold found also coming back into the company's coffers. The whole scheme smacked of chicanery as it was widely promoted in the newspapers as something special, a deal that would bring fortune to those fortunate enough to become involved. This created a boom in the sale of the company's shares and dredging claims when its shares were listed on the stock exchange and heavily traded.

## CONSTRUCTION OF THE DAM

By 1924, with the capital and permits required to construct the dam in place, tenders were called and construction began. By the end of the year there were 20 men working on the Kawarau Falls site, which had been designed to incorporate a bridge over the river. The engineers involved knew that the flow of the Kawarau River could not be stopped unless the Shotover and Arrow rivers were also dammed, and to the credit of the Kawarau Goldmining Company, attempts were made to gain permission to dam both rivers. Shutting them off, however, would have had a different effect from stopping the flow from Lake Wakatipu. At the time it was thought that closing the exit of Lake Wakatipu would only involve a lift in the level of the lake, while dams on the two rivers would have meant extensive flooding of surrounding land as waters of the Shotover and the Arrow backed up. Local landowners were either opposed to this flooding or wanted considerable compensation, and the plan to dam the Shotover and the Arrow was dropped. Even though the Kawarau Falls Dam engineers and the directors of the company knew that the Kawarau River could not be dried out without controlling the Shotover and Arrow rivers, the company was by 1925 so deeply involved that construction at Kawarau Falls carried on to its inevitable result.

Building the dam involved the construction of 10 gates supported against piers that were anchored to the rocks in the river at Kawarau Falls. Each pier was a little over 2 m wide, 10 m high and 16 m long. By August 1925 two piers had been completed, and those investors who had been successful in securing the dredging claims began to invent schemes to raise enough capital to finance those claims. Every few kilometres of the river bed had its own company floated, both in New Zealand and overseas, to raise the money required. The Consolidated Kawarau Company owned 60 claims and employed three managers, while the Nevis Junction Company had a paid-up capital of 6500 pounds in 2/6d shares. All that was needed was for the dam to be completed and the gates closed.

The big day arrived on 23 August 1926, and excited spectators watched while all the gates were closed. Nothing happened. There was no noticeable drop in the river that first day or during the following night. The level of the river did drop by 1 m, but this was meaningless in a river whose depth averaged 12 m over its entire length. As the engineers had known, the flow of the Shotover and Arrow rivers into the Kawarau was large enough to keep

To enable the concrete foundations of the Kawarau Dam to be built, the Kawarau River had to be diverted. This was done in stages. As the boxing for foundations was put in place and the ground excavated, the river was diverted around them by the construction of temporary walls and channels.

HOCKEN COLLECTIONS S05-044H,
UNIVERSITY OF OTAGO, DUNEDIN

RIGHT ABOVE Once the foundation of each section of the Kawarau Falls Dam was secured, it was then extended to the height required to take the steel beams to support the bridge that would eventually be built across the full width of the dam.

HOCKEN COLLECTIONS S05-045F, UNIVERSITY OF OTAGO, DUNEDIN

RIGHT CENTRE A 1925 view of the partly completed Kawarau Falls Dam.

HOCKEN COLLECTIONS S05-044, UNIVERSITY OF OTAGO, DUNEDIN

RIGHT BELOW The Kawarau Falls Dam was a clever combination of dam and bridge. This 1926 photograph shows the layout of the bridge that would eventually span the Kawarau River at Frankton. The bridge, when completed, linked Queenstown with Southland and provided access to the south side of Lake Wakatipu at this point — an area that was later known as Kelvin Heights.

HOCKEN COLLECTIONS S05-044L, UNIVERSITY OF OTAGO, DUNEDIN

**LEFT ABOVE** This photograph, taken in March 1926 from the Queenstown or upriver side of the dam, shows how and where the metal gates that were intended to stop of flow of the Kawarau River were placed between each concrete pillar.

HOCKEN COLLECTIONS S05-044G, UNIVERSITY OF OTAGO, DUNEDIN

**LEFT BELOW** A second photograph, also taken in March 1926, this time from the Cromwell or downriver side of the dam, shows the opposite side of the concrete pillars. It was here that the pulleys to operate the wire ropes that raised or lowered the metal gates on the upriver side were located.

HOCKEN COLLECTIONS S05-044H, UNIVERSITY OF OTAGO, DUNEDIN

it flowing permanently. Added to this was seepage from Lake Wakatipu through the Frankton Flat and the Nevis River, which deposited a large volume of water into the Kawarau, downstream near Cromwell.

Even if these rivers had been dammed, nobody involved in the construction at Kawarau Falls had made allowance for the fact that the level of Lake Wakatipu rose alarmingly, threatening to flood Queenstown, when the gates were closed for only a short period of time. There was a partial loss of water in the river bed as far downstream as the Shotover River, but when this short length was explored it was found that the current over this distance had been too swift to deposit any gold in the river bed. The whole project was a white elephant.

## THE AFTERMATH

In spite of the shambles, the investors still did not give up. At a meeting in Dunedin in 1927 a new company called the Amalgamated Kawarau Company was formed to control all the claims and find new ways to make the project work. The new company soon learnt that this task was not as simple as it appeared. There were financial complications when it was found that many of the claims had changed hands several times since the project was first mooted and many of the claim holders still owed money to the original Kawarau Goldmining Company. This situation was further aggravated by the terms of these claims, which provided that, if and when gold was dredged from the river, the original company still held the right to claim a percentage under its agreement.

Even if these complications could have been ironed out and the Shotover and Arrow rivers had been dammed, the seepage from the lake at Frankton Flat and the various small tributaries downstream would still have resulted in the Kawarau having a substantial flow of water. In the event, the new company was unable to raise the necessary capital to build any new dams.

The Public Works Department eventually took control of the dam. Because the Kawarau Goldmining Company claims were protected by an Act of Parliament, attempts were made in later years to have the dam gates closed, particularly during hard winters when the level of Lake Wakatipu was low. Legal problems relating to the company's claims put a stop to these attempts. By the time these legalities were overcome, the snow on the mountains that fed the lake had usually melted, returning the lake level to normal.

The Kawarau Goldmining Company, with no income and with shareholders unwilling to become further involved financially, fell behind with rates and rents payable for claims. After briefly raising its head with a failed prospectus to raise 125,000 pounds capital during the revival of mining by the government during the depression of the 1930s, it faded into obscurity. It was only then that the complete Kawarau Falls Dam venture was finally written off as an expensive fiasco.

# BIBLIOGRAPHY

Adamson, Irene, *From Meetings to Mountains*. 2001.

Anderson, Atholl, *When All the Moa-Ovens Grow Cold*. Otago Heritage Books, 1983.

Baker, Catherine Jean, *Memories of Walter Peak, Mt Nicholas & Fernhill Stations*. 1999.

Beaton, Eileen, *Macetown*. John McIndoe Ltd, 1971.

Beattie, Herries, *Otago Place Names*. Otago Daily Times, 1948.

Cowan, J., *Down the years in The Maniototo*. Otago Centennial Historical Publications, 1948.

Duff, Geoffrey P., *Sheep May Safely Graze*. Cadsonbury Publications, 1998.

Duff, Roger, The *Moa Hunter Period of Maori Culture*. Govt. Printer, 1956.

Duncan, A.H., *The Wakatipians*. Reprint by Capper Press, 1984.

Griffiths, G.J., *King Wakatip*. John McIndoe Ltd., 1971.

Hall-Jones, John, *Mr Surveyor Thomson: Early Days in Otago and Southland*. AH & AW Reed Ltd, 1971.

Leaske, Ken, *Ophir Memories*. 1995.

Mackenzie, N.S., *Gateway to Maniototo, A History of Kyeburn & Kokonga Districts*. 1996.

Martin, John (ed.), *People, Politics & Power Stations*. Bridget William Books, 1991.

McAra, Jill, *Stand for New Zealand: Voices from the Battle of Crete*. Wilson Scott Publishing, 2004.

Miller, F.W.G. and Wheeler, Colin, *Historic Central Otago*. AH & AW Reed Ltd, 1970.

Murray, J.S. and R.W., *Costly Gold*. AH & AW Reed Ltd, 1978.

Newman, Robyn, *Lines from Central*. 2003.

Nicholson-Garrett, Gladys, *St Bathans*. John McIndoe Ltd., 1977.

Parcell, J.C., *Heart of the Desert*. Otago Centennial Publications, 1951.

Pascoe, John, *Great Days in NZ Exploration*. AH & AW Reed Ltd, 1959.

Peat, Neville, *Southern Land, Southern People*. University of Otago Press, 2002.

Ramage, Gordon, *Alexandra, A Place in the Sun*. Central Otago District Council, 1990.

Ross, Angus, *23rd Battalion*. War History Branch, Dept. of Internal Affairs, 1959.

Roxburgh, Irvine, *Wanaka Story*. Otago Centennial Historical Publications, 1957.

Thomson, Jane, *Southern People*. Dunedin City Council, Longacre Press, 1998.

Todd, Dennis, *Ranfurly, the Centennial History*. 1998.

Veitch, Isobel, *Clyde on the Dunstan*. Square One Press, Dunedin, 2003.

Webster, A.H.H, *Teviot Tapestry*. Otago Centennial Historical Publications, 1948.

Women's Division of Federated Farmers, Tarras, *A Tapestry of Tarras*. John McIndoe Ltd, Dunedin, 1993.

# INDEX

2nd New Zealand Expeditionary Force (2NZEF) 24
23rd Battalion 82; see also D Company
28th (Maori) Battalion 82

Abbey St Bathans 24
Abel Ferris Domini 148
African American 140, 141
A & G Price Ltd 203
Ah Quay 200
Ahuriri River 35
Albert Town 150-151
Alexandra 11, 43, 55, 65-67, 69-70, 72, 80, 90-91, 96-97, 98, 99, 107-111, 113, 114, 119, 122, 138, 141-143, 174, 188-189, 193, 204, 206
Alexandra bridge 47
Alexandra courthouse 113
Alexandra, Princess of Denmark 107
Allies, The 83-84, 86-87, 89
Amalgamated Kawarau Co. 223
Ancient Briton Hotel 159
Annan, William 97, 99
antimony 11
apples 97
apricots 93, 95-96, 115
archeology 15
Arrow River 32, 123-124, 126, 177, 219-220, 223
Arrowtown 11, 29, 60, 114, 123-125, 127, 129-131, 177
art deco 169, 171-172, 173, 175
Arthurs Point 194-195
Auripo 71, 73
Australia 21, 28, 31, 36, 40-41, 48, 74, 91-93, 99-100,
117, 140, 144, 157, 176
Australia–New Zealand Mining Co. 154, 176

Balclutha 23, 188
Bald Hill Flat 96
Ballarat Hotel 139
Bamborough Castle 23, 25
Bank of New South Wales 47, 138-139, 169
Bannockburn 15, 43, 49-50, 176-177, 181, 183-186, 206
Bannockburn Creek 177, 183
Bannockburn Terraces 178
Barry's Tea Rooms 112
Battle of Crete 81-84, 86, 88-89
Battle of the Somme 78
Battle of Vinegar Hill 134
Beale, Joe 123
Beale, John 123
Beaumont 25, 95, 118, 122
Beaumont Water 25
Bendigo 26, 35, 43, 49-50, 66, 193
Bendigo Hotel 69
Bendigo Mine 50, 150, 180

Berwickshire 26
Bishop of Lindisfarne 25
Black, Charles 140-141
Black, Harold 170
Black Knob mountain 24; see also Grandview
Black Peter 45
Black, Thomas 140
Black, William 140-141
Blacks 140, 142
Blacks cemetery 144
Blacks homestead 141
Blacks Hotel 142-143, 144-145
blacksmiths 69, 110, 133, 143, 169
Blackstone Hills 26
Blackton 142
Blue Lake 48, 132, 134-135
Blue Slip 199
Boer War 108, 186
Booth Road 140, 141, 145
Bourdeau, Julien 196, 200
Bragato, Signor 93
Bridge Hill 109
Britain 81-83, 98, 100; see also United Kingdom
Bullendale 49, 194, 200-201, 204
Bullen, George 200
Bullock Creek 152
bullocks 40
  drivers 40
Bungalow, The 61
bungy jumping 194, 200
butchering camps 15
Butchers Dam 97, 111-112
Butchers Gully 110
Butchers River 112

California 10, 45, 48, 56, 99
  goldfields 45, 129
Cairnmuir Range 15, 176
Cambrians 49, 133-134
Cardrona 26, 31, 49, 151
Cardrona River 151, 153-154
Cargill, Captain 21
Cargill, John 116
Carrick Range 22, 50, 176-177, 183, 185
Carricktown 183
Castle Rock 197
Cecil Peak 32
cemeteries 80, 129
  Blacks 144
  Hamiltons 187
  Kyeburn 162, 163, 165
  St Bathans 132
  Swinburn 161, 165
Centennial Refreshment Rooms 170, 173, 175
Central Otago Fruit Growers Assoc 99
Central Otago News 189
Chalet Community Trust 175

Chalet Home for the Aged 175
Chalmers, Alexander 21
Chalmers, Gerit 117
Chalmers, Nathanael 21-23, 116-117
Chalmers, William 21
Charlemont Street 168
Chatto Creek 26, 111
  water race 113
Chatto Creek Hotel 111
Chatto Creek Post Office 111
Cheong Shing Tong 59
cherries 96, 126
China 56-57, 61, 97
Chinatown 56, 59-60, 181
Chinese
  coffins 58–59
  merchants 58
  miners 55-56, 57-61, 118, 126-127, 160, 162-163, 181, 191, 200
  opium addiction 57-58
  shantytowns 59
Christchurch 39, 82, 95, 103, 216
Clarke, Jack 155
Clarke, Joseph (Big) 117
Clarke, William 117
climate 10, 62, 97
Clutha Development (Clyde Dam) Empowering Bill 210, 212
Clutha district 21
Clutha Dredging Co. 206
Clutha River 11, 12, 15, 22, 24-26, 31, 35, 43, 45-46, 48, 51-52, 54-55, 57, 62, 75, 90, 93, 95, 99, 107-112, 115-122, 148-150, 154-156, 176-179, 187-188, 189, 193, 204, 207, 209-210, 218
Clyde 26, 43, 69-70, 72-74, 90-91, 97-98, 107, 121, 182, 187-190, 192, 206, 210-212
Clyde Bridge 188
Clyde Dam 69, 73, 99, 176, 179, 192-193, 211, 212
Clydesdale horses 41
coal 11, 121, 123, 135-136, 162, 201, 204
Coal Creek 92-93, 95, 119-120, 121-122, 205, 209
Cobb & Co. 68-69, 121, 152
codlin moth 95
Colville, Dan (Yankee) 150
Commissioners Flat 209
Conroy's Gully 98-99
Conroys River 112
Consolidated Kawarau Co. 220
Cook Islands 13
Cook, James (Captain) 13, 62
Cook Strait 82
Corbie 26
Corbies Rock 26
Corcoran, John 172
Corners, The 197

Cornish Point  177
Coronet Peak  32, 195, 197
Cowan, James  177
Craig, James  121
Crete  83, 85-86, 87-89
Cromwell  12, 22-23, 26, 31, 43, 45, 51, 55-56, 59-60, 64-65, 69-70, 73, 97, 114, 149, 150-152, 176-177, 178-179, 180-182, 206-207, 210, 222
Cromwell Argus  151, 180
Cromwell Bridge  51, 180
Cromwell Gorge  22, 35, 46, 54, 62, 69, 72, 99, 182
Cromwell Guardian  180-181
Cromwell Quartz Mining Co.  50, 150, 180
Cromwell Railway Station  72
Crossan's Gully  121

D Company, 23rd Battalion  81-82, 84-85, 89
Daisybank  166
Dalgety & Co.  100-102, 106, 133
Dalgety & NZ Loan  102
Dalgety Crown  102
Dalgety, Frederick  37, 41, 100-102, 132-133
Dalgety Rattray  100
dams see Butchers, Clyde, Poolburn, Roxburgh, etc  wing  109
Daniel O'Connell Bridge  145, 188
Dansey, W.H.  161
Danseys Pass  159, 161, 163
Danseys Pass Hotel  161-162, 163-164
Dart River  32
Dawson, Mrs  97, 98-99
Dawson cherry  98-99
Dawson, Richard, 98-99
Dawson's orchard  98
Dead Horse Pinch  68
Deep Creek  197
deer  154-155
Department of Conservation  50, 59, 73, 165
Depression, 1880s  70, 103, 117, 134, 151-152
   1930s  55, 101, 131, 136, 156, 170, 223
Devils Elbow  197, 199
Diamond Lake  32
dogs, wild  37, 114, 188
   Goat & Dog Nuisance Ordinance  114
Domini, Abel Ferris (alias Henry Norman)  148
Domini, Robert  148
Don, Alexander (Rev.)  60, 61, 118, 127
Don, Amelia  61
Donald Reid & Co.  100, 102-103
Donald Reid Otago Farmers Ltd  103
Donnelly family  146
Drake brothers  150
Drake, Murdoch  151
Drake, Reverend  150
dredges
   current wheel  52, 55, 119

spoon  51, 119
   steam  52, 55, 119, 121
   see also gold dredges
dredge elevators  55
dredging  51, 53-54, 70, 99, 108-109, 119-121, 154, 158, 162, 196, 199, 204, 207, 219, 223; see also dredges
Drummey, J.  138
Duggan, Teddy  146
Dumbarton  93, 95, 205
Dunedin  9, 24, 29, 36-37, 43, 45-46, 54, 58-59, 61, 64, 66-68, 70-71, 74, 91, 95, 97, 100, 102-105, 106, 115, 121, 141, 148, 153, 164-165, 171, 179, 182, 187-189, 193, 203, 218, 223
Dunedin Diocesan Trust Board  133
Dunning brothers  95
Dunstanburgh Castle  25
Dunstan Creek  133, 140
Dunstan electorate  73-74, 187
Dunstan Flat  90
Dunstan goldfield  46, 74
Dunstan Hotel  193
Dunstan Jockey Club  192
Dunstan Lead  51
Dunstan Mountains  25-26, 35, 41, 140
Dunstan News  189
Dunstan Times  189

Earnscleugh  26, 99, 109, 206
Earnscleugh Station  62, 189
Edwards, Peter  45
Eichardts Hotel  34
electrical dredging  52, 55, 204
electricity generation  10, 115, 121, 156, 200-201, 203, 205, 209-210, 215
elevating  48, 119, 134-135
England  51, 74, 77-78, 83, 101, 133, 144, 157, 203, 213
Ettrick  26, 92, 115, 120, 205
Evans, Fred  200-203
Eweburn  25
Eweburn Township reserve  168
Ewing, John  48, 120, 132, 134, 150, 153

Falls Dam  88, 136
Fenwick, George  181
Feraud, Jean Desire  90-91, 97-98, 191
Fernhill  31
ferrets  20, 63
Fifth Earl of Ranfurly  168
Fillyburn  25
floods  151
Forty-Niners  45
Frankton  29, 32, 206, 218, 221
Frankton Arm  218
Frankton Flat  222-223
Fraser River  112, 204, 206
Fraser, William  187, 189

Frenchman's Point  90
frost  10, 94, 97, 128, 176
   oil pots  94
Fruit Control Board  95
fruit growing  92-99, 108, 115, 120; see also apples, apricots, etc.
Fruitlands  96-97

Gabriels Gully  12, 31, 43, 45, 149
Gallagher, John  139
Galloway  141
Galloway Station  98, 188
Gammie, George  28-29
Garrett, William  51
Garvie, Alexander  25, 33
Gault, James  18
Gentle Annie stream  192
geology  197
   scheelite  11
   shaft tors  197
   see also quartz; schist
George, Edwin  162
German parachutists  85, 89
German 12th Army  83
Gibraltar Rock  181
Gibson, Hector  42
Gilbert, Frances see Rees, Frances
Gilchrist family  170
Gimmerburn  25
gin traps  64
Glendhu Bay  148
Glenorchy  29, 31, 43, 49
Glenshee Park  164
Goat & Dog Nuisance Ordinance  114
gold  11, 28, 45, 50-52, 56, 67, 97, 100, 102, 109, 115, 117-119, 123, 133-134, 141, 149, 152-153, 157-158, 162-163, 165, 167, 176, 183, 187, 189, 193-194, 209, 218-219, 222-223
   alluvial gold  48, 49, 56, 58, 108-109, 118, 124, 177, 196
   discovery  37, 121
   prospecting  28, 123, 209
gold dredges
   *Fourteen-mile Beach*  204
   *Golden Treasure*  52
   *Lowburn*  154
   *Molyneux* electric  54; *see also* dredges
gold mines
   Achilles  204
   Golden Progress  49, 143
   Invincible  49
   Kildare Hill Claim  48
   Nicholson  135
   Phoenix  201, 204
   Premier Mine  125
   Young Australian  50
gold miners  12, 21, 23, 31-33, 37, 67, 98, 102, 108, 194

miners' rights  46
Golden Canyon  199
Golden Reward Gold Dredge Co.  53
Goldfields Act 1858  46
Goldfields Mining Centre  57, 59-60, 181
Goodger, George  51, 178, 189
Gorge Creek  115, 118
Graham, Alex  155
Grandview  24, 36; see also Black Knob
Grant, William (Colonel)  28
grapes  90-91, 93-94, 97-98, 176, 186; see also wine, vineyards
grazing licences  27
rights  27, 31, 35-37
greenstone  16, 115, 148
Greenstone River  31
Griffiths, Thomas  139

Haast  115
Haast Road  156
Haast's eagle  18, 20
Halfway House Hotel  182
Hallenstein, Bendix  35, 178
Hall Jones, John  26
Hamiltons  43, 49, 167
Harliwich, N.J.  121
Hartley, Horatio  35, 43 45-46, 187, 189
Hartley's Township  187; see also Clyde
Hassing, George  149-150, 178
Hawea Flat  148, 150-151, 153-154, 156
Hawea River  148
Hawk Heights  26
Hawkdun irrigation scheme  88
Hawkdun Range  10, 25-26, 159-161
Hawkdun Station  102
Hawkesburn  15
Hayes Engineering Works  213-214, 215, 216-217
Hayes, Ernest  214-217
Hayes, Hannah  213-215, 217
Head, Bernard (Captain)  155
health camp  115
Heavens Gate  197
Hebden, Joe (Charcoal)  51, 150
Hector Mountains  22
Hedditch, Charles (Captain)  150
Hells Gate  197
Historic Places Trust  142, 146, 216
Hogburn  25, 157
Holland & Hannen consortium  209
Holloway, John  193
Holly Lea  39
Hore, Eden  164
Hore, Frank  88
Horn, James  185
Horseburn  25
horses  41, 69-70, 105, 114, 152
Horseshoe Bend  118, 122

Houndburn  25
House of Representatives  102
Hoy Yow Ku  200
hunting
by Maori  14-16
deer  154-155
Hyde  9, 74, 171
Hyde Harris, John  157
Hyde, J.G. (Dr)  99

Ida  25
Idaburn stream  25
Ida Valley  15, 49, 67-68, 70, 72, 77, 79-80, 161, 216
Inspector of Nuisances  114
Invercargill  23-24, 26, 206
Ireland  134, 178
Irish miners  145
irrigation  11, 50, 88, 90, 94, 97-99, 136, 153, 174, 185, 191, 204-206
Iversen, Andreas  97, 99
Iversen, Jane  99

Jenkins, Billy  131
J.G. Ward & Co.  117
Jolly, D.A.  178-179,181
Junction, The (Alexandra)  107, 176-177

Kaikoura (Maori explorer)  22
Kakanui Mountains  10, 165
Kawarau Falls  33, 220, 222
Kawarau Falls Dam  218, 220-221, 223
Kawarau Goldmining Co.  218-219, 223
Kawarau Gorge  22, 60, 181, 206
Kawarau River  11, 22-23, 33, 54, 183-184, 207, 218-220, 221-223
Kawarau Station  176-177, 185
Kearney, Ned  145-146
Kelvin Heights  221
Kildare Consolidated Mining Co.  135
Kingston  9, 31-32, 177
kiore  18, 20
Knobby, The  10
Kokonga  161, 165-166
Kye Burn river  24-25, 68, 161-162, 164
Kyeburn  9, 15, 49, 68, 161–166
Kyeburn Bridge  161
Kyeburn Diggings  161-162, 163-166
Kyeburn Hotel  163
Kyeburn 200 runs  165

Ladysmith Gold Dredging Co.  205
Laird of Earnslaw  23
Lake Dunstan  10, 73, 99, 179-182, 193
Lake Hawea  9, 10, 22, 25, 35, 147-148, 150, 152, 154-156, 193, 207, 208
Lake House, Hawea  155
Lake Onslow  10

Lake Wakatipu  9, 10, 16, 22, 24, 28-29, 31-34, 75, 155, 206, 210, 218-220, 221-223
Lake Wanaka  9, 10, 22, 25, 29, 31, 147-148, 150-155, 178, 193, 207, 210, 218
Lammermoor Range  25
Lammermuir Hills  25
land reforms  158
Lane, Joseph  111
Lanes Dam  109
Lauder  26, 71, 73, 140, 206
Lauder Station  41
Lawrence  9, 11, 12, 26, 43, 49, 59, 61, 64, 95, 121-122
Leaning Rock Creek  35
leasehold  27, 63, 90, 100, 102, 117, 140-141, 148, 169, 185
Legislative Council  39, 165
Lighthouse, The  197
Lindisfarne  23
Lindis Pass  9, 16, 24-25, 29, 40, 102, 156
Lindis River  26, 149
Livingston  162
Logan, Thomas  50-51, 180
Logantown  35, 50
Long Gully  197
Long Valley  152
Lowburn  75, 206
Lowburn Terrace  178
Lower Township (Alexandra)  107
Low, John  121
Luggate  153, 182, 210
Lye Bow  97, 111

Macandrew, James  142
Mace brothers  123
Mace, Charles  123
Mace, Harry  123
Mace, John  123
Macetown  11, 49, 123-124, 125-131, 204
Macintosh, J W  143
Mackenzie, James  116
Macraes Flat  9, 49
Maerewhenua diggings  162
Maisey's Kyeburn Hotel  162
Makarora  150, 153, 178
Maniototo County Council  135
Maniototo Early Settlers Museum  164
Maniototo Hospital  170
Maniototo irrigation scheme  174
Maniototo Plain  10, 15-16, 24, 31, 70, 72, 133, 157-158, 167-168, 170, 189
Manorburn Dam  11, 25
Manuherikia  107
Manuherikia River  11, 24, 72, 109-110, 136, 140, 145
Manuherikia Suspension bridge  110
Manuherikia Valley  15, 68, 132, 140, 187, 206
Manuherikia Viaduct  73

Maori  7, 9, 12-17, 20-23, 29, 33, 36, 38, 45, 115, 147-148, 188, 199
  hunting  14-16
ovens  15, 115
Maori Point  199
Mareburn  25
market gardening  92, 97-98, 111
matagouri  11, 22, 27, 63
Matakanui  26, 43, 49, 146
Matarua River  22
Matthews, Henry  168
Matthews, William  181
Mathewson, Donald  79
Matukituki River  150
Matukituki Valley  152
McBreen, Andrew  76-77, 78-80
McKay, James  178
McKenzie, John  75
McKenzie, Scobie  165
McKerrow, James  25, 32, 148
McKnight Bros  143
McKnight family  143
McKnight, Jimmy  143
McLean, Allan  28, 37, 39
McLean family  35, 37, 39, 41
McLean, John (Jock)  28, 36-37, 39
Melmore Terrace  179-180, 181
members of Parliament  70, 165, 189, 210
mercury poisoning  126
middens  15
Middlemarch  9, 67, 70-72, 164
Mill Creek  150, 205
Miller, Walter  116
Millers Flat  52, 95, 115, 121-122
Millers Flat bridge  119
Milton  95
mines see gold mines, quartz mining
miners' right  46
moa  12, 14-15, 17-18, 20, 115, 148
Moa Creek,  77
Moa Flat Station  117
Moke Creek  32
Moke Lake  32
Molyneux Dredging Co.  206
Monte Christo  90-91, 98, 191
Morrison–Knudson Inc.  209
Morven Downs  42
Morven Hills Station  35-37, 40-42, 63-64, 102, 153
Moutere Station  67, 188
mountains
  Aspiring  25-26, 155
  Burster  159-160
  Buster  160
  Cook (Aoraki)  25
  Difficulty  22
  Earnslaw  24
  Ida  25

Nicholas  31
Olympus  82-83
Pisa  177
Thomson  26
Turnbull  26
Mt Arum Station  200
Mt Morgan Sluicing Co.  146
mudbrick  72, 123, 132, 139, 146, 215, 217
mules  88, 160-161
Murihiku block  22
Murray Roberts & Co.  117
Muster on the Buster  88, 160-161
musterers  38, 160-161; see also shepherds
Mutton Town Gully  188

Naseby  11, 26, 43, 49, 99, 133, 157-159, 161-162, 164, 167-169
National Mortgage & Agency Co. (NMA)  100, 103-106
Nees, Alfred  150
Nevis Junction Co.  220
Nevis River  184, 122
Nevis Valley  22, 43, 50, 176-177, 181, 185
Newtown Tavern  146
New Zealand Company  21
New Zealand Fruit Growers Assoc  95
New Zealand Railways  161
Ngai Tahu  12, 16
Nichols, Charles  41
Nicholson, Neil  134
Norman, Henry (also Abel Ferris)  148
Northern Ireland  178
North Island  17, 20, 129, 156
North Otago  161, 124
North Taieri  102
nor'wester (wind)  10, 178

Oamaru  36, 39, 148, 162
Old Dunstan Road  67
Old Man Range  10, 15
Old Woman Range  10
Omakau  26, 61
One Mile Creek  205-206
Ophir  10, 49, 61, 66, 126, 142-143, 144-145, 146, 188, 213
Ophir courthouse  142-143, 144
Ophir hall  143
Ophir Union church  143
opium addiction  57-58
orchardists  92, 97, 111
orchards  92-95, 96-97, 99, 122, 153, 193
Oreti  21
Otago  9, 21, 23-26, 43, 56-57, 58, 102-103, 105, 129, 138, 148, 181, 210
Otago Central Electric Power Board  205-206
Otago Central Fruitlands  97
Otago Central Land League  75
Otago Central Rail Trail  73, 175

Otago Central Railway  64, 67, 69-70, 72-75, 94, 110, 122, 161, 166, 168, 170, 174, 175, 182, 214
Otago Free Church settlement  21
Otago Goldfields Park  113
Otago Infantry Regiment  77
Otago Provisional Council  56, 102, 181, 190
Otago Provincial Government  45, 74
Otago School of Mines  134
Otago Superintendent  142, 157
Otago Witness newspaper  133
Otakau  9
Otekaieke Run  161
Oturehua  15, 47, 49, 136, 139, 143, 213-217
Oturehua Historical Society  139

Palmerston  9, 68
Parker, B.R. & W.C.  157
Parkers (Naseby)  157
Patearoa  166
peaches  95
Pelton wheel  68, 203, 207, 213
Pembroke  150-156
pests see deer, ferrets, rabbits, sweet briar, etc
Pigroot  68, 164
Pinchers Bluff  197-198, 199
pinot noir  94, 176
Pisa  10, 25
Pitches, Charles  141
Pitches, William  141
plums  95
poison  63-65, 66, 214; see also rabbits
  1080  64
poison cutter  214
poll tax  58
Poolburn  140
Poolburn Dam  11
Poolburn Gorge  71, 73
Poolburn hall  79
Poolburn Stream  25
Poolburn viaduct  73
poppet head  49, 135
Port Chalmers  46, 58, 104, 178, 213
Port Molyneux  46, 117
powerhouses  201, 203, 207, 209, 211
power stations  204, 206
  Clyde Dam  209–12
  Roxburgh Dam  207-210
Presbyterian Church  60, 61, 102, 118, 127, 130-131, 175
Prince, Walter  203
Public Works Dept  204, 223
Puketoi Station  166, 189
Pyke, Frances  74
Pyke, Vincent  70, 73-75
Pyne Gould Guinness & Co.  103
quartz  11, 49-50, 134, 197
  mining  35, 50, 58, 70, 126, 180, 194, 196, 200-201

230    INDEX

quartzite 15
Quartzville 183
Queenstown 23, 28-29, 31-32, 34-35, 114, 122, 130, 177, 205-207, 218, 221-222
Queenstown Borough Council 205
Quinnat salmon 155

rabbit 20, 31, 35, 37, 41, 62-65, 66, 102, 108, 112, 126, 141, 151-152, 214
  boards 64, 66
  buyers 65
  canning 65
  pelts 64-66
Rabbit Calicivirus Disease (RCD) 66
Rabbit Nuisance Act 1876 64
rabbiters 63-64
Raggedy Range 10, 26, 140
Ranfurly 72, 74, 157, 159, 164, 167-174
Ranfurly Hotel 172
Rapid Creek 204
rats 20
  kiore 18, 20
Rattray, James 102
Read, Gabriel 26, 43, 45, 149; see also Gabriels Gully
Redcastle 36
Redfern, Harry 194
Rees, Cecil Walter 32
Rees, Frances (nee Gilbert) 28, 29, 32
Rees River 32
Rees, William 28-29, 31-33, 34-35, 194
Reid, Donald 100-103
Reid, John 79
Reilly, Christopher 35, 43, 45-46, 189
Reko (Maori explorer) 21-24, 116
Remarkables, The (mountains) 10, 33, 177
remittance men 129
Richardson, Jim 47
Richardson, John (Sir) 32
Ritchie, George 103-104
Ritchie, James 104
Ritchie, John 100, 103-104
Roaring Meg Power Station 22-23, 206-207
Roaring Meg stream 206-207
Robertson, James 12
Robertson, Robert 105
Rock and Pillar Range 10, 26, 67
Ross, J.D. 150
Rough Ridge 10, 26, 213
Roxburgh 26, 43, 48, 52, 55, 74, 92-93, 95-96, 111, 115, 118-122, 134, 204-207, 209
Roxburgh Dam 122, 207, 208, 209-210
Roxburgh Gorge 57
Roxburgh hydro village 209
Roxburgh railway 122
Roxburghshire 26
Roy, John 148
runholders 17, 27, 31, 37-38, 40, 62, 64, 67, 100, 102-103, 115-117, 121, 133, 141, 149, 151-152, 187
runs 2, 23, 25, 27-29, 31, 35, 40-41, 75, 116, 157, 165, 166, 177, 189
runs by number:
  200 (Kyeburn) 165
  215 117
  219 158
  235 35
  236 35
  237 35
  238 35
  244 140
  346 29
  350 31
  356 29, 35
Russell Ritchie & Co, 100, 103
Russell, Theodore 150, 153
Ryan, Teddy 145-146

Salisbury 77
Salisbury Estate 102
Salisbury House 102
Sandhills Goldmining Co. 204
Sargood, Percy (Sir) 153-154
Savage, Michael Joseph (Mickey) (Hon) 81
scab 31, 35
Scandinavian Water Race Co. 134
scheelite 11
schist rock 11, 41, 57, 71-72, 166, 188
schools
  Albert Town 150
  Bannockburn 183
  Blacks 142
  Clyde 191
  Kyeburn 164
  Macetown 128
  Ranfurly 168-169, 173
  Rough Ridge 213
  Skippers 200
  St Bathans 137, 139
Scotland 36, 82, 102, 154, 176, 188
Scotland Point 54
Scott, Robert (Sir) 165
sealers 12, 188
Seddon, Richard (Hon) 122, 200
Semple, Richard (Hon) 206
Serpentine Church 165
Seventh Viscount Charlemont 168
shaft tors 197
Shag Point 9
Shaky Bridge 110
shantytowns 59
shearers 37, 38
sheep 21, 23, 25, 27, 29, 37-38, 40, 63-64, 97, 109, 112, 126, 149, 152, 158-161, 173, 176, 188
  Border Leicester 23
  half-bred
  merino 31-32, 35, 42, 117, 188-189
  transport 72-73
sheep runs see runs
Shennan, Alexander 187-188
Shennan, Watson 187, 189
shepherds 27, 37
ships (see also transport; steamers)
  *Aboukir* 178
  *Althone Castle* 83
  *Andes* 82
  *Athenic* 78
  *Calcutta* 83
  *Cameronia* 83
  *Dunedin* 119
  *Equator* 28
  *Glengyle* 83
  *Marbs* 117
  *Mary Anne* 28
  *Opawa* 78
  *Otago* 21
  *Phoebe* 83
  *Taranaki* 213
  *Ventnor* 59
Shotover House 29
Shotover River 26, 29, 43, 194-195, 199, 203-204, 219-220, 222-223
Shum, Joe 162
Simpson's Creek 32
Skippers 43, 49, 194-195, 196-197, 199-200, 203
Skippers Bridge 194, 199-200
Skippers Gorge 196
Skippers Road 194-195, 196-198, 200-204
Skippers Saddle 195
sluicing 48-49, 58, 70, 119, 134, 136, 157-158, 163, 176-177, 184-185-196
  claims 94
  guns 49
Smith, Asher 153
Smith, Gideon 121
snow 10, 86, 159-160, 200
snow poles 121, 162, 196
soldiers' syndicate 88, 160
Southern Alps 10, 26, 155
Southland 21-24, 61-62, 105, 221
Sowburn 25
St Albans the Martyr Church 102, 133
St Bathans 43, 47- 48, 49, 79, 88, 102, 120, 132-139
St Bathans Goldmining Co. 135
St Bathans Range 132
St Cuthbert 25
St Dunstans Church 191
St Kevins College 36, 39
St Marys Church 191
Stafford, Kathleen 141
Staircase, The 197
stamper batteries 49-50, 126, 201

INDEX 231

steam-powered dredging see dredging
steamers, lake (see also ships)
   *Antrim* 75
   *Earnslaw* 24, 32-33, 155
   *Elswick* 155
   *Kura* 155
   *Makarora* 147, 152, 155
   *Surprise* 150
   *Theodore* 152-153, 155
   *Tilikum* 155
Stephenson, John 100, 104-105
stock agents 101, 105
Stock Exchange, 49
stock firms 37, 101
stock & station industry 100, 102-104, 106
Stotburn 25
Straw Cutting 74, 171
strawberries 95
Strode A.C. 189
Styx 26, 67
Styx Hotel 68
subdivision 42
Sun Kum Shan 57
Supreme Court 168, 210
sweet briar (wild rose) 11
Swinburn 25
Swinburn cemetery 161, 165
Swinney, John 79

Taieri Gorge 70-71
Taieri Lake 24
Taieri Plain 102
Taieri River 11, 15, 24-26, 67-68, 71, 158, 161, 166
Tamblyn, John 92-93, 95
Tamblyn, Joseph 92
Tarbet Street 107-108
Tarras 42
Te Houka 13
Teviot 15, 115-120, 122, 206
Teviot & Alexandra Fruitgrowers Assoc 95
Teviot District Electric Lighting-Power & Irrigation Board 205
Teviot Electric Power Board 205
Teviot Fruitgrowers Assoc 95
Teviot Molyneux Goldmining Co. 120
Teviot River 121, 204
Teviot Valley 92, 94-96
Thomas, Arthur 194

Thompson, James 23
Thomson, Archibald 148
Thomson, John Turnbull 23-26, 24, 36, 148, 152, 158, 167, 199
Thomson's Gorge 26, 31
thyme 11, 60
Tiger Hill 26
tourism 12, 152-155, 194, 209
trout 154-155
   hatchery 155
Tuapeka 118, 210
tuberculosis 63, 164
Turnbull Thomson Falls 26
Turnbull Thomson, John see Thomson, John Turnbull
tussock 11, 27, 63, 161, 217
tutu 37
Twelve Apostles 129
Twizel River 25
typhoid fever 113-114

unemployment 55, 131, 136
United Kingdom 28, 62, 66, 126
Upper Clutha 25
Upper Clutha Railway League 182
Upper Kye Burn River 162
Upper Roaring Meg Power Station 206

Vincent County 73, 75, 191
Vincent County Council 179
Vincent Flour Mill 213
Vinegar Hill 134
vineyards 184, 186; *see also* grapes; Monte Christo
viticulture 90-91, 93-94
von Haast, Julius 148, 154
Von River 31
von Tunzelmann, John 31
von Tunzelmann, Nicholas 28-29, 31
Vulcan Hotel 132, 139

Waikerikeri Valley 90-91
Waikouaiti 29, 68, 188
Waipiata 15, 24, 71, 79, 158, 161
Waipiata TB Sanatorium 167
Waipuna Springs 90
Waitaki River 24, 155, 207
Waitaki Valley 22, 24-25, 29, 161, 163
Waldron, Honora 144

Waldron, John 144
Walter Peak 31-32
Wanaka 22, 75, 114, 122, 148-150, 154-156
Wanaka Shipping Co. 155
Wanaka Station 153
war
   World War I 77, 79-80, 82, 97, 120, 145, 156, 160, 217
   World War II 79-80, 89, 121-122, 131, 146, 207
Ward, Joseph (Sir) (Hon) 138-139
Waste Land Board 37
Waste Lands Act 1855 27, 75
water races 43, 49-50, 94, 97, 99, 111, 113, 119, 160, 177, 184, 203
water rights 191, 210
water supply 111-112, 163, 190, 201, 203, 215, 217
water wheels 49-50
Wedderburn 15
Welcome Home Hotel 198-199
Wellington 26, 28, 39, 59, 77-78, 122, 148-149
Welsh 49, 133
Welshtown 35, 49-50
West Coast, The 16, 53, 56, 129, 144, 148, 155-156, 182
West Wanaka Station 149
Wetherburn 25
whalers 12, 188
Whitmore, (Colonel) 41
Wilkin River 150
Wilkin, Robert 148
Wilkinson, Jack 135
Williams, William 140-141
wine 126; see also viticulture; grapes
   industry 90
Wingatui 70-71
wing dams 109
Woodhouse, James 118
wool 12, 100-103, 106, 172-173, 188
Wright, John 100, 104-105
Wrightson NMA 102, 104-105, 106
Wright Stephenson & Co. 100, 104-105, 117
Wye Creek 206

Young, Andrew 118

Zublin-Williamson Consortium 212